MW01116435

Second Print Edition [2.0] -1433 h. (2012 c.e.)

Copyright © 1433 H./2012 C.E.
Taalib al-Ilm Educational Resources

http://taalib.com
Learn Islaam, Live Islaam.ᔆᴹ

ISBN EAN-13:   978-1-938117-11-4   [Soft cover Print Edition]
Library of Congress Control Number: 2012939609

From the Publisher

GOLDEN WORDS UPON GOLDEN WORDS...FOR EVERY MUSLIM.

"Imaam al-Barbahaaree, may Allaah have mercy upon him said:

May Allaah have mercy upon you! Examine carefully the speech of everyone you hear from in your time particularly. So do not act in haste and do not enter into anything from it until you ask and see: Did any of the Companions of the Prophet, may Allaah's praise and salutations be upon him, speak about it, or did any of the scholars? So if you find a narration from them about it, cling to it, do not go beyond it for anything and do not give precedence to anything over it and thus fall into the Fire.

Explanation by Sheikh Saaleh al-Fauzaan, may Allaah preserve him:

'Do not be hasty in accepting as correct what you may hear from the people, especially in these later times. As now there are many who speak about so many various matters, issuing rulings and ascribing to themselves both knowledge and the right to speak. This is especially the case after the emergence and spread of new modern day media technologies. Such that everyone now can speak and bring forth that which is, in truth, worthless; by this, meaning words of no true value - speaking about whatever they wish in the name of knowledge and in the name of the religion of Islaam. It has even reached the point that you find the people of misguidance and the members of the various groups of misguidance and deviance from the religion speaking as well. Such individuals have now become those who speak in the name of the religion of Islaam through means such as the various satellite television channels. Therefore be very cautious!

It is upon you, oh Muslim, and upon you, oh student of knowledge, individually, to verify matters and not rush to embrace everything and anything you may hear. It is upon you to verify the truth of what you hear, asking, 'Who else also makes this same statement or claim?', 'Where did this thought or concept originate or come from?', 'Who is its reference or source authority?' Asking what are the evidences which support it from within the Book and the Sunnah? And inquiring where has the individual who is putting this forth studied and taken his knowledge from? From who has he studied the knowledge of Islaam?

Each of these matters requires verification through inquiry and investigation, especially in the present age and time. It is not every speaker who should rightly be considered a source of knowledge, even if he is well spoken and eloquent and can manipulate words captivating his listeners. Do not be taken in and accept him until you are aware of the degree and scope of what he possesses of knowledge and understanding. Perhaps someone's words may be few, but possess true understanding, and perhaps another will have a great deal of speech yet he is actually ignorant to such a degree that he doesn't actually possess anything of true understanding. Rather he only has the ability to enchant with his speech so that the people are deceived. Yet he puts forth the perception that he is a scholar, that he is someone of true understanding and comprehension, that he is a capable thinker, and so forth. Through such means and ways he is able to deceive and beguile the people, taking them away from the way of truth.

Therefore, what is to be given true consideration is not the amount of the speech put forth or that one can extensively discuss a subject. Rather, the criterion that is to be given consideration is what that speech contains within it of sound authentic knowledge, what it contains of the established and transmitted principles of Islaam. Perhaps a short or brief statement which is connected to or has a foundation in the established principles can be of greater benefit than a great deal of speech which simply rambles on, and through hearing you don't actually receive very much benefit from.

This is the reality which is present in our time; one sees a tremendous amount of speech which only possesses within it a small amount of actual knowledge. We see the presence of many speakers, yet few people of true understanding and comprehension.' "

[The eminent major scholar Sheikh Saaleh al-Fauzaan, may Allaah preserve him- 'A Valued Gift for the Reader Of Comments Upon the Book Sharh as-Sunnah', page 102-103]

❴ *Is not He better than your so-called gods, He Who originates creation and shall then repeat it, and Who provides for you from heaven and earth? Is there any god with Allaah? Say: 'Bring forth your proofs, if you are truthful.'* ❵-(Surah an-Naml: 64)

Explanation: ❴ *Say: "Bring forth your proofs.."* ❵ This is a command for the Prophet, may Allaah's praise and salutation be upon him, to rebuke them immediately after they had put forward their own rebuke. Meaning: '*Say to them: bring your proof, whether it is an intellectual proof or a proof from transmitted knowledge, that would stand as evidence that there is another with Allaah, the Most Glorified and the Most Exalted*'. Additionally, it has been said that it means: '*Bring your proof that there is anyone other than Allaah, the Most High, who is capable of doing that which has been mentioned from His actions, the Most Glorified and the Most Exalted.*' ❴ *...if you are truthful.* ❵ meaning, in this claim. From this it is derived that a claim is not accepted unless clearly indicated by evidences."

[*Tafseer al-'Aloosee: vol. 15, page 14*]

Sheikh Rabee'a Ibn Hadee Umair al-Madkhalee, may Allaah preserve him said,

'It is possible for someone to simply say, "*So and so said such and such.*" However we should say, "*Produce your proof.*" So why did you not ask them for their proof by saying to them: "*Where was this said?*" Ask them questions such as this, as from your weapons are such questions as: "*Where is this from? From which book? From which cassette?...*" '

[*The Overwhelming Falsehoods of 'Abdul-Lateef Bashmeel' page 14*]

The guiding scholar Imaam Sheikh 'Abdul-'Azeez Ibn Abdullah Ibn Baaz, may Allaah have mercy upon him, said,

'It is not proper that any intelligent individual be misled or deceived by the great numbers from among people from the various countries who engage in such a practice. As the truth is not determined by the numerous people who engage in a matter, rather the truth is known by the Sharee'ah evidences. Just as Allaah the Most High says in Surah al-Baqarah, ❴ *And they say, "None shall enter Paradise unless he be a Jew or a Christian." These are only their own desires. Say "Produce your proof if you are truthful."* ❵-(Surah al-Baqarah: 111) And Allaah the Most High says ❴ *And if you obey most of those on the earth, they will mislead you far away from Allaah's path. They follow nothing but conjectures, and they do nothing but lie.* ❵-(Surah al-'Ana'an: 116)'

[*Collection of Rulings and Various Statements of Sheikh Ibn Baaz -Vol. 1 page 85*]

Sheikh Muhammad Ibn 'Abdul-Wahaab, may Allaah have mercy upon him, said,

'Additionally, verify that knowledge held regarding your beliefs, distinguishing between what is correct and false within it, coming to understand the various areas of knowledge of faith in Allaah alone and the required disbelief in all other objects of worship. You will certainly see various different matters which are called towards and enjoined; so if you see that a matter is in fact one coming from Allaah and His Messenger, then this is what is intended and is desired that you possess. Otherwise, Allaah has certainly given you that which enables you to distinguish between truth and falsehood, if Allaah so wills.

Moreover, this writing of mine- do not conceal it from the author of that work; rather present it to him. He may repent and affirm its truthfulness and then return to the guidance of Allaah, or perhaps if he says that he has a proof for his claims, even if that is only a single statement, or if he claims that within my statements there is something unsupported, then request his evidence for that assertion. After this if there is something which continues to cause uncertainty or is a problem for you, then refer it back to me, so that then you are aware of both his statement and mine in that issue. We ask Allaah to guide us, you, and all the Muslims to that which He loves and is pleased with.'

[Personal Letters of Sheikh Muhammad Ibn 'Abdul-Wahaab- Conclusion to Letter 20]

Sheikh 'Abdullah Ibn 'Abdur-Rahman Abu Bateen, may Allaah have mercy upon him, said, 'And for an individual, if it becomes clear to him that something is the truth, he should not turn away from it and or be discouraged simply due to the few people who agree with him and the many who oppose him in that, especially in these latter days of this present age.

If the ignorant one says: "*If this was the truth so and so and so and so would have been aware of it!*" However this is the very claim of the disbelievers, in their statement found in the Qur'aan ﴾ *If it had truly been good, they would not have preceded us to it!*"﴿-(Surah al-Ahqaaf: 11) and in their statement ﴾ *Is it these whom Allaah has favored from amongst us?*"﴿-(Surah al-Ana'am: 53). Yet certainly, as Alee Ibn Abee Taalib, may Allaah be pleased with him, stated "*Know the truth and then you will know it' people.*" But for the one who generally stands upon confusion and uncertainty, then every doubt swirls around him. And if the majority of the people were in fact upon the truth today, then Islaam would not be considered strange, yet, by Allaah, it is today seen as the most strange of affairs!"

[Durar As-Sanneeyyah -vol. 10, page 400]

al-Waajibat: The Obligatory Matters

A Twenty Part Educational Course w/ Assessment Quizzes & Lesson Benefits
[Self Study/Teachers Edition]

What it is Decreed that Every Male and Female Muslim Must Have Knowledge Of -from the statements of
Sheikh al-Islaam Muhammad ibn 'Abdul-Wahaab

Compiled and Translated by:
Umm Mujaahid Khadijah Bint Lacina Al-Amreekeeyah

Table of Contents

Publisher's Introduction

In the name of Allaah, The Most Gracious, The Most Merciful

All praise is due to Allaah, Lord of the Worlds, peace and salutations be upon the Messenger of Allaah, his household, his Companions, and all those who follow his guidance until the day of Judgment. To proceed:

The Final Messenger sent to guide humanity, the Prophet Muhammad, may Allaah's praise and salutation be upon him, is authentically narrated to have said to his Companions, *{ Indeed I have left you upon a white path of clarity; its night is like its day. No one deviates away from it after me except that he will be ruined. Those among you who live for some time will come to see widespread differing. So adhere firmly to that which you know of my Sunnah and the sunnah of my rightly guided successors; cling to it with your molar teeth. And hold closely to obedience to the legitimate Muslim authority, even if he is an Abyssinian slave, as indeed the believer is like a submissive camel, in that it goes where it is directed. }* (Silsilaat al-Hadeeth as-Saheehah Hadeeth: 937)

Our Prophet, by the permission of Allaah, guided and taught this Ummah to understand and practice the revealed guidance of Islaam which came from the Lord of the worlds, such that its clarity was undeniable and recognized as it spread forward into the world. Yet without question the state of confusion, separation, and differing he also knew and informed us would reach us, is now apparent to a greater degree than at any other time in history. How many people do not even recognize the basic need of humanity for the blessing of revealed guidance? Yet consider what Sheikh al-Islaam Ibn Taymeeyah reminds us:

"The message of guidance for worshipers of Allaah, is a necessity that they truly require, and their genuine and real need for it surpasses their need for any and everything else. This message is the spirit of the world, its light, and its life, and how could this world attain a state of correctness and rectification without having its spirit, light, and life?? The world is indeed a dark and cursed place except when the sun of the message of guidance rises over it. Likewise you find that the state of the worshipper is similar; if the light of the message of guidance does not shine within and spread throughout the life and spirit of his heart, then he sits in darkness. And this is clearly a type of death. Allaah the Most High says, ◈ Is he who was dead without faith by ignorance and disbelief and We then gave him life by knowledge and faith and set for him a light whereby he can walk amongst men, like him who is in the darkness of disbelief, associating others with Allaah and hypocrisy from which he can never come out? ◈ –(Surah Al-An'am: 122). This is the description of the believer, that he was dead and stood in the darkness of ignorance, and then Allaah gave him life through the light of guidance and the light of imaan, or faith, and blessed him with a light by which he could then proceed upon guidance among the people. But as for the disbeliever then his heart remains dead and sits in darkness.

Allaah, the Most High described His message of guidance as a spirit or a soul. As the spirit or soul if it is absent, then one is in fact deprived of life. As Allaah the Most High, says, ❧ And thus We have sent to you the spirit of Our Command. You knew not what was the Book, nor what is Faith. But We have made this Qur'aan a light wherewith We guide whosoever of Our slaves We will.❧ –(Surah Ash-Shuraa: 52) Thus Allaah here has mentioned two fundamentals: the spirit and light, the spirit means life itself, and light which is the light of guidance. Additionally, Allaah makes other examples of the revelation which He has sent down in order to bring life to the hearts and enlighten them, by comparing it to the rain which descends from the heavens bringing life to the earth, and to a fire which brings forth light in darkness…" (Majmou al-Fataawa 19/93)

Certainly, the heart and soul of that message of guidance is and will always be- tawheed, the affirmation by one's heart, tongue, and limbs, in belief and deeds, inwardly and outwardly- that there is nothing worthy of worship except Allaah alone. It is for that reason that I am pleased to offer our first course related book, *"Al-Waajibaat: The Obligatory Matters"*.

The origin and basis for this format of study which we have developed is from the excellent book of the guiding scholar Sheikh Saleeh Ibn Fauzaan al-Fauzaan, may Allaah preserve him, in his book *"Mulkhis fee Sharh Kitaab at-Tawheed"*. In the introduction he states (page 5),

"This is an abridged commentary of the work "Kitaab at-Tawheed" of Sheikh al-Islaam Muhammad 'Abdul-Wahaab, may Allaah have mercy upon him, which I have composed upon a modern educational methodology, in order to make it easier to understand for the beginners in their studies. I hope that Allaah will bring benefit through it, and grants it a contributing role in the spreading of knowledge and the correction of the beliefs of the Muslims…"

His basic framework for the beginner's study of that essential book, was initially the foundation for the (ongoing) development of an extended course on *"Kitaab at-Tawheed"*, as as well later being further adapted and modified in different ways for other knowledge based projects - including the present course –by incorporating some of those same beneficial characteristics. This specific course *"Al-Waajibaat: The Obligatory Matters"* was also first developed for and taught by Umm Mujaahid to a group of over twenty Muslim sisters in Sana'a Yemen, and by Allaah's grace alone was very successful. It has since been revised and further modified to enable its study by both the single individual or, preferably, a group of Muslims wherever in the world they may be. May Allaah reward our sister Umm Mujaahid for her efforts to contribute to the call to worship Allaah without associates, and raising the crucial awareness of the necessity of the Muslims making that foundation the essential basis of every aspect of their lives inwardly and outwardly.

The student who undertakes the course should please take note of the following:

1. The hadeeth are only mentioned with a general reference of source and status, except in specific situations in which additional information may have been brought forth. The compiler has indicated the clear ruling of the status of the hadeeth narrations from the scholars whenever that was possible. In general the scholars' reliance of the hadeeth in the original text was relied upon.

2. Regarding any minor issues of independent judgment or positions in which the scholars have differed about, the compiler has presented the evidenced position that she believes is the strongest from the sources reviewed; this does not dismiss the fact that there may be other positions from those whose scholarship we recognize, and whom we take as our scholars and love for Allaah's sake. Therefore for any related questions or differences that someone may encounter, we first encourage them to ask any of the recognized people of knowledge throughout the world regarding any matter that is not clear to them. Secondly we encourage them to return to the original works of the scholars quoted as well as all other recognized scholars who have produced works in this essential area of knowledge to further investigate the evidences and explanations related to such issues according to their ability.

In closing we hope that the publication of this book contributes to the efforts of the Muslims around the world to step by step gain a better basic understanding and practice of the foundations of the religion of Islaam. And I ask Allaah to grant every sincere believer a firm hand hold upon that essential knowledge of the worship of Allaah alone without associate or partner, so that that we all may be successful in this life and the Hereafter, and I end with His praise.

Abu Sukhailah Khalil Ibn-Abelahyi
Taalib al-Ilm Educational Resources

Compilers Introduction

All praise is due to Allaah, Lord of the Worlds, peace and salutations be upon the Messenger of Allaah, his household, his Companions, and all those who follow his guidance until the day of Judgment. To proceed:

The matter of sound Islamic beliefs, or *'aqeedah*, is a vital one, both to each individual Muslim, as well as the society as a whole. It is the foundation upon which all else is built- so if it is weak, that which is built upon it is weak, and in danger of falling, while if it is sound, that which is above it will be sound, if Allaah so wills. Sheikh Saalih Fauzaan, may Allaah preserve him, said, concerning this,

"It is obligatory upon the Muslim to understand all of the matters of his religion, both of belief and that which is legislated. With that he learns the matters of 'aqeedah, and that which it makes obligatory, and that which opposes it, and that which completes it, and that which makes it deficient, until his 'aqeedah is the correct, sound, 'aqeedah. And it is obligatory upon him to learn the rulings of his religion concerning actions, until he performs that which Allaah has made obligatory upon him, and leaves that which Allaah has made forbidden for him, with insight." ("al-Muntaqa", Volume 1, Page 310)

As if our knowledge is not sound, than the actions which follow will not be sound, as Sheikh Fauzaan says, *"If the 'aqeedah is correct, then the legislated actions are correct; and that which is not based upon the correct 'aqeedah, then the action will not be correct."* ("al-Muntaqa", Vol. 1 Page 301)

Along with this, is calling the people to *at-tawheed*, and educating them as to the correct beliefs. Sheikh Bin Baaz, may Allaah have mercy upon him, says, concerning this,

"It is obligatory for you, Oh Slave of Allaah: if you understand that which has been presented, that you expend every effort in explaining and clarifying this foundational principle, and to spread it amongst the people, and to make it apparent to mankind, until they are educated from their ignorance…" ("Rasaail fee at-Tawheed", Page 51)

When teaching this course to my students here in Sana'a, I told them that it could have been called, "Survival Islaam"; as through this excellent compilation *'al-Waajibaat'* one may attain a basic understanding of many of the most important aspects of our belief system, I stressed to them, as I do to you all, that all of this knowledge will not benefit you unless you act upon it. And so I tried, throughout the explanations, to choose quotes from the scholars of both our times and the past, and to give examples and clarifications that will, insh'Allaah, assist the student in implementing these foundational principles in their own lives. Along with that, I made them each keep a journal in which they took accounting of themselves and their thoughts, speech and actions, in order that they be aware of their conditions, and see how they add up in the scales of good and bad. Armed with self- knowledge, one can see more clearly where improvements have to be made, insh'Allaah. I recommend that the reader also keep one of these little reckoning notebooks, at least for the duration of the course, and that he be honest with himself and take account at least once or twice a week, if not every day.

How to use this Book

One can, of course, just read through it. Insh'Allaah this will bring some benefit; however there are ways to make use of it in a much more effective manner than this.

First of all, a student may study it on her own, without a teacher or someone to guide her through it. In this case, the student should read the lessons, making notes as desired on the lines provided for this. After each lesson, she should do the homework in a separate notebook, and check her answers in the answer key provided at the back of the [Self Study\Teachers Edition].

As for the quizzes, she should study for them and take them without her notes, as this is how they are intended to be used. She can use these to assess her progress, and see what things she may need to go over again before proceeding to the next section. The final test, as well, is intended to be taken without referring to any notes or the course text. Again, it should be used to see what areas may require further study before continuing on to any further books in the series, insh'Allaah.

Secondly, a group of students may get together in person or over the internet, and study it together. In this case, one trustworthy reliable person of good character should be designated as the study group leader, and she reads the lessons to the students. Students should be flexible yet consistent in scheduling their group study of the course. Everyone involved proceeds through the course together, discussing issues and assisting each other in gaining a firm understanding. If they have any questions that are not answered in the text, then, as with the single student above, they should write them down in order to later direct them to any recognized student of knowledge or scholar who might answer them upon evidence and sound understanding. The study group leader administers and checks all homework, quizzes and tests from the answer key which is available at the back of this [Self Study\Teachers Edition]; and might suggest to the other students areas which they may have to review before going on to the next lesson. The smaller [Directed Study edition] does not contain an answer key and is only intended only for those who are studying it together with a study group or a teacher who has the teachers edition to refer to.

The difference between the Level 1 [required] questions and the Level 2 [supplementary] questions are the following. The Level 1 [required] questions are those which everyone in the class should definitely complete and fully comprehend before moving on to the next lesson. These are directly linked to the required comprehension of that specific lesson, which the next lesson will be built upon. However, the Level 2 [supplementary] questions are a little more detailed and require a little more understanding and may not be understood by everyone, or some people may be able to answer some of them, or only parts of some of them- without that failure to understand every aspect of those Level 2 [supplementary] questions then becoming a reason for them to not proceed further. It is one way of ensuring the fundamental and core comprehension is gained by everyone, while still addressing the differing levels of comprehension among people in a single learning circle.

Lastly, the book can also be used in a class or seminar situation, which in many ways is the most recommended but often not feasible. In this case, there is a teacher who has a greater and more in depth understanding than the students and can answer their additional questions and assist them in understanding that which is presented. She may be able to clarify matters for them, based on sound knowledge and understanding of the subject, and provide them with examples and additional information as necessary. She grades all the homework, quizzes, and the test using the answer key, and can clearly show the students where they need to review in order to have a more complete understanding of the subject. She also checks their journals, if they are doing them, by looking at the dates of their entries, rather than reading what has been written. Again, the class can meet in person, or over the internet in any way the conforms to Shari'ah guidelines. For sisters who have purchased the book, there is the added option of possibly taking the free online course, at **study. taalib.com,** insh'Allaah. Please refer to the site for more information and scheduling.

Beneficial comments and knowledge based corrections would be appreciated, as if there is a mistake we would like to correct it in future editions of the work, insh'Allaah. Send specifics to *kitaabwaajibaat@taalib.com.*

May Allaah make us all steadfast in gaining knowledge of our Lord, our Prophet, and this beautiful and complete way of life, Islaam. May He assist us in passing on our knowledge and implementing it in our lives, and the lives of our families. I ask that Allaah forgive me for any mistakes I may have made in this compilation, and that He accept this from me, and that it be a benefit to the people in this life and the next.

Umm Mujaahid Khadijah Bint Lacina
al-Amreekiyyah as-Salafiyyah
Shihr, Yemen
Sha'baan 1430

Bismillaah ir Rahman ir Raheem

The Three Principles which it is Obligatory upon every Male and Female Muslim to Understand

They are: That the servant knows his Lord, his religion, and his Prophet, Muhammad, may Allaah's praise and salutations be upon him.

If it is said to you: Who is your Lord? Then say: My Lord is Allaah, who has nurtured me and all of the creation with His blessings and beneficence. He is the only one I worship, there is nothing worthy of being worshipped other than Him.

If it is said to you: What is your religion? Then say: My religion is al-Islaam, and it is to submit to Allaah alone, with *at-tawheed-* joining none along with Him in worship, and complying with Him with obedience, and being free from associating others with Allaah and those who do so.

If it is said to you: Who is your Prophet? Then say: Muhammad ibn 'Abdullah ibn 'Abdal-Mutalab ibn Haashim; and Haashim is from the tribe of Quraish, and Quraish is from the Arabs, and the Arabs are from the descendents of Ismaa'eel ibn Ibraaheem, upon them both, and upon our Prophet the best of praise and salutations.

The Principles of the Religion and its Fundamentals Consist of Two Matters:

The First: The command to worship Allaah alone, without associating any partners with Him, and being motivated by that, and inciting others towards it, and support and loyalty due to it, and to know that the one who leaves it has disbelieved.

The Second: Warning away from *ash-shirk* (associating others along with Allaah in worship) in the worship of Allaah, and strength upon that, and enmity due to it, and knowing that the one who engages in it has disbelieved.

The Conditions of *ash-Shahadah* (*la ilaha ila Allaah*) None has the Right to be Worshipped but Allaah Alone

The First: Knowledge, encompassing negation and verification

The Second: Certainty, and knowledge is perfected through it, and it negates doubt and uncertainty

The Third: Sincerity, which negates *ash-shirk*, which is associating others along with Allaah in worship

The Fourth: Truthfulness, which negates insincerity

The Fifth: Love for the statement, and that which it signifies, and contentment with that

The Sixth: Compliance with all that is required by these words, and that is, the obligatory acts, sincerely for Allaah alone, seeking His pleasure

The Seventh: Acceptance, which negates rejection

The Evidences of these Conditions from the Book of Allaah, the Most High, and from the Sunnah of the Messenger of Allaah, may Allaah's praise and salutations be upon him

From the Proofs for Knowledge:

His, the Most High's, saying, ﴿ *So know (Oh Muhammad) that la ilaha ila allaah (none has the right to be worshipped but Allaah)* ﴾ –(Surah Muhammad, from Ayat 19)

And His saying, ﴿ *...except for those who bear witness to the truth knowingly (i.e. believed in the Oneness of Allaah, and obeyed His Orders and they know (the facts about the Oneness of Allaah)...* ﴾ –(Surat az-Zakhroof, from Ayat 86). Meaning, with "*la ilaha ila Allaah*". ﴿ *...and they know (the facts about the Oneness of Allaah)* ﴾ –(Surah az-Zakhroof, from Ayat 86) (know) with their hearts, that which they say with their tongues.

And from the Sunnah: The hadeeth found in *"as-Saheeh"* on 'Uthmaan, may Allaah be pleased with him, wherein he said, "Allaah's Messenger, may Allaah's praise and salutations be upon him, said, {*He who died, knowing with certainty that there is none worthy of worship except for Allaah, entered Paradise.*}" (*"Saheeh Muslim"*, No. 26)

From the Proofs for Certainty:

His, the Most High's, saying, ❴ ***Only those are the believers who have believed in Allaah and His Messenger, and afterward doubt not but strive with their wealth and their lives for the Cause of Allaah. Those! They are the truthful.*** ❵ –(Surat al-Hujuraat, Ayat 15)

And it is a condition of truthfulness, their belief in Allaah and His Messenger, may Allaah's praise and salutations be upon him, making it a reality without any skepticism; that is to say, without doubting. As for the one who doubts, then he is from the hypocrites.

And from the Sunnah: The hadeeth found in *"as-Saheeh"* from Abee Hurairah, may Allaah be pleased with him, that he said, "The Messenger of Allaah, may Allaah's praise and salutations be upon him, said, {*I bear testimony to the fact that there is none worthy of worship except Allaah, and I am the Messenger of Allaah. The servant who would meet Allaah without entertaining any doubt about these two would enter heaven.*}' (*"Saheeh Muslim"*, No. 27)

And in another narration, {*The servant who would meet Allaah without any doubt about these two statements (the shahadatan), would never be kept from Paradise.*} (*"Saheeh Muslim"*, No. 28)

And on Abee Hurairah also, from a long hadeeth, {*The one who you meet behind this garden, who bears witness that there is none worthy of worship but Allaah, and his heart is firm upon that, then give him glad tidings of Paradise.*} (*"Saheeh Muslim"*, No. 31)

From the Proofs of Sincerity:

The saying of the Most High, ❴ ***Surely, the religion (i.e. the worship and the obedience) is for Allaah only...*** ❵ –(Surat az-Zamr, from Ayat 3)

And His saying, Glorified is He, ❴ ***And they were commanded not, but that they should worship Allaah, and worship none but Him Alone (abstaining from ascribing partners to Him)...*** ❵ –(Surat al-Bayyinah, from Ayat 5)

And from the Sunnah, the hadeeth found in *"as-Saheeh"* on the authority of Abee Hurairah, may Allaah be pleased with him, on the Prophet, may Allaah's praise and salutations be upon him, *{The most pleased of the people with my intercession is the one who said la ilaha ila Allaah sincerely from his heart (or his self)}* ("Saheeh al-Bukhaari", No.99)

And in the *Saheeh*, on the authority of 'Utbaan ibn Maalik, may Allaah be pleased with him, from the Prophet, may Allaah's praise and salutations be upon him, that he said, *{Verily Allaah has made the Fire forbidden for the one who said, la ilaha ila Allaah, seeking by that the Face of Allaah, the Glorified, the Most Exalted.}* ("Saheeh al-Bukhaari", No. 425, "Saheeh Muslim", No. 33)

And from an-Nasaa'i, in his book, *"al-Yawm wa al-Layl"*, from a hadeeth of two men of the Companions, from the Prophet, may Allaah's praise and salutations be upon him, that he said, *{The one who says, 'There is none worthy of worship except Allaah Alone, without associating any partners with Him, to Him is the dominion over everything, and to Him is due all praise, and He has power over all things', and his heart is sincere upon it, and his tongue is truthful in saying it, except that Allaah will split the heavens open for him, until he sees the ones who say it from the people of the Earth. And the right of the servant is that Allaah looks upon him to grant him his request.}* (This is a weak narration. See *"Da'if at-Targheeb"*, No.932)

From the Proofs of Truthfulness:

The saying of The Most High,

❀ **Alif-Laam-Meem.**[These letters are one of the miracles of the Qur'aan, and none but Allaah (Alone) knows their meanings.]

Do people think that they will be left alone because they say: "We believe," and will not be tested?

And We indeed tested those who were before them. And Allaah will certainly make (it) known (the truth of) those who are true, and will certainly make (it) known (the falsehood of) those who are liars, (although Allaah knows all that before putting them to test).❀ –(Surat al-'Ankaboot, Ayat 1-3)

And the saying of The Most High,

And of mankind, there are some (hypocrites) who say: "We believe in Allaah and the Last Day," while in fact they believe not.

They (think to) deceive Allaah and those who believe, while they only deceive themselves, and perceive (it) not!

In their hearts is a disease (of doubt and hypocrisy) and Allaah has increased their disease. A painful torment is theirs because they used to tell lies. —(Surat al-Baqarah, Ayats 8-10)

And from the Sunnah: that which is found in the two Saheehs, on the authority of Mu'aadh ibn Jabal, may Allaah be pleased with him, that the Prophet, may Allaah's praise and salutations be upon him, said, *{There is no one who testifies that there is none worthy of worship except Allaah, and that Muhammad is His servant and Messenger, truthfully from his heart, except that Allaah makes the Fire forbidden for him.}* (al-Bukhaari, No. 128, and Muslim, No.32)

From the Proofs of Love:

The saying of the Most High, *And of mankind are some who take (for worship) others besides Allaah as rivals (to Allaah). They love them as they love Allaah. But those who believe, love Allaah more (than anything else).* —(Surat al-Baqarah, from Ayat 165)

And His saying, *O you who believe! Whoever from among you turns back from his religion (Islaam), Allaah will bring a people whom He will love and they will love Him; humble towards the believers, stern towards the disbelievers, fighting in the way of Allaah, and never fear the blame of the blamers* —(Surat al-Maa'idah, from Ayat 54)

And from the Sunnah: That which is found in the *Saheeh*, on the authority of Anas ibn Maalik, may Allaah's praise and good mention be upon him, that he said, "Allaah's Messenger, may Allaah's praise and salutations be upon him, said,:

{Whoever possesses the following three qualities will have the sweetness (delight) of faith:

1. The one to whom Allaah and His Messenger becomes dearer than anything else.

2. Who loves a person and he loves him only for Allaah's sake.

3. Who hates to revert to disbelief as he hates to be thrown into the fire.}"

(Found in the two Saheehs: al-Bukhaari, No. 16, and Muslim, No. 43)

From the Proofs of Compliance:

The saying of The Most High is a proof for it: ❨*And turn in repentance and in obedience with true Faith (Islamic Monotheism) to your Lord and submit to Him (in Islaam) before the torment comes upon you, (and) then you will not be helped.*❩ –(Surat az-Zumar, from Ayat 54)

And His saying, ❨*And who can be better in religion than one who submits his face (himself) to Allaah (i.e. follows Allaah's religion of Islamic Monotheism); and he is a Muhsin (a good-doer)*❩ –(Surat an-Nisaa`, from Ayat 125)

And His saying, ❨*And whosoever submits his face (himself) to Allaah, while he is a Muhsin (good-doer, i.e. performs good deeds totally for Allaah's sake without any show-off or to gain praise or fame and does them in accordance with the Sunnah of Allaah's Messenger Muhammad), then he has grasped the most trustworthy handhold [la ilaha ila llaah (none has the right to be worshipped but Allaah)].*❩ –(Surat Luqmaan, from Ayat 22) Meaning, to the statement, *"la ilaha ila Allaah".*

And His, The Most High, saying, ❨*But no, by your Lord, they can have no Faith, until they make you (O Muhammad) judge in all disputes between them, and find in themselves no resistance against your decisions, and accept (them) with full submission.*❩ –(Surat an-Nisaa`, Ayat 65)

And from the Sunnah, his, may Allaah's praise and salutations be upon him, saying, *{One of you does not believe until his desires come after that which I have come with.}* (This hadeeth is weak, see verification of *"al-Mushkaat"*, No. 167)

And this is from the completeness of compliance, and its purpose.

From the Proofs of Acceptance:

His, the Most High, saying,

❨*And similarly, We sent not a warner before you (O Muhammad) to any town (people) but the luxurious ones among them said: "We found our fathers following a certain way and religion, and we will indeed follow their footsteps."*❩

(The warner) said: "Even if I bring you better guidance than that which you found your fathers following?" They said: "Verily, we disbelieve in that with which you have been sent."

So We took revenge on them, then see what was the end of those who denied (Islamic Monotheism). –(Surat az-Zukhruf, Ayats 23-25)

And His saying, the Most High, *Truly, when it was said to them: "La ilaha illallaah (none has the right to be worshipped but Allaah)," they puffed themselves up with pride (i.e. denied it).*

And (they) said: "Are we going to abandon our (gods) for the sake of a mad poet? –(Surat as-Saaffaat, Ayats 35-36)

And from the Sunnah: That which is found in the *Saheeh* from Abi Moosaa, may Allaah be pleased with him, from the Prophet, may Allaah's praise and salutations be upon him, that he said, { *The example of guidance and knowledge with which Allaah has sent me is like abundant rain falling on the earth, some of which was fertile soil that absorbed rain water and brought forth vegetation and grass in abundance. Another portion of it was hard and held the rain water and Allaah benefited the people with it and they utilized it for drinking, making their animals drink from it and for irrigation of the land for cultivation. Another portion of it was barren which could neither hold the water nor bring forth vegetation (then that land gave no benefits). The first is the example of the person who comprehends Allaah's religion and gets benefit (from the knowledge) which Allaah has revealed through me (the second) is the one who learns and then teaches others. The last example is that of a person who does not care for it and does not take Allaah's guidance revealed through me (He is like that barren land.)}* (Found in the two Saheehs: al-Bukhaari, No. 79, and Muslim, No.2282)

From the Things which Nullify Islaam

Know that there are ten things which nullify Islaam:

The First: Associating others in the worship of Allaah, the Most High.

Allaah, the Most High, says, *Verily, Allaah forgives not that partners should be set up with Him (in worship), but He forgives except that (anything else) to whom He wills...* –(Surat an-Nisaa, from Ayat 48)

And He says, ❨*Verily, whosoever sets up partners (in worship) with Allaah, then Allaah has forbidden Paradise to him, and the Fire will be his abode. And for the polytheists and wrong doers there are no helpers.*❩ –(Surat al-Maa'idah, from Ayat 72)

And from this is sacrificing to other than Allaah, such as the one who sacrifices to the *jinn*, or to the graves.

The Second: One who sets up between himself and Allaah intermediaries, and supplicates to them and asks them for intercession and relies upon them: all of this is disbelief (*kafara*)

The Third: The one who does not say that the ones who associate others along with Allaah in worship are disbelievers, or has doubt as to their disbelief, or who says that their way is correct, has himself disbelieved.

The Fourth: The one who believes that other than the guidance of the Prophet, may Allaah's praise and good mention be upon him, is more complete than his guidance, or that rulings other than his are better than his rulings, such as the one who places the judgments of the *tawagheet* (anything that is worshipped other than Allaah) before his (the Prophet's) rulings-than he is a disbeliever.

The Fifth: The one who hates something which the Messenger, may Allaah's praise and good mention be upon him, came with, even if he acts upon it, has disbelieved.

The Sixth: The one who ridicules something from the religion of the Messenger, may Allaah's praise and good mention be upon him, or the reward or punishment of Allaah concerning it, has disbelieved.

And the proof is the saying of Allaah, the Most High, ❨*If you ask them (about this), they declare: "We were only talking idly and joking." Say: "Was it Allaah and His Ayat (proofs, evidences, verses, lessons, signs, revelations, etc.) and His Messenger that you were mocking?"*

Make no excuse; you disbelieved after you had believed.❩ –(Surat at-Tawbah, Ayats 65-66)

The Seventh: Magic, and from it is *as-sarf* and *al-'atf*; as the one who performs it, or is pleased with it has disbelieved.

And the proof is the saying of Allaah, the Most High, ❨*...but they could not thus harm anyone except by Allaah's Leave. And they learn that which harms them and profits them not...*❩ –(Surat al-Baqarah, from Ayat 102)

The Eighth: Assisting those who associate others in worship with Allaah, and supporting them against the Muslims.

The proof is the saying of the Most High, ❴ *And if any amongst you takes them (the Jews and Christians) as Auliyaa' (friends, helpers, protectors), then surely, he is one of them. Verily, Allaah guides not those people who are the polytheists and wrong doers and unjust.*❵ –(Surat al-Maa'idah, from Ayat 51)

The Ninth: The one who believes that some of the people are able to be exempt from the legislation of Muhammad, may Allaah's praise and good mention be upon him, just as al-Khidr made it possible to leave the legislation of Moosaa, may Allaah's praise be upon him- as he is a disbeliever.

The Tenth: Abandoning the religion of Allaah, the Most High; not learning about it or acting upon it.

The proof is the saying of Allaah, the Most High, ❴ *And who does more wrong than he who is reminded of the Ayat (proofs, evidences, verses, lessons, signs, revelations, etc.) of his Lord, then turns aside from them? Verily, We shall exact retribution from the criminals, disbelievers, polytheists, sinners.* ❵ –(Surat as-Sajdah, Ayat 22)

And there is no difference in any of these things which nullify Islaam between the one who is joking, or the one who is in earnest, and the one who is afraid- except for the one who is forced. And all of them are from the greatest of the grave things, and of the most prevalent matters. So it is necessary that the Muslim be cautious of them, and be afraid of them for himself, and we ask Allaah's protection from anything that will bring about His wrath and the torment of His punishment.

At-Tawheed is of Three Categories

The First: Tawheed ar-Ruboobiyah (Tawheed in the Lordship of Allaah)

This is the one which the disbelievers at the time of the Messenger of Allaah, may Allaah's praise and good mention be upon him, affirmed, and yet it did not enter them into Islaam, and the Messenger of Allaah, may Allaah's praise and good mention be upon him, killed them, and made their blood and wealth permissible for the Muslims. It is the belief of Allaah by His actions.

The proof is the saying of the Most High, ❋ *Say (O Muhammad: "Who provides for you from the sky and the earth? Or who owns hearing and sight? And who brings out the living from the dead and brings out the dead from the living? And who disposes the affairs?" They will say: "Allaah." Say: "Will you not then be afraid of Allaah's punishment (for setting up rivals in worship with Allaah)?* ❋ –(Surat Yoonus, Ayat 31) And there are many verses concerning this.

The Second: Tawheed al-Uloohiyah (Tawheed in worship)

It is that which conflict has occurred concerning it, in past ages and in modern times. It is the belief of Allaah by the actions of the worshipper, such as supplication, making a vow, slaughtering, hope, fear, reliance, desire, reverence, and turning to Allaah. Each category from these categories of worship is supported by proofs from the Qur'aan. *The Third: Tawheed adh-Dhaat wa al-Asmaa wa as-Sifaat (Tawheed in Allaah's being, His names and His attributes– and that they apply to Him Alone in perfection)*

Allaah, the Most High, says, ❋ *Say: "He is Allaah, (the) One.*

Allaah-us-Samad [Allaah – the Self-Sufficient Master, Whom all creatures need, (He neither eats nor drinks)].

He begets not, nor was He begotten.

And there is none coequal or comparable to Him. ❋ –(Surat *al-ikhlaas*, Ayats 1-4)

And His, the Most High, saying, ❋ *And (all) the Most Beautiful Names belong to Allaah, so call on Him by them, and leave the company of those who belie or deny (or utter impious speech against) His Names. They will be requited for what they used to do.* ❋ –(Surat al-A'raaf, Ayat 180)

And He, the Most High says, ❋ *There is nothing like Him, and He is the All-Hearer, the All-Seer.* ❋ –(Surat ash-Shooraah, From Ayat 11)

The Opposite of *at-Tawheed* (the worship of Allaah Alone) is *ash-Shirk* (associating others along with Him in worship)

It is of three categories: greater *shirk*, lesser *shirk*, and hidden *shirk*

The First Category from the Categories of ash-Shirk:

ash-Shirk al-Akbar- The Greater Shirk

Allaah, the Most Glorified, Most Exalted, says, ❬ *Verily, Allaah forgives not (the sin of) setting up partners (in worship) with Him, but He forgives whom He wills, sins other than that, and whoever sets up partners in worship with Allaah, has indeed strayed far away.* ❭ –(Surat an-Nisaa, Ayat 116)

And He, Glorified is He, says, ❬ *Surely, they have disbelieved who say: "Allaah is the Messiah (Jesus), son of Maryam (Mary)." But the Messiah said: "O Children of Israel! Worship Allaah, my Lord and your Lord." Verily, whosoever sets up partners (in worship) with Allaah, then Allaah has forbidden Paradise to him, and the Fire will be his abode. And for the polytheists and wrong doers there are no helpers.* ❭ –(Surat al-Maa'idah, Ayat 72)

And He, the Most High, says, ❬ *And We shall turn to whatever deeds they (disbelievers, polytheists, sinners) did, and We shall make such deeds as scattered floating particles of dust.* ❭ –(Surat al-Furqaan, Ayat 23)

And He, Glorified is He, says, ❬ *And indeed it has been revealed to you (O Muhammad), as it was to those (Allaah's Messengers) before you: "If you join others in worship with Allaah, (then) surely, (all) your deeds will be in vain, and you will certainly be among the losers.* ❭ –(Surat az-Zumar, Ayat 65)

And He, Glorified and Exalted, says, ❬ *But if they had joined in worship others with Allaah, all that they used to do would have been of no benefit to them.* ❭ –(Surat al-An'aam, from Ayat 88)

The Greater Shirk is of Four Categories:

The First: Shirk of Supplication

The Proof is His, the Most High, saying, ❬ *And when they embark on a ship, they invoke Allaah, making their Faith pure for Him only, but when He brings them safely to land, behold, they give a share of their worship to others.* ❭ –(Surat al-'Ankiboot, Ayat 65)

The Second: Shirk of Intention, Desire, and Purpose

The proof is His, the Most High, saying, ❧ *Whosoever desires the life of the world and its glitter, to them We shall pay in full (the wages of) their deeds therein, and they will have no diminution therein.*

They are those for whom there is nothing in the Hereafter but Fire, and vain are the deeds they did therein. And of no effect is that which they used to do. ❧ –(Surah Hood, Ayats 15-16)

The Third: Shirk of Obedience

The proof is His, the Most High, saying, ❧ *They (Jews and Christians) took their rabbis and their monks to be their lords besides Allaah (by obeying them in things that they made lawful or unlawful according to their own desires without being ordered by Allaah), and (they also took as their Lord) Messiah, son of Maryam, while they (Jews and Christians) were commanded to worship none but One Ilaah (God – Allaah), La ilaaha ila Huwa (none has the right to be worshipped but He). Glorified is He (far above is He) from having the partners they associate (with Him).* ❧ –(Surat at-Tawbah, Ayat 31)

And the explanation of it which has no ambiguity in it: Following the scholars and the worshippers in wrongdoing, not calling them their gods, as is explained by the Prophet, may Allaah's praise and good mention be upon him, to 'Adee ibn Haatim when he asked him when he said, "We did not worship them." He (the Prophet, may Allaah's praise and good mention be upon him, said, {*Indeed your worship of them was your obeying them in wrongdoing.*} ("as-Saheehah", Number 3293)

The Fourth: Shirk of Love

The proof is His, the Most High, saying, ❧ *And of mankind are some who take (for worship) others besides Allaah as rivals (to Allaah). They love them as they love Allaah.* ❧ –(Surat al-Baqara, from Ayat 165)

The Second Category from the Categories of Shirk:

ash-Shirk Asghar- the Lesser Shirk, and it is ar-riyaa' (this is engaging in acts for the sake of the recognition by the people)

The Second Category from the Categories of Shirk:

ash-Shirk Asghar- the Lesser Shirk, and it is ar-riyaa' (this is engaging in acts for the sake of the recognition by the people)

The proof is His, the Most High, saying, ﴾*...So whoever hopes for the Meeting with his Lord, let him work righteousness and associate none as a partner in the worship of his Lord.*﴿ –(Surat al-Kahf, from Ayat 110)

The Third Category from the Categories of ash-Shirk

ash-Shirk khafee- the hidden shirk:

And the proof of it is the saying of the Messenger of Allaah, may Allaah's praise and good mention be upon him, *{Ash-Shirk in this Ummah (nation) is more hidden than the creeping black ant on a black piece of wood in the darkness of the night.}* ("*Musnad*" of Imaam Ahmad No. 18781)

And the expiation for it is his, may Allaah's praise and good mention be upon him, saying, *{Oh Allaah, indeed I ask You for protection from associating any partners along with You in worship, and I am aware of it, and I ask Your forgiveness for the sins which I am not aware of.}* ("*Saheeh al-Jaami'*" No.3731)

Kufr, (Disbelief) is of Two Types

The First Type: Disbelief which takes one out of the religion

And it is five categories:

The First Category: Kufr of Falsehood and Denial

The proof is His, the Most High, saying, ﴾ *And who does more wrong than he who invents a lie against Allaah or denies the truth (Muhammad and his doctrine of Islamic Monotheism and this Qur'aan), when it comes to him? Is there not a dwelling in Hell for the disbelievers (in the Oneness of Allaah and in His Messenger Muhammad)*﴿ –(Surat al-Ankaboot, Ayat 68)

The Second Category: Kufr of Rejection and Pride, along with Affirmation of the Truth

The proof is the saying of Allaah, the Most High, ﴿ *And (remember) when We said to the angels: "Prostrate yourselves before Aadam." And they prostrated except Iblees, he refused and was proud and was one of the disbelievers (disobedient to Allaah).* ﴾ –(Surat al-Baqarah, Ayat 34)

The Third Category: Kufr of Doubt, and it is Kufr of Uncertainty

The proof is the saying of Allaah, the Most High, ﴿ *And he went into his garden while in a state (of pride and disbelief), unjust to himself. He said: "I think not that this will ever perish.*

And I think not the Hour will ever come, and if indeed I am brought back to my Lord (on the Day of Resurrection), I surely shall find better than this when I return to Him."

His companion said to him during the talk with him: "Do you disbelieve in Him Who created you out of dust, then out of Nutfah (mixed drops of male and female sexual discharge), then fashioned you into a man?

But as for my part, (I believe) that He is Allaah, my Lord, and none shall I associate as partner with my Lord." ﴾ –(Surat al-Kahf, Ayats 35-37)

The Fourth Category: Kufr of Abandonment

The proof is the saying of the Most High, ﴿ *But those who disbelieve, turn away from that whereof they are warned.* ﴾ –(Surat al-Ahqaaf, from Ayat 3)

The Fifth Category: Kufr of Hypocrisy

The proof is His, the Most High, saying, ﴿ *That is because they believed, and then disbelieved; therefore their hearts are sealed, so they understand not.* ﴾ –(Surat al-Munaafiqoon, Ayat 3)

The Second Type from the Types of Disbelief: It is lesser disbelief, and it does not remove one from the religion, and it is the disbelief in Allaah's beneficence

The proof is the saying of Allaah, the Most High, ﴿ *And Allaah puts forward the example of a township (Makkah), that dwelt secure and well-content; its provision coming to it in abundance from every place, but it (its people) denied the Favors of Allaah (with ungratefulness). So Allaah made it taste extreme of hunger (famine) and fear, because of that (evil, i.e. denying Prophet Muhammad) which they (its people) used to do.* ﴾ –(Surat an-Nahl, Ayat 112)

Categories of Hypocrisy

Hypocrisy is of two categories: hypocrisy of belief, and hypocrisy of action

Hypocrisy of Belief

It is of six categories: The one who engages in them is from lowest depths of the Hellfire:

The First: Denial of the Messenger, may Allaah's praise and good mention be upon him

The Second: Denial of some of what the Messenger, may Allaah's praise and good mention be upon him, came with

The Third: Hatred of the Messenger, may Allaah's praise and good mention be upon him

The Fourth: Hatred of some of what the Messenger, may Allaah's praise and good mention be upon him, came with

The Fifth: Happiness with a lowering of the religion of the Messenger, may Allaah's praise and good mention be upon him

The Sixth: Dislike with the victory of the religion of the Messenger, may Allaah's praise and good mention be upon him

Hypocrisy of Action

The hypocrisy of action is of five types:

And the proof is the saying of the Messenger of Allaah, may Allaah's praise and good mention be upon him, "The Prophet said, *"The signs of a hypocrite are three: Whenever he speaks, he tells a lie. Whenever he promises, he always breaks it (his promise). If you trust him, he proves to be dishonest. (If you keep something as a trust with him, he will not return it.)"* ("Saheeh al-Bukhaari", No. 33, and "Saheeh Muslim", No.59)

And in another narration, *"...Whenever he makes a covenant, he proves treacherous and whenever he quarrels, he behaves in a very imprudent, evil and insulting manner."* ("Saheeh al-Bukhaari".No. 34, "Saheeh Muslim", No. 58)

The Meaning of *at-Taaghoot* and the Foremost of its Categories

Know, may Allaah, the Most High have mercy upon you: Indeed the first thing that Allaah made obligatory upon the sons of Aadam was the disbelief in *at-taaghoot* and belief in Allaah.

The proof is the saying of the Most High, *And verily, We have sent among every Ummah (community, nation) a Messenger (proclaiming): "Worship Allaah (Alone), and avoid taaghoot (all false deities, i.e. do not worship anything besides Allaah).* –(Surat an-Nahl, from Ayat 36)

As for the description of disbelief in *at-taaghoot:* To believe that worship of anything other than Allaah is false, and to leave it, to dislike it, and to know that the ones who engage in it are disbelievers, and are enemies.

As for the meaning of belief in Allaah: To believe that Allaah is the only god worthy of worship, without anything other than Him being worthy of worship, and to make all acts of worship intended solely for Allaah alone, and to deny all that is worshipped other than Him, and to love the people of faith and devotion (*al-Ikhlaas*) and to have hatred for the people who associate others with Allaah and make them enemies.

This is the religion of Ibraaheem, and the one who turns away from it has shown himself to be devoid of good sense and judgment. And this is the example which Allaah informed us of in His saying, the Most High, *Indeed there has been an excellent example for you in Ibraaheem and those with him, when they said to their people: "Verily, we are free from you and whatever you worship besides Allaah, we have rejected you, and there has appeared between us and you, hostility and hatred for ever until you believe in Allaah Alone," – except the saying of Ibraaheem to his father: "Verily, I will ask forgiveness (from Allaah) for you, but I have no power to do anything for you before Allaah." "Our Lord! In You (Alone) we put our trust, and to You (Alone) we turn in repentance, and to You (Alone) is (our) final Return.* –(Surat al-Mumtahanah, Ayat 4)

And *at-taaghoot* is general: as everything which is worshipped other than Allaah, and is pleased with that worship, from that which is worshipped, followed, or obeyed with other than obedience to Allaah and His Messenger, may Allaah's praise and good mention be upon him; it is a *taaghoot.* And they are many, and the foremost of them are five:

The First: ash-Shaytaan, the one who calls to the worship of other than Allaah

The proof is the saying of the Most High, *Did I not command you, O Children of Aadam, that you should not worship Shaytaan? Verily, he is a plain enemy to you.* –(Surah YaaSeen, Ayat 60)

The Second: the unjust judge who alters the rulings of Allaah, the Most High

The proof is the saying of Allaah, the Most High, ❴ *Have you not seen those (hypocrites) who claim that they believe in that which has been sent down to you, and that which was sent down before you, and they wish to go for judgment (in their disputes) to the taaghoot (false judges) while they have been ordered to reject them. But Shaytaan wishes to lead them far astray.*❵ —(Surat an-Nisaa, Ayat 60)

The Third: The one who judges by other than that which Allaah revealed

The proof is the saying of Allaah, the Most High, ❴ *And whosoever does not judge by what Allaah has revealed, such are the Kaafiroon (disbelievers).* ❵ —(Surat al-Maa'idah, from Ayat 44)

The Fourth: The one who professes to have knowledge of the unseen other than Allaah

The proof is the saying of the Most High, ❴ *(He Alone is) the All-Knower of the Ghaib (Unseen), and He reveals to none His Ghaib (Unseen)."*

Except to a Messenger whom He has chosen (He informs him of the Unseen as much as He likes), and then He makes a band of watching guards (angels) to march before him and behind him. ❵ —(Surat al-Jin, Ayats 26-27)

And His, the Most High, saying, ❴ *And with Him are the keys of the Ghaib (all that is hidden), none knows them but He. And He knows whatever there is in the land and in the sea; not a leaf falls, but He knows it. There is not a grain in the darkness of the earth nor anything fresh or dry, but is written in a Clear Record.* ❵ —(Surat al-An'aam, Ayat 59)

The Fifth: The one who is worshipped other than Allaah and he is pleased with that worship

The proof is the saying of the Most High, ◈ **And if any of them should say: "Verily, I am an ilaah (a god) besides Him (Allaah)," such a one We should recompense with Hell. Thus We recompense the polytheists and wrong-doers.** ◈ –(Surat al-Anbiyaa, Ayat 59)

And know that mankind cannot become true Believers in Allaah without disbelieving in *at-taaghoot.*

The proof is the saying of the Most High, ◈ **There is no compulsion in religion. Verily, the Right Path has become distinct from the wrong path. Whoever disbelieves in taaghoot and believes in Allaah, then he has grasped the most trustworthy handhold that will never break. And Allaah is All-Hearer, All-Knower.** ◈ –(Surat al-Baqarah, Ayat 256)

ar-rushd (the right path): the religion of Muhammad, may Allaah's praise and good mention be upon him.

al-ghay (the wrong path): the religion of Abee Jahl

al-'urwat al-wuthqa: (the trustworthy handhold that will never break): to testify that there is none worthy of worship except for Allaah.

And this includes negation and affirmation. The negation of every category of worship to other than Allaah, the Most High, and affirmation of every aspect of worship, all of them, to Allaah alone, without associating any partners with Him.

All praise is due to Allaah, by whose blessing good deeds are completed.

LESSON ONE

What is 'aqeedah?

Simply put, *'aqeedah* is beliefs. It is the system of belief which should guide the life of every Muslim and Muslimah. The correct *'aqeedah* is found in the Qur'aan, the Sunnah of the Messenger of Allaah, may Allaah's praise and salutations be upon him and his household, based upon the understanding of the Companions and the Pious Predecessors who came after him, may Allaah's praise and salutations be upon him and his household. This is the creed of *ahl-us-sunnah wa al-jamaa'ah*, or those who have always followed the Prophet, may Allah's praise and salutations be upon him, adhered to the way of his noble Companions, as well as the succeeding generation who learned Islaam from the Companions, and that third generation who learned Islaam from those who had themselves learned from the Companions, and so are described as Salafis. This is vitally important for every Muslim to understand, as the calls to other beliefs and methodologies that differ from their clear way abound. It is clear that in order to follow the correct beliefs, one must look to the source of those beliefs; anyone who comes after them and claims to have a better understanding or insight into what has been revealed is calling to a false ideology.

al-Haafidh ibn Katheer mentions in his *tafseer* of the Qur'aan the explanation of the verse regarding the one who leaves the way of the first believers, which is found in Surat an-Nisaa:

❦ *And whoever contradicts and opposes the Messenger after the right path has been shown clearly to him, and follows other than the believers' way, We shall keep him in the path he has chosen, and burn him in Hell; what an evil destination!* ❧ –(Surah an-Nisaa, Ayat 115)

❦ *And whoever contradicts and opposes the Messenger after the right path has been shown clearly to him.* ❧ *This refers to whoever intentionally takes a path other than the path of the Law revealed to the Messenger after the truth has been made clear, apparent and plain to him.*

Allaah's statement, ❦ *...and follows other than the believers' way...* ❧ *refers to a type of conduct that is closely related to contradicting the Messenger. This contradiction could be in the form of contradicting a text (from the Qur'aan or Sunnah) or contradicting what the ummah of Muhammad has agreed upon. The ummah of Muhammad is immune from error when they all agree on something, a miracle that serves to increase their honor, due to the greatness of their Prophet. There are many authentic ahadeeth on this subject.*

Allaah warned against the evil of contradicting the Prophet and his ummah, when He said, ❦ *We shall keep him in the path he has chosen, and burn him in Hell --- what an evil destination!* ❧ *meaning, when one goes on this wicked path, We will punish him by making the evil path appear good in his heart, and will beautify it for him so that he is tempted further."* [End of translation from *"Tafseer Ibn-Katheer"*]

34

The Messenger of Allaah, praise and salutations be upon him and his family, made clear the importance of sticking to his guidance and that of the rightly guided predecessors in the following authentic hadeeth, on the authority of al-Irbaad ibn Saaryah who said: *{ Allaah's Messenger, may Allaah's praise and His salutations be upon him, gave us an admonition which caused our eyes to shed tears and the hearts to fear, so we said, "O Messenger of Allaah, may Allaah's praise and salutations be upon him, this is as if it were a farewell sermon, so with what do you counsel us?"*

So he, may Allaah's praise and His salutations be upon him, said, "I have left you upon clear guidance, its night is like its day, no one deviates from it except one who is destroyed, and whoever lives for some time from amongst you will see great differing. So stick to what you know from my Sunnah and the Sunnah of the rightly guided caliphs. Cling to that with your molar teeth, and stick to obedience even if it is to an Abyssinian slave since the believer is like the submissive camel; wherever he is led, he follows. }

(An authentic hadeeth found in *"Sunan Abu Dawud"* 4607, *"Sunan Ibn Majah"* 43,44, *"Sunan at-Tirmidhee"* 2676, *"al-Musnad"* of Imaam Ahmad vol. 4/126 and other collections)

The scholar Abu Shaamah said,

> *"The order to adhere to the Jamaa'ah means adhering to the truth and its followers; even if those who adhere to the truth are few and those who oppose it are many; since the truth is that which the first Jamaa'ah from the time of the Prophet and his Companions, may Allaah be pleased with them, were upon. No attention is given to the great number of the people of futility coming after them."* ("al-Baa'ith 'alaa Ahl-Bida'h wal-Huwaadith", Page 19).

And a last word on the subject from Imaam Barbahaaree, may Allaah have mercy upon him:

> *"May Allaah have mercy upon you. Know that the Religion is what came from Allaah, the Blessed and Most High. It is not something left to the intellect and opinions of men. Knowledge is that which comes from Allaah and His Messenger, so do not follow anything based upon your desires and so deviate away from the Religion and leave Islaam. There will be no excuse for you since Allaah's Messenger explained the Sunnah to his ummah and made it clear to his Companions and they are the Jamaa'ah, and they are the Main Body (as-Sawaad ul-A'dham), and the Main Body is the truth and its followers."*

And he said:

> *"The ummah approached ruin in a number of ways, and some disbelieved in a number of ways, became heretical in a number of ways, went astray in a number of ways and innovated in a number of ways, except for those who remained firm upon the sayings of the Messenger of Allaah, praise and salutations be upon him, what he was upon and what his Companions were upon, not declaring any of them to be in error, nor overstepping what they were upon.*

> *He finds sufficiency in what they sufficed with, he does not turn away from their way and position, and he knows that they were upon correct Islaam and correct Faith; so*

35

he follows them in his religion and finds calmness and knows that the religion lies in following. Those who are meant to be followed are the Companions of Muhammad, praise and salutations be upon him."

And he, may Allaah have mercy upon him, said:

"He who limits himself to the Sunnah of the Messenger of Allaah, praise and good mention be upon him, and that which his Companions and the Jamaa'ah were upon is successful and triumphs over all the people of innovation and is saved, and his religion is preserved, if Allaah wills, since the Messenger of Allaah, praise and salutations be upon him) said, "My ummah will split..." and the Messenger of Allaah, praise and salutations be upon him, told us which would be the saved sect, saying, "That which I and my Companions are upon". This is the cure, the explanation, the clear affair and the straight and distinct road."

(End of translation from Imaam Barbahaaree)

For a more complete discussion on seeking knowledge and the correct methodology, see my article on the 'Female Students of Knowledge' at www.taalib.com.

Why do we have to study 'aqeedah?

Sheikh Saalih ibn Fauzaan ibn 'Abdullah al-Fauzaan, may Allaah preserve him, answered this question beautifully when he answered this question on *'aqeedah*:

Question: Why are many of the Muslims concerned with the knowledge of *'aqeedah*, and what is the meaning of *al-'aqeedah*, and *al-eemaan* (faith), and *at-tawheed* (oneness of Allaah, worshipping Him alone)? Is there a difference between these expressions? What is your opinion concerning the one who says: Some of the matters of *al-'aqeedah* and its position are already finished and passed in our time, and consequently do not open public classes in it?

Answer: *"The successful ones from the Muslims are concerned with the knowledge of 'aqeedah, following the examples of the messengers, may Allaah's praise and salutations be upon all of them. Considering that they began their call with correcting the 'aqeedah; because it is the foundation upon which the actions proceed. If the 'aqeedah is correct, then the legislated actions are correct, and that which is not based upon correct 'aqeedah, then the action will not be correct.*

Allaah, the Most High, says, ❧ **And indeed it has been revealed to you (O Muhammad), as it was to those (Allaah's Messengers) before you: "If you join others in worship with Allaah, (then) surely, (all) your deeds will be in vain, and you will certainly be among the losers."** ❧ –(Surah az-Zamr, Ayat 65)

And He, the Most High, says, ◈ But if they had joined in worship others with Allaah, all that they used to do would have been of no benefit to them. ◈ – (Surat al-An'aam, From Ayat 88)

And what is meant by al-aqeedah, al-eemaan, and at-tawheed is the same thing, as all of them are actions of the heart. And al-eemaan is increased by connecting along with that- that is to say, its form as a belief in the heart- in that it also comprises the saying of the tongue, and the action of the limbs.

All of the matters of al-'aqeedah and its position are undoubtedly from that which must be understood, and that which the people must concern themselves with in every time and place. Acting upon them never ends until the Hour comes. The one who says that the matters of 'aqeedah and that which it encompasses end at a certain time- he does not fall outside of one of two cases (i.e. he falls into one of these two categories):

Either he is ignorant and does not understand the position of al-'aqeedah and its importance

Or he has a deficiency in his 'aqeedah, and he wants to cover this deficiency so that it not be uncovered.

Like the ones who say: Abstain from speaking about matters of tawheed al-uloohiyyah (tawheed of worship), because this causes a difference between the Muslims. Be content with speech concerning tawheed ar-ruboobiyyah (tawheed of Lordship) and confirming the existence of Allaah, They repulse the atheist and the communists, while not opposing the worshippers of the graves and the tombs!!

And like the ones who say: Abstain from speaking about the confirmation of the names and attributes of Allaah, and refrain from refuting the one who opposes them by negating them or interpreting them…and other than that.

All of this speech is false; it is necessary to expose its falsity and clarify its significance, and uncover its false content and that which it implies about the evil of the ideology! And the Messenger, may Allaah's praise and salutations be upon him, came to the people with the clear explanation of al-'aqeedah, and a clear explanation of that which corrupts it, before everything. And many of the verses of the Qur'aan and its chapters are concerned with clarifying this matter and the obligation of clarifying it for the people. So do they want from us that we leave the Qur'aan and that which is with it explaining al-'aqeedah?"

("al-Muntaqa", from fatawa of the esteemed Sheikh Saalih al-Fauzaan, from Volume 1, Page 301)

Sheikh Fauzaan, may Allaah preserve him, also said, when asked about what it is obligatory that a Muslim understand about his religion, concerning belief and legislation:

"It is obligatory upon the Muslim to understand all of the matters of his religion, both of belief and that which is legislated. With that he learns the matters of al-'aqeedah, and that which it makes obligatory, and that which is opposite to it, and that which completes it, and that which makes it deficient, until his 'aqeedah is the correct, sound 'aqeedah. And it is likewise obligatory upon him to learn the rulings of his religion concerning actions, until he performs that which Allaah has made obligatory upon him, and leaves that which Allaah has made forbidden for him, with insight.

Allaah, the Most High, says, ❨ **So know (O Muhammad) that La ilaaha illallaah (none has the right to be worshipped but Allaah), and ask forgiveness for your sin, and also for (the sin of) believing men and believing women.** ❩ – (Surah Muhammad, From Ayat 19)

So He begins with knowledge, before the speech and the action.

It is necessary that from the knowledge comes the action, as knowledge without action is not sufficient, even if it hated by the one who does it, and it is a proof upon the people. And the action without the knowledge is not correct, because it is going astray. And Allaah has commanded us to ask protection from the way of those who incur His anger, and those who are astray at the end of Surat al-Faatihah in every rak'at in our Salaat."

("al-Muntaqa", from *fatawa* of the Esteemed Sheikh Saalih al-Fauzaan, Vol. 1, Page 310)

Having the correct *'aqeedah* allows us to put things in perspective. In Western thought and ideology, the center of all things is the self- "me". Everything else revolves around that…family, job, religion, household…everything is based on self, and what that self desires. In Islaam, we must know that we were put upon this Earth for one thing, and one thing only- the worship of Allaah. Allaah, the Most High, says, ❨ **I did not create the jinn and mankind except to worship Me** ❩ –(Surat adh-Dhaariyaat, Ayat 56) And He has given us the *halal* (that which is permissible) and *haram* (that which Allaah has forbidden), defining the borders of our actions in this life, while clearly explaining the rewards and punishments that await us in the next life. So, the correct way to look at our lives, is with Allaah at the center, and ourselves and all that we do and plan and want seen in relationship to Him. We should be surrounded by Islaam, engulfed in it- it should not be just a segment of our lives, put to one side until it is wanted.

So you see, Islaam is the roadmap for our lives. Allaah has already decreed our state in life, and knows how we will end…and in His infinite mercy He has given us Islaam as a guidebook for every situation we face, every decision we have to make. And al-'aqeedah? 'Aqeedah is the key to that map. If we understand our 'aqeedah and live by it, then the map will be clear and easy to follow. If we do not, we will be like the one who was given a lamp to guide him in the darkness, and blew it out, deciding to find his own way through the hazards of the night.

Who is Sheikh Muhammad ibn 'Abdul Wahaab?

It is always beneficial to learn about the lives of the pious people, the scholars, the judges, the carriers of the banner of Islaam throughout history and in our time. We gain respect and love for these people through knowing more about them, insh'Allaah. They are an inspiration for us, and an encouragement, and excellent examples for us to follow. We should share their stories with our children, so that they, too, can benefit from knowing about these great men and women through the history of Islaam.

As for Sheikh Muhammad ibn 'Abdul Wahaab, *rahimahu Allaah*: His full name was Muhammad ibn 'Abdul Wahaab ibn Sulaymaan ibn 'Alee ibn Muhammad ibn Ahmad ibn Raashid ibn Burayd ibn Muhammad ibn Mushrif ibn 'Umar, of a branch of the tribe of Tameem

He was born in 'Uyaynah (also at times listed as 'Unayzah), in Saudi Arabia, in 1115 H, which corresponds to 1703 C.E.. Both his grandfather and father were scholars, and his father was also a judge. The sheikh memorized the totality of the Qur'aan by the age of ten, as well as eventually memorizing books from every branch of knowledge, including Islamic jurisprudence, hadeeth studies, and Qur'aanic explanation, or *tafseer*.

He travelled throughout Najd seeking knowledge, studying in Makkah and Madinah with the scholars there. From among his teachers are Sheikh 'Abdullah ibn Ibraaheem ash-Shammaree and his son, and Muhammad Hayat as-Sindee, a scholar of hadeeth. He was known to memorize and record any points of benefit he came across in his studies, and he devoted most of his time to his studies. He eventually went to Basrah, where his knowledge and wisdom became well known. He called to the principles set down in the Qur'aan and called to by the Prophet, Muhammad, may Allaah's praise and salutations be upon him and his family- he called to *at-tawheed* and took a firm stance against the Sufism and paganism that the Hijaaz was steeped in at that time. He took a firm stance against all innovations, and gained many students and followers. Outsiders referred to his followers as *Wahaabis*, a derogatory term still in use today. They made it clear, though, that they were Muslims, only, *Muwahideen*- those who worship Allaah alone without any partners. When his prestige grew to greater heights, he was banished from Basrah.

He went and lived in Hasa, then to Huraimila, where his father lived. When his father died, Sheikh Muhammad may have become a judge there. At any rate, he alienated many powerful people by telling them to leave their sinful practices. At last some of these people attacked his home, only to be driven off by his neighbors. Sheikh Muhammad ibn 'Abdul Wahaab then went back to 'Uyaynah, where he had been born and raised.

In 'Uyaynah, he gained as a student the ruler, 'Uthmaan ibn Hamad. With his support, they leveled graves, and tore down trees that had become idols, and destroyed tombs that people worshipped at. At one point he destroyed a large and much visited tomb himself. The people were sure the Sheikh would be destroyed- when he appeared the next day, healthy and whole, many more people followed him and his call to *at-tawheed*. Eventually, though, many people turned against him when he ordered an adulteress who would not take back her confession to be stoned. The people thought the act barbaric, and a powerful supplier of food and merchandise to the city called for the death of the Sheikh. 'Uthmaan was afraid to lose this man's support, and so banished Sheikh Muhammad ibn 'Abdul Wahaab from his home.

The Sheikh went to Diriya, where the house of Sa'ud was in charge. The leader at that time was Muhammad ibn Sa'ud. He settled there in 1744 or 1745. He again began to gather students around him, and people who wanted to follow Islaam as it was meant to be followed, and turn away from the false practices that so many were engaging in. Two of Muhammad ibn Sa'ud's brothers, along with his wife, called for the ruler to extend his protection to the Sheikh. He put down two conditions: one, that the Sheikh stay in Diriya, and the second, that he not oppose a tax that ran against the Islamic *Shari'ah*, or legislation. Sheikh Muhammad ibn 'Abdul Wahaab agreed the first; he did NOT agree to the second. Muhammad ibn Sa'ud gave him his protection, and became a staunch supporter. He, and his son 'Abdul 'Azeez, and grandson, Sa'ud, supported and assisted the Sheikh through the rest of his life, as they strove to bring the message of *at-tawheed* to the whole of the Hijaaz, with great success, by the grace and mercy of Allaah.

Sheikh Muhammad ibn 'Abdul Wahaab was a prolific writer, following in the footsteps of another great reviver of the religion, Sheikh al-Islaam ibn Taymiyyah, and his student Ibn Qayyim al-Jawziyyaah, may Allaah have mercy upon them all. He published many works, the most famous of which are probably *"Kitaab at-Tawheed","* *Usool ath-Thalaathah"*, *"Usool as-Sittah"*, *"Kashf ash-Shubahaat"*, and *"Qawa'id al-Arba"*. Insh'Allaah we will be studying many of his works in this and other series of classes, as they are of great benefit to any Muslim or Muslimah who is striving to understand the correct beliefs of Islaam and to live by them.

The Meaning of "al-Waajibaat"

The first book in our series is actually a compilation by Sheikh 'Abdullaah ibn Ibraaheem al-Qar'awi, of some of the great points of benefit from various books by Sheikh Muhammad ibn 'Abdul Wahaab. It is titled "al-Waajibaat" - its whole title translates as, "What it is Decreed that Every Male and Female Muslim must have Knowledge of" The key word is "must".

Waajib, in Arabic, means obligatory. In Islaam, all actions can be broken down into five categories: *waajib, mustahab, mubah, makrooh, and haraam.*

Waajib: if an act is *waajib*, it is obligatory that the Muslim carry it out. He will be punished if he does not perform it, and rewarded for performing it. One example would be the five daily prayers.

Mustahab: These acts are recommended. They are pleasing to Allaah, and the doer will be rewarded if he does them. He will not, however, be punished if he does not do them. An example of this is would be the night prayers.

Mubah: These are neutral acts…the doer is neither rewarded nor punished for doing them; for example, choosing to eat from that which is *halal* for us, such as to choose either chicken or beef for a meal.

Makrooh: These acts are disliked. It is something that does not please Allaah, but there is no specific punishment set aside for it. An example would be drinking while standing up or wearing one shoe, or unnecessary movement in the *salaat*.

Haraam: These are the forbidden acts. If one does them, he is punished by Allaah, and if he leaves them, he is rewarded for obedience to Allaah. An example would be to drink alcohol, or to tell a lie.

This book lays out many of the beliefs that it is obligatory that the Muslim understand and act upon. It is divided into small, easy to understand sections, which make it ideal for the beginning student of *'aqeedah*. Insh'Allaah, we will begin with the text of the book in our next class.

NOTES

Key Terms in this Lesson

Define these terms:

'aqeedah:

al-eemaan

at-tawheed:

waajib:

mustahab:

mubah:

makrooh:

haraam:

Lesson Questions

Level 1: [required]

1. What is 'aqeedah?
2. What is the ruling on learning correct 'aqeedah?
3. Where was Sheikh Muhammad ibn 'Abdul Wahaab born?
4. What did he call to?
5. List the five categories that all actions fall into, and briefly describe them.

Level 2: [supplementary]

1. How does 'aqeedah help a Muslim in everyday life?
2. Why is a sound 'aqeedah so important?
3. Why was it clearly a blessing from Allaah that Sheikh Muhammad ibn 'Abdul Wahaab was so successful in his call?
4. Give an example of each type of the five categories of actions
5. Briefly explain the sources for learning the correct 'aqeedah, and the importance of taking them as our guides

LESSON TWO

> *Bismillaah ir Rahman ir Raheem*

Explanation: Beginning the book with the *Basmalah* is following that which Allaah, the Most High, does in the Qur'aan, as the Qur'aan begins with *al-Fatihah*, and *al-Fatihah* begins with the *Basmalah*.

It is *Mustahab* to begin a book with the *Basmalah*, as it was the practice of the Messenger of Allaah, may Allaah's praise and salutations be upon him and his family, to do so when writing letters.

As for the well-known hadeeth of Abee Hurairah, may Allaah be pleased with him, that says, "Every important matter which is not begun with the name of Allaah is devoid of good." Then know that Sheikh al-Albaani, may Allaah have mercy upon him, has declared it to be weak, as it is related to az-Zuhri as *mursal*, meaning that there is a gap between him, a *tabi'* (a person from the generation after the Companions) and the Prophet, may Allaah's praise and salutations be upon him and his family- and that which is related on az-Zuhri in a *mursal* condition is generally not accepted.

And saying the *Basmalah* contains within it that which is not spoken, which completes the meaning. This unspoken part is a specific verb, as in, "In the name of Allaah, I write", or, "In the name of Allaah I read." Sheikh al-Utheimeen, may Allaah have mercy upon him, says in his explanation of *"Usool ath-Thalaathah"*, that the verb comes after the name of Allaah, for two reasons:

1. To seek blessing by beginning with the name of Allaah, the One Free from all Imperfections, the Most High

2. That this is a way of expressing the fact that this is the only cause for the writing

All of the facets of *at-tawheed* are found in the *Basmalah: Tawheed ar-Ruboobiyah, Tawheed al-Uloohiyah*, and *Tawheed al-Asmaa wa as-Safaat*. We are acknowledging Allaah's Lordship and His dominion and power over all things, we are making our act an act of worship by making our intention solely for Allaah alone, and we are calling upon Allaah by His names.

NOTES

The Three Fundamentals which it is Obligatory that all Male and Female Muslims Understand

Explanation: We discussed the meaning of *wajaba/yajibu/waajib* in the first lesson.

It is important to understand that these are not the *only* fundamentals that it is obligatory that a Muslim learn. Rather, they are the ones that the Sheikh, rahimahu Allaah, is focusing on in this writing. This is a well-known device used by the scholars to make the knowledge more understandable to the student. By doing this, the scholar shows us the relationship between these things and their relationship to the *deen* (religion) as a whole. For example, later in the text it states, "The Principles of the Religion and its Fundamentals Consist of Two Matters". This is another case where the Sheikh chose these two fundamental matters to explain in this way, so we see the relationship between them and their importance- it does not mean that there are not other matters that are considered principles of the religion.

In the title it is also stated clearly, "male and female Muslim." This is because in most matters, the men and the women have the same requirements. It is only in specific matters in which they differ, such as *jihaad*, inheritance, rulings regarding the menses, and their roles within the household and other matters. In most matters, such as *aqeedah*, and the general obligations of prayers and fasting, they are equal.

They are: That the servant knows his Lord, his religion, and his Prophet, Muhammad, may Allaah's praise and salutations be upon him.

Explanation:

Question: Where do these three principles come from?

Answer: Their foundation is the hadeeth of al-Baraa' ibn 'Aazib, which is found in the two Saheehs of Muslim and al-Bukhaari in shortened form, and in Ibn Abee 'Aasim and Ibn Abee Shaybah in their works. Sheikh Muqbil ibn Haadee al-Waadi'ee, may Allaah have mercy upon him, in his *"Saheeh al-Musnad"* mentions it in its longer form. It is narrated on Anas in *"Saheeh al-Bukhaari"*.

This hadeeth refers to the three principles each person will be asked about in his grave. After his burial, when the people have left him, two angels will come to him and make him sit up, and will ask him, "Who is your Lord?", "What is your religion?" and "Who is your Prophet?" The Believer will reply, "My Lord is Allaah, my religion is Islaam, and my Prophet is Muhammad." The one who doubts, or the hypocrite, will say, "Aaah, Aaah, I don't know. I heard the people saying something, so I said it also."

> If it is said to you: Who is your Lord? Then say: My Lord is Allaah, who has nurtured me and all of the creation with His blessings and beneficence. He is the only one I worship, there is nothing worthy of being worshipped other than Him.

Explanation: The word in the Arabic is "*rub*" which comes from the same root as "*tarbiyyah*" – nurturing, sustaining, educating. So we are acknowledging belief in *tawheed ar-ruboobiyyah*, which will be discussed in detail later, insh'Allaah.
"He is the only one I worship, there is nothing to be worshipped other than Him": This encompasses *tawheed al-uloohiyyah*, or *tawheed* in worship of Allaah alone.

Question: How do we learn about Allaah?

Answer: We learn about Him from His book, al-Qur'aan, and through His Prophet, may Allaah's praise and salutations be upon him and his household. We learn about Allaah through His signs, and that which He has created. We understand all of this in the way that it was understood by the Pious Predecessors, may Allaah have mercy upon them all. From the explanation of *"Usool ath-Thalathah"* by Sheikh 'Utheimeen, may Allaah have mercy upon him, regarding the Ayat (signs) of Allaah:

"Signs are that which indicate something and make it clear. Then the signs of Allaah, the Most High, are of two types: signs in creation, and signs in His Shari'ah, or revealed way. The signs in creation are those things which He created, and the signs in His Shari'ah are that which is found in His Revelation, which Allaah sent down to His Messengers... so whichever is the case, then knowledge of Allaah, the Mighty and Majestic, is arrived at through His signs in the creation, the magnificent things contained within it which are wondrous creations and clear proofs of perfect wisdom. Likewise, through the signs in His Shari'ah, and the justice to be seen in it and how it comprises all that is beneficial and repels all that is corrupt." (From *"Jaami' Sharooh al-Usool ath-Thalathah"* Page 220-221)

It is important to consider the creation of Allaah. The mountains, the rain, the cycles of life- through all of these things we can see His Wisdom and Perfection. Allaah says in the Qur'aan:

❨ *Indeed in the heavens and the earth, and the alternation of the night and the day there are clear signs for people of understanding.* ❩ –(Surat aal-'Imraan, Ayat

46

190)

And He, the Most High, says:

❝ *Indeed in the alternation of the day and the night, and in that which Allaah has created in the heavens and the earth there are clear signs for those who fear the punishment of Allaah.*❞ –(Surah Yoonus, Ayat 6)

And the verses concerning this are many, alhamdulillah.
There are also the signs of His legislation, the message that He sent down to all of the Messengers to teach the people. In this one sees Allaah's knowledge and infinite wisdom and mercy, alhamdulillah.

For example, look at the command of the *hijaab*. The purposes of the *hijaab* are many. From them are the protection of the woman, both her physical self and her modesty and honor. From them is the protection of the man's honor as well. From them is the protection and betterment of society, as there is much less opportunity for illegal sexual intercourse and children without fathers to claim them. The *hijaab* serves these purposes and many more. And you see with your own eyes what happens when the *hijaab* is corrupted or absent- immorality, a loosening in the relationships between women and strange men, and a general bringing down of society to a lower level, based on the whims and desires of the people.

Sheikh Fauzaan, may Allaah preserve him, said concerning the corruption of society:

"The man and the woman each cover their 'awraat with an abundant covering, because in that is that which preserves moral character. As for the immorality and nakedness, then they are causes for the corruption of the moral character, and loss of the safeguards, and the spreading of immorality." (From *"Beneficial Advice to the Muslim Woman"* by Sheikh Fauzaan, as quoted in, *"My Hijaab, My Path"* from our publications)

We see clearly the benefits of the *hijaab*, and see Allaah's wisdom at work in its legislation, alhamdulillah.

The third branch of *at-tawheed, tawheed adh-dhaat wa al-asmaa wa as-sifaat* (*tawheed* in Allaah's being, His names and His attributes- and that they apply to Him Alone in perfection), is the one this lesson will focus on, as truly one of the best ways to know who our Lord is, is to learn about Him from His Excellent names and perfect attributes.

Innovations and misunderstandings concerning the names and attributes of Allaah are many. Some of these are:

al-Jahmiyyah: The people of this sect believe that whoever describes Allaah with anything of what He has described Himself in His book or with anything His Messenger mentioned about him, is a disbeliever, and likens Allaah to His creation.

al-Mu'tazilah: They affirmed Allaah's most excellent names and denied the attributes that these names referred to.

al-'Asharees: They believe that one must interpret the attributes of Allaah beyond that which is clear from the texts. For example, they would say that His hand, means His power. They say that anything else is likening Allaah to His creation.

al-Baatiniyyah: This people do not affirm anything or deny anything from the names and attributes of Allaah.

The principles of *ahl-as-Sunnah wa al-Jama'ah* concerning the names and attributes of Allaah:

1. They affirm that which Allaah and His Messenger, may Allaah praise and salutations be upon him, affirmed concerning the names and attributes of Allaah, without distortion, interpretation, or negation
2. They believe that all the names and attributes of Allaah are most excellent, and all His attributes are perfect
3. The elevation of Allaah, the Blessed, the Exalted, above His attributes being likened to the attributes of His creation, and above any attribute of imperfection
   Allaah, the Most High, says, ❮ *There is nothing like unto Him, He is the All-Hearing, the All-Seeing* ❯ (Surat ash-Shuraa, Ayat 11)
4. The attributes are understood according to their clear and apparent meaning
5. General terms are used for negating (one of Allaah's attributes) while detail is used for affirming. (i.e. in the verse, ❮ *There is nothing like unto Him* ❯ –(Surat ash-Shuraa, Ayat 11)
6. *Al-waqf* in regards to the names and attributes of Allaah- that is, not naming Him by any name other than those He gave Himself or the Prophet, may Allaah's praise and salutations be upon him, named Him by, and not giving Him attributes that He did not give Himself or the Messenger, may Allaah's praise and salutations be upon him, did not describe Him with

7. Abandoning investigation into the reality of the Divine Essence and the attributes it necessitates. We see how the *Salaf as-Saalih* detested this question of "how" or "in what manner, in the *athar* of Imaam Maalik, may Allaah have mercy upon him, related in various forms by Abu Na'im in "*al-Hilyah*", by ad-Daarimee in "*ar-Rad 'ala al-Jahmiyyah*" and by al-Bayhaqee in "*al-Asmaa wa as-Sifaat*" and others: *A man came to Maalik ibn Anas and asked about the verse,* ❬ **ar-Rahmaan is over His Throne istaawa** ❭. *He asked, "How is that istaawa?" The narrator said, I saw him (Maalik) get angry like never before, due to his question and he started to sweat and he lowered down his head. The people waited for the reply, and when he had regained his composure, he said, "How it is, is not known. However, the istaawa is known, and eemaan in it is obligatory, and questioning concerning it is an innovation. Indeed I fear that you may be misguided." and he had him removed from the circle.*

8. Not committing heresy with respect to Allaah's names and attributes

Before continuing with the discussion on Allaah's names and attributes, another benefit from the narration of how Imaam Maalik dealt with the question of "How?" should be brought forth. We must look at how he dealt with his anger. He did not yell at or strike out at the questioner. Instead, he lowered his head and waited to speak until he had regained his composure. He then answered the man in a controlled, concise manner. This is in contrast to so many of the people, who, as soon as they are angry or upset, they explode, or "give the person a piece of their minds". Later in the course we will cover, insh'Allaah, how one of the signs of the hypocrite is that when he gets angry, he overreacts and responds in an evil manner. Look at the contrast of this, with the example of Imaam Maalik. Insh'Allaah we must all try to learn from his excellent example in our everyday lives.

We see also how Imaam Maalik followed that which Allaah commanded in His Book, concerning separating from the one who belies or denies Allaah's names. Allaah says in His book:

❬ *And (all) the Most Beautiful Names belong to Allaah, so call on Him by them, and leave the company of those who belie or deny (or utter impious speech against) His Names. They will be requited for what they used to do.* ❭ –(Surat al-A'raaf, Ayat 180) So Allaah says, ❬ *And (all) the Most Beautiful Names belong to Allaah, so call on Him by them...* ❭

There are several benefits mentioned by the scholars concerning understanding and knowing the names and attributes of Allaah. From them are:

1. Knowledge of the names and attributes of Allaah is the way to knowledge of Allaah
2. Purification and correction of the souls through the worship of the One, the Unique
3. Knowledge of His names and attributes is of the most excellent and virtuous types of knowledge
4. Knowledge of the names and attributes of Allaah is the root and origin of knowledge of everything other than Him
5. Increase of faith
6. The greatness of the reward for whoever memorizes and comprehends the names of Allaah
7. Exaltation and glorification of Allaah and supplication of Him with His names and attributes

By learning and understanding the names and attributes of Allaah, and using them to call upon Him, we increase in faith. If we know, for example, that Allaah is *ar-Rahman.* the Most Merciful, and that He bestows His Mercy as He wills, then this should give us calmness and a feeling of security in times of upheaval and stress in our lives. Likewise, if we remember that He is *ash-Shaafee,* the One who Heals, then this should help us through times of illness and illness in our family and friends.

There are many specific *du'a* (supplications) which use the names and attributes of Allaah in them. The student is urged to look these up in one of the excellent Arabic *du'a* books and memorize them- I am giving you the translation to make understanding easy, insh'Allaah, and get you started in learning them:

It is related from Abee Hurairah, may Allaah be pleased with him, that the Messenger of Allaah, may Allaah's praise and salutations be upon him, said, *{If anyone extols Allaah after every prayer thirty-three times, and praises Allaah thirty-three times, and declares His Greatness thirty-three times, ninety-nine times in all, and says to complete a hundred: "There is no god worthy of worship but Allaah, having no partner with Him, to Him belongs sovereignty and to Him is praise due, and He is Potent (Qadeer) over everything," his sins will be forgiven even If these are as abundant as the foam of the sea.}* ("Saheeh Muslim", No. 597)

It is related from 'Aishah, may Allaah be pleased with her, that the Messenger of Allaah, may Allaah's praise and salutations be upon him, when he would finish with his *salaat*, he would ask Allaah's forgiveness three times, and then say, *{Oh Allaah, you are as-Salaam, and from you is all peace, blessed are You, Oh Possessor of majesty and honor.}*

And from a hadeeth in "*Saheeh Muslim*", that the Prophet said, *{Oh Allaah, Lord of mankind, take away the severe sickness, and cure. You are the One Who Cures (ash-Shaafee); there is no cure except Your cure, a cure that leaves behind no sickness.}*

Key Terms in this Lesson

Define these terms:

basmalah:

usool:

du'a:

Lesson Questions:

Level 1: [required]

1. What is the ruling on beginning a book with the *basmalah*?

2. What are the three principles stated in the text that it is obligatory on every male and female Muslim to understand?

3. Where do these three principles come from?

4. What is the stance of *ahl-as-Sunnah wa al-Jama'ah* in regards to the names and attributes of Allaah?

5. What are the benefits of learning and understanding the names and attributes of Allaah?

Level 2: [supplementary]

1. Why does the Sheikh specify both male and female Muslims?

2. What are some of the ways that we can know about our Lord?

3. What are some of the deviations and innovations concerning the beliefs in Allaah's names and attributes?

4. List five names of Allaah in Arabic and English. You may want to use your translation of the Qur'aan for this. Memorize these names and understand their meanings so that you can use them in your *du'a*.

5. Is it permissible to ask about the "how" of Allaah's attributes? Why or why not? How do we understand His names and attributes?

LESSON THREE

> If it is said to you: What is your religion? Then say: My religion is al-Islaam, and it is to submit to Allaah Alone, with *at-tawheed*- joining none along with Him in worship, and complying with Him with obedience, and being free from associating others with Allaah and those who do so.

Explanation: *al-istislaam*: this means submission; in this case, submitting to the will and command of Allaah, alone.

bi at-tawheed: That is to say, submitting to Allaah alone, with *at-tawheed*- that is, joining none along with him in worship. Later in the course, we will discuss the categories of *ash-shirk*, which is associating others along with Allaah in worship, insh'Allaah.

al-inqiyaad lahu: compliance, yielding, submitting to Him, that is, to Allaah alone. This is a willing compliance, done to seek the pleasure of Allaah, alone.

bi at-taa'a: with obedience- we obediently comply with the boundaries and legislation that Allaah has set forth for us, alhamdulillah.

wa al-baraa': disassociation; separating and freeing oneself from something. The opposite of this is *al-walaa'*.

min ash-shirk wa ahlihi: from *ash-shirk*, associating others with Allaah, and its people.

Submission to Allaah Alone, with *at-Tawheed*

In this we see the reality of being the *ghuraba*, the strangers.

It is related in *"Saheeh Muslim"* on Abee Hurairah, as well as with the same meaning in other sources on 'Abdullah ibn 'Amr al 'Aas and 'Abdullah ibn Mas'ood, may Allaah be pleased with all of them, that the Prophet, may Allaah's praise and salutations be upon him and his family, said, *{ Islaam began as something strange, and it will end as it came, and tooba is for the strangers. }* (*tooba* has been explained as a tree in Paradise, and Allaah knows best) In the narration on Ibn Mas'ood, which is authentic through support from other narrations, they ask him, may Allaah's praise and salutations be upon him, *{ Who are the strangers, Oh Messenger of Allaah?" He, may Allaah's praise and salutations be upon him and his family, said, "Those who remain upright around the corruption of the people. }*

The one who submits to Allaah in all things, is truly a stranger in this life, where the normal thing for the people is to follow their whims and their desires. Submission is a strong word, mash'Allaah, implying complete obedience and humility. Submission can be difficult for a person, but the rewards are well defined in the Qur'aan, alhamdulillah. Submitting with love, and certainty, and purity of intention, and the other conditions of *ash-shahadah*, can lead us to increase in faith, and brings us contentment, insha'Allaah. And the success is truly from Allaah alone.

Complying with Allaah with Obedience

{ Adhere to obedience, even if it be to an Ethiopian slave, for the believer is but like the camel's nose, wherever you point it he goes. } (Recorded by ibn Maajah, Ahmad, al-Haakim, and others. It was graded authentic by Sheikh al-Albaani in *"Saheeh al-Jaami'"*, no. 4369)

The meaning of this hadeeth, and Allaah knows best, is the believer must yield obediently to Allaah, and be led by that which He has set forth in His book, and that which the Messenger of Allaah, may Allaah's praise and salutations be upon him and his family, was sent with and set forth for us as an example. It is not for the true believer to come up with his own path that he thinks will lead to goodness or salvation. Rather, he is to follow the guidance of Allaah in all matters. Islaam is a complete religion, alhamdulillah, a complete way of life, and we can find guidance for anything that occurs to us in life within it, alhamdulillah.

The scholars have said that an act of worship will only count as a righteous or accepted action when two conditions are fulfilled. They are:

1. Purity of intention- it is being done for the pleasure of Allaah

2. Following the Qur'aan and the Sunnah of the Messenger of Allaah, may Allaah's praise and good mention be upon him, in that act. It must remain within the limits of that which has been revealed and legislated.

Sheikh 'Utheimeen, may Allaah have mercy upon him, mentioned six conditions that an action must fulfill in order for it to conform to the *Shari'ah*, or Islamic legislation, in his treatise concerning innovation:

1. The action must be done for the correct reason. If a person were to worship Allaah, trying to get closer to him with a reason that is not from the guidance of Islaam, then his worship would be an innovation which is to be thrown back upon his face. (An example of this is celebrating the birthday of the Prophet, may Allaah's praise and good mention be upon him)

2. The action must be done with the correct type of material or accessory that is associated with that action. (The Sheikh uses as an example, the sacrificing of a horse rather than the types of animals that it is legislated to sacrifice)

3. The amount of the action must be correct. (For example, making the *maghrib* prayer four *raka'at* instead of the legislated three)

4. The action must be done in the correct form or manner. (The sheikh brings forth the example of the one who makes *wudhoo* for *as-salaat* in an order other than that which has been legislated)

5. The action must be done at the right time. (The sheikh brings the example of someone making the sacrifice for the *hajj* during the first few days of *Dhul-*

Hijjah)

6. The action must be done in the correct place. (The sheikh brings the example of someone making *I'tikaaf* for the last ten days of *Ramadhaan* in his house, rather than in the *masjid*)

For an excellent example of how the companions of the Messenger of Allaah, dealt with this, look at that which 'Amr ibn Salmah said:

"We used to sit by the door of 'Abdullah ibn Mas'ood before the morning prayer, so that when he came out we would walk with him to the mosque. One day Abu Moosaa al-Ash'aree came to us and said, "Has Abu 'AbdurRahmaan come out yet?" We replied, "No." So he sat down with us until he came out. When he came out, we all stood along with him, so Abu Moosaa said to him, "O Abu 'AbdurRahmaan! I have just seen something in the masjid which I deemed to be evil, but all praise is for Allaah, I did not see anything except good." He inquired, "Then what is it?" (Abu Moosaa) replied, "If you live you will see it. I saw in the masjid people sitting in circles awaiting the prayer. In each circle they had pebbles in their hands and a man would say 'repeat Allaahu Akbar a hundred times.' So they would repeat it a hundred times. Then he would say, 'say Laa ilaaha illallaah a hundred times.' So they would say it a hundred times. Then he would say, 'say Subhaanallaah a hundred times.' So they would say it a hundred times." (Ibn Mas'ood) asked, "What did you say to them?" (Abu Moosaa) said, "I did not say anything to them. Instead I waited to hear your view or what you declared." (Ibn Mas'ood) replied, "Would that you had ordered them to count up the evil deeds they acquired and assured them that their good deeds would not be lost!" Then we went along with him (Ibn Mas'ood) until he came to one of these circles and stood and said, "What is this which I see you doing?" They replied, "O Abu 'AbdurRahmaan! These are pebbles upon which we are counting takbeer, tahleel and tasbeeh." He said, "Count up your evil deeds. I assure you that none of your good deeds will be lost. Woe to you, O ummah of Muhammad, praise and salutations be upon him! How quickly you go to destruction! These are the Companions of your Prophet and they are widespread. There are his clothes which have not yet decayed and his bowl which is unbroken. By Him in Whose Hand is my soul! Either you are upon a religion better guided than the Religion of Muhammad, praise and salutations be upon him, or you are opening the door of misguidance." They said, "O Abu 'AbdurRahmaan! By Allaah, we only intended good." He said, "How many there are who intend good but do not achieve it. Indeed Allaah's Messenger said to us, "A people will recite the Qur'aan but it will not pass beyond their throats." By Allaah! I do not know, perhaps most of them are from you." Then he left them.

Umar ibn Salmah (the sub-narrator) said: We saw most of those people fighting against us on the day of Nahrawaan, along with the Khawaarij."

(ad-Daarimee in his *"Sunan"*: 1/79 Authenticated by Sheikh Saleem al-Hilaalee)

The great scholar, Ibn Qayyim, said, *"al-Islaam is tawheed Allaah (belief in the Oneness of Allaah) and worshipping Him alone without associating any partners with Him, and belief in His Messenger, and following him in that which he came with."* (*"Fatawa al-*

A'imat an-Najdiyyah", Vol. 1, Page 94)

So we see that if we intend good, and we want our actions to be correct, we have to follow that which is put forth in the Qur'aan and the Sunnah of the Messenger of Allaah, may Allaah's praise and salutations be upon him, upon the way of the first generations.

Separation from ash-Shirk and its People

One of the best examples of this is Prophet Ibraaheem, may Allaah's praise and salutations be upon him. Allaah says in the Qur'aan,

❴ *Indeed there has been an excellent example for you in Ibraaheem and those with him, when they said to their people: "Verily, we are free from you and whatever you worship besides Allaah, we have rejected you, and there has appeared between us and you, hostility and hatred for ever until you believe in Allaah Alone"; except the saying of Ibraaheem to his father: "Verily, I will ask forgiveness (from Allaah) for you, but I have no power to do anything for you before Allaah." "Our Lord! In You (Alone) we put our trust, and to You (Alone) we turn in repentance, and to You (Alone) is (our) final Return.* ❵ –(Surat al-Mumtahinah, Ayat 4)

This means removing yourself from *ash-shirk* and those who are infected by it as much as possible. This is a protection for us from their evil, and from sitting in the evil sitting, and it sets us apart from them, alhamdulillah. This will be discussed in more detail in a later lesson, insh'Allaah.

Conversely, we should have *al-walaa* with the Muslims. This is the opposite of *al-baraa*, and it means to associate and have allegiance with them and support them in good. There are many ways to do this, all with a basis in the Qur'aan and Sunnah and the practices of the *Salaf as-Saalih*, alhamdulillah. For example, the rights of the neighbor are well defined in Islaam. If we abide by these rights and do our best to fulfill them, then we will, insh'Allaah, have good relations with our neighbors. If we have a choice to buy from an upright Muslim, then perhaps we should buy from him, rather than from someone else simply because they are a little closer to us or a little cheaper. We should support our fellow Muslims in every form of good, and help them in righteousness. And Allaah knows best.

The Conditions for Islaam to be Correct and Accepted

Sheikh Muhammad ibn 'Abdul Wahaab, may Allaah have mercy upon him, said, in his book, *"ad-Durur as-Sunniyyah"*, Vol. 10, Pages 87 and 88:

Know, may Allaah have mercy upon you: Verily the religion of Islaam is upon the heart with belief, with love and hatred (for the sake of Allaah). And it is upon the tongue by the pronunciation and leaving off speaking the speech of disbelief. And it is upon the limbs through performing the pillars of Islaam, and leaving the actions of disbelief. If one leaves one of these three, then he has committed disbelief (kufr) and apostated... and it is the meaning of the saying of Allaah, the Most High, **"Whoever disbelieved in Allaah after his belief, except him who is forced thereto and whose heart is at rest with Faith; but such as open their breasts to disbelief, on them is wrath from Allaah, and theirs will be a great torment."**

Up until His saying, ﴾ **That is because they loved and preferred the life of this world over that of the Hereafter. And Allaah guides not the people who disbelieve.** ﴿ *—(Surat an-Nahl, Ayats 106-107) And the one who understands this, understands the danger, the great, extreme danger, and understands the strength of the necessity of learning and remembering and contemplating. .."* (From *"Fataawa al-A'imat an-Najdiyyah"*, Vol. 1, Pages 87-88)

The Difference between Disbelief and al-Islaam

Fatwa Number 10,684 of the Permanent Committee of Major Scholars, as found in *"Fataawa al-Lajnat ad-Daa'imah lilbahooth al-'Ilmiyah wa al-iftaa'"*, Vol. 2, Numbers 45 and 46

Question: What is the boundary that separates disbelief from Islaam, and does the one who pronounces the *shahaadatain* (there is no god worthy of worship except Allaah, and Muhammad is the Messenger of Allaah), then puts forth actions which are in opposition to them, enter into the ranks of the Muslims in spite of (the deficiencies in) his prayers and his life?

Answer: *"All praise is due to Allaah alone, and may His praise and salutations be upon His Messenger, his family, and his companions...to proceed:*

The boundary between disbelief and Islaam is the pronunciation of the shahaadatain with truthfulness and sincerity while he makes that a reality in his life- then he is a Muslim, a true believer. As for the hypocrite, then he is not truthful, and is not sincere and he is not a believer. And likewise the one who pronounces them and enters into that which nullifies them from ash-shirk. For example, the one who calls on the dead for help in times of hardship or ease, and the one who prefers the ruling by the laws of the establishment over ruling by that which Allaah, the Most High, revealed, and the one who makes fun of the Qur'aan or that which is established in the Sunnah of the Messenger of Allaah, may Allaah's praise and salutations be upon him- then this is a disbeliever, even though he says the shahaadatain and prays and fasts.

And with Allaah is success, and may Allaah's praise and salutations be upon His Prophet, Muhammad, his family, and his companions."

(End of their ruling)

Key Terms in this Lesson

Define these terms:

al-inqiyaad:
at-taa'a:
ash-shirk
al-baraa':

Lesson Questions

Level 1: [required]

1. What is the religious definition of *al-Islaam*?

2. What are the two conditions put forth by the scholars for an act to be considered a righteous action?

3. How did ibn Qayyim, may Allaah have mercy upon him, define *al-Islaam*?

4. Why is Ibraaheem a good example for us concerning *al-baraa'* from *ash-shirk* and its people?

5. What is a main difference between a believer and a disbeliever?

Level 2: [supplementary]

1. Why is the one who submits totally to Allaah alone considered one of the *ghuraba* (the strangers)?

2. Why did Ibn Mas'ood chastise the ones who were making *dhikr* in the *masjid* collectively with the stones?

3. A man wants to please Allaah so he decides to wear *hijaab*. Will his act be accepted? Why or why not?

4. A woman wants to please Allaah so she swears that she will live a life of austerity. She wears old clothes and eats only old rice and regularly prays an extra prayer after *'Asr*. She does not consult her husband about this. Will her action be accepted? Why or why not?

5. Explain how *al-Islaam* is a matter of the heart, the tongue, and the limbs.

LESSON FOUR

> If it is said to you: Who is your Prophet? Then say: Muhammad ibn 'Abdullah ibn 'Abdal-Mutalab ibn Haashim; and Haashim is from the tribe of Quraish, and Quraish is from the Arabs, and the Arabs are from the descendents of Ismaa'eel ibn Ibraaheem, upon them both, and upon our Prophet the best of praise and salutations.

Explanation:

dhuriyah: descendents

Alhamdulillah, this topic is covered at length in "*'Usool ath-Thalaathah*", so we will only briefly touch on some important points here, insh'Allaah, and study it more deeply in that part of the series, insh'Allaah.

Sheikh 'Utheimeen, may Allaah have mercy upon him, states in his explanation of "*Usool ath-Thalaathah*", five matters that are covered in the knowledge of the Prophet, may Allaah's praise and good mention be upon him:

1. *His lineage.* This includes his name. If someone asks you about who your prophet is, and you say, simply, Muhammad, then this is not very specific. To be more specific, then you should know his name, and that of his father, and that of his grandfather, and so on, as stated in the *matn*, or text of the work. He is from the tribe of Quraish, which was at that time the most powerful tribe in Makkah, and one of the most powerful tribes in the area that we know as Saudi Arabia today. Concerning his names, there is a hadeeth in Saheeh al-Bukhaari and Muslim which addresses this.

Narrated Jubair ibn Mut'im, may Allaah be pleased with him, Allaah's Messenger, may Allaah's praise and salutations be upon him, said, { *I have five names: I am Muhammad and Ahmad; I am al-Maahee through whom Allaah will eliminate al-kufr (disbelief); I am al-Haashir who will be the first to be resurrected, the people being resurrected after that; and I am also al-'Aaqib (there will be no prophet after him).* } ("*Saheeh al-Bukhaari*", Vol. 4, No. 732)

2. *The age he attained,* the place he was born, and where he migrated to. He was born in Makkah, in Saudi Arabia, to a man named 'Abdullaah, who died before he was born, and a woman named Aaminah, who died when he was a young boy. He lived in Makkah for fifty-three years, alhamdulillah, before migrating to al-Madinah, where he completed his life. He lived to be sixty-three years old, may Allaah's praise and good mention be upon him and his family.

3. *Knowledge about his life as a Prophet.* This covered a period of twenty-three years, beginning when he was forty years old. We should read about the persecution and trials that he went through in the first thirteen years of his call to *at-tawheed*, as well as how he established Islaam once he migrated to al-Madinah.

4. *Through what did he become a prophet and a messenger.* He was given the

prophethood first, with the revelation of the first verses of Surat al-'Alaq, and the messengership with the first verses of al-Muddaththir. This is related in an authentic hadeeth in Saheeh al-Bukhaari and other than that:

{ Narrated 'Aishah, the mother of the believers: The commencement of the Divine Inspiration to Allaah's Messenger was in the form of good dreams which came true like bright day light, and then the love of seclusion was bestowed upon him. He used to go in seclusion in the cave of Hira' where he used to worship (Allaah alone) continuously for many days before his desire to see his family. He used to take with him the journey food for the stay and then come back to (his wife) Khadijah to take his food again till suddenly the Truth descended upon him while he was in the cave of Hira'. The angel came to him and asked him to read. The Prophet replied, "I do not know how to read.

The Prophet added, "The angel caught me (forcefully) and pressed me so hard that I could not bear it any more. He then released me and again asked me to read and I replied, 'I do not know how to read.' Thereupon he caught me again and pressed me a second time till I could not bear it any more. He then released me and again asked me to read but again I replied, 'I do not know how to read (or what shall I read)?' Thereupon he caught me for the third time and pressed me, and then released me and said, ❀ Read in the name of your Lord, who has created (all that exists) has created man from a clot. Read! And your Lord is the Most Generous.❀ –(Surat al-'Alaq, Ayats 1-3) Then the Messenger of Allaah returned (home) with the Inspiration and with his heart beating severely. Then he went to Khadijah bint Khuwailid and said, "Cover me! Cover me!" They covered him till his fear was over and after that he told her everything that had happened and said, "I fear that something may happen to me." Khadijah replied, "Never! By Allaah, Allaah will never disgrace you. You keep good relations with your family ties, help the poor and the destitute, serve your guests generously and assist the deserving ones who are afflicted with calamity."

Khadijah then accompanied him to her cousin Waraqa bin Naufal bin Asad bin 'Abdul 'Uzza, who, during the Pre-Islamic Period became a Christian and used to write the writing with Hebrew letters. He would write from the Gospel in Hebrew as much as Allaah wished him to write. He was an old man and had lost his eyesight. Khadijah said to Waraqa, "Listen to the story of your nephew, O my cousin!" Waraqa asked, "O my nephew! What have you seen?" Allaah's Messenger described that which he had seen. Waraqa said, "This is the same one who keeps the secrets (angel Jibreel), whom Allaah had sent to Moosaa. I wish I were young and could live up to the time when your people would turn you out." Allaah's Messenger asked, "Will they drive me out?" Waraqa replied in the affirmative and said, "Anyone who came with something similar to what you have brought was treated with hostility; and if I should remain alive till the day when you will be turned out then I would support you strongly." But after a few days Waraqa died and the Divine Inspiration was also paused for a while.

Narrated Jaabir bin 'Abdullah Al-Ansaari while talking about the period of pause in revelation reporting the speech of the Prophet "While I was walking, all of a sudden I heard a voice from the sky. I looked up and saw the same angel who had visited me at the cave of Hira' sitting on a chair between the sky and the earth. I got afraid of him and came back home and said, 'Wrap me (in blankets).' And then Allaah revealed the following Holy Verses:

Oh you wrapped up in garments!' Arise and warn (the people against Allaah's Punishment)"... up to "and desert the idols. –(Surah Muddaththir, Ayats 1-5) After this the revelation started coming strongly, frequently and regularly. }*

There are many benefits to be found in this hadeeth, alhamdulillah. One of them is the excellent example of Khadijah, may Allaah be pleased with her. She is an example for the women, to look and see how she supported her husband, alhamdulillah. Before the revelation, she was patient with his long absences. After the first revelation she calmed him and affirmed him, and took him to her cousin seeking advice.

Secondly, look at the way that Khadijah, may Allaah be pleased with her, described the Prophet, may Allaah's praise and good mention be upon him:

"Never! By Allaah, Allaah will never disgrace you. You keep good relations with your family ties, help the poor and the destitute, serve your guests generously and assist the deserving ones afflicted with calamity."

She also had faith in Allaah, that the good deeds and character of the Prophet, may Allaah's praise and good mention be upon him, would never be lost. And all of the things she described him with are characteristics that we should foster within ourselves, as Muslims, insh'Allaah. So in this amazing hadeeth, we see many examples of how knowing about and following the way of the prophets and Companions can benefit our characters and our lives as a whole, insh'Allaah.

5.   *What was the message he was sent with,* may Allaah's praise and salutations be upon him, and why was he sent? He was sent with the call to *at-tawheed,* worshipping Allaah alone, doing that which He orders, and leaving that which He forbids. Likewise, he was sent as a warner, against *ash-shirk* and all that it encompasses. He was sent as a mercy to all of mankind, to show them the way to truth and eternal reward, alhamdulillah.

The Difference between a Prophet and a Messenger

One of the common statements concerning this difference is that a prophet has revelation sent to him, but he is not told to propagate that message, while a messenger has revelation and is told to spread it amongst the people. However, many of the scholars say that this is incorrect, as the revelation would not be given, and then kept secret.

Sheikh al-Islaam ibn Taymiyyah says, concerning this, that they both receive revelation, but that a prophet is one who teaches and spreads the *shar'iah* (legislation) of the prophet who came before him, while a messenger is given a new *shar'iah* to teach the people. So, all messengers are prophets as well, because they both receive revelation; but not every prophet is a messenger, as he is not given a new *shar'iah*.

Insh'Allaah, for the remainder of this lesson, I would like to share some characteristics of our Prophet, Muhammad, may Allaah's praise and salutations be upon him. Through knowing about him, we can increase in our love of him, and truly he is the best example for us in how to live our lives as Muslims. To make things easier, I took them all from *"al-Lu'lu al Marjaan"*, which is a collection of *ahaadeeth* that are found in both *"Saheeh Muslim"* and *"Saheeh al-Bukhaari"*, and have noted where they are found in al-Bukhaari. It has been translated into English, alhamdulillah.

Some of the Physical Characteristics which have been Related Concerning Him:

Anas, may Allaah be pleased with him, narrated, *{ I have never touched silk or deebaaj (a thicker type of silk) softer than the palm of the Prophet, may Allaah's praise and good mention be upon him, nor have I smelled perfume which smelled better than the sweat of the Prophet, may Allaah's praise and good mention be upon him. }* (al-Bukhaari, Vol. 4, No. 761)

al-Baraa' ibn 'Aazib, may Allaah be pleased with him, narrated, *{ The Prophet, may Allaah's praise and good mention be upon him, was of medium height, having broad shoulders, and (long) hair which reached his ear lobes. Once I saw him in a red cloak, and I had never seen a more handsome person than him. }* (al-Bukhaari, Vol. 4, No. 751)

He also said, *{ The Messenger of Allaah was the most handsome of people, and had the best appearance. He was neither very tall nor short. }* (al-Bukhaari, Vol. 4, No 749)

Anas, may Allaah be pleased with him, narrated, *{ The hair of the Messenger of Allaah, may Allaah's praise and salutations be upon him, was neither very straight, nor very curly, and it used to hang down to between his shoulders and his ears. }* (al-Bukhaari, Vol. 7, No. 791)

His Character and Manners:

Anas, may Allaah be pleased with him, said, *{ I served the Prophet, may Allaah's praise and salutations be upon him, for ten years, and he never said to me, "Uff" (an expression of impatience or displeasure) and never blamed me by saying, "Why did you do such and such, or why didn't you do so! }* (al-Bukhaari, Vol8. No. 64)

This shows his general character and behavior, his patience in dealing with people, his gentleness, and his kindness towards the young, alhamdulillah.

Ibn 'Abbaas, may Allaah be pleased with him, said, *{ The Messenger of Allaah was the most generous of all people, and he used to reach the peak of generosity during the month of Ramadhaan, when Jibreel met with him. Jibreel used to meet with him every night of Ramadhaan to teach him the Qur'aan. Allaah's Messenger, may Allaah's praise and good mention be upon him, was the most generous person, even more generous than the fair winds sent by Allaah with glad tidings (of rain).}* (al-Bukhaari, Vol. 1, No. 5)

Jaabir, may Allaah be pleased with him, said, *{ Never was the Prophet, may Allaah's praise and salutations be upon him, asked for anything to be given for which his answer was, "No." }* (al-Bukhaari, Vol. 8, No. 60)

This shows his generosity, and the hadeeth regarding his generosity are many, alhamdulillah.

Anas, may Allaah be pleased with him, said, *{ The Prophet, may Allaah's praise and good mention be upon him, was the best and bravest of the people. Once the people of al-Madina were terrified at night, so they went in the direction of the noise (that had frightened them). The Prophet, may Allaah's praise and good mention be upon him, met them (on his way back) after he had found out the truth (what the noise had been). He* *was riding an unsaddled horse belonging to Abi Talhah, and a sword was hanging by his neck, and he was saying, "Don't be afraid! Don't be afraid!" He also said, "I found it (the horse he was riding) very fast," or he said, "This horse is very fast. }* (al-Bukhaari, Vol. 4, No. 156)

Here we see his courage, and his love and care for his people. There are also many *ahaadeeth* concerning these two things. It also shows that he was an active man, and a good horseman.

Abu Sa'eed al-Khudree, may Allaah be pleased with him, said, *{The Prophet was more modest than a veiled virgin girl. }* (al-Bukhaari, Vol. 4, No. 762)

Narrated 'Aishah, may Allaah be pleased with her, *{ A Bedouin came to the Prophet, may Allaah's praise and good mention be upon him, and said, "You (people) kiss the (young) boys! We don't kiss them." The Prophet, may Allaah's praise and good mention be upon him, said, "I cannot put mercy in your heart after Allaah has taken it away." }* (al-Bukhaari, Vol. 8, No. 27)

He was merciful and kind to the children, alhamdulillah. We also see his manners in dealing with the Bedouin. He was patient with him, and simply guided him, rather than insulting him or being rough.

I previously translated a story from Umm Shu'ayb, one of the wives of Sheikh Muqbil, and he was a scholar, and so an inheritor of the Prophet, in his knowledge and his manners, may Allaah have mercy upon him, which shows how we can have mercy to the people. She said that when he would come into the courtyard the children would all run up to him and pluck at his pockets and his garments. She said that he always gave them whatever he had, even if it was only some dates. He also set aside time each day to spend with his family, and sometimes when there was company he would even go in and offer to help the women if he thought they needed it.

The example of the Prophet, may Allaah's praise and salutations be upon him, is the best example for us- we should try to emulate as many of his characteristics, and the characteristics of his Companions, who he described as the best of people after the prophets, in our lives, insh'Allaah, as well as the examples of the righteous people after them, as in the example of Imaam Maalik in the last lesson. We should all try to have as many books containing the correct story of the life of the Prophet, may Allaah's praise and salutations be upon him, and these righteous people in our homes as we are able, insh'Allaah, and read them, and contemplate them, and put them into action, as well as teaching them to our children so that they have the examples of strong, righteous people to follow as well, insh'Allaah.

Know, also, that Allaah's Messenger, may Allaah's praise and salutations be upon him, was the last prophet and messenger, there will be none to come after him.

Narrated Abu Hurairah, may Allaah be pleased with him, Allaah's Messenger, may Allaah's praise and salutations be upon him, said, *{ My example and the example of the other prophets that came before me, is that of a man who has built a house nicely and beautifully, except for a place of one brick in a corner. The people go around it and are amazed by its beauty, and say, "If only this brick were put in its place." So I am that brick, and I am the last of all the prophets. }* *("Saheeh al-Bukhaari",* Vol. 4, No. 735)

NOTES

Key Terms in this Lesson

Define these terms:

dhariyah:

shar'iah:

Lesson Questions:

Level 1: [required]

1. What are the five matters that Sheik Utheimeen mentions that make up knowledge of the Prophet?

2. What is the Prophet's, may Allaah's praise and salutations be upon him, name and his lineage?

3. Where was he born? What age was he when prophethood came to him? When he died?

4. What Message was he, may Allaah's praise and salutations be upon him, sent with?

5. What is the difference between a prophet and a messenger, according to Sheikh al-Islaam ibn Taymiyyah?

Level 2: [supplementary]

1. How did revelation of the Qur'aan descend upon the Prophet, may Allaah's praise and salutations be upon him, the first time?

2. How did Khadijah react to this? How is she a good example for all of us? If there is anything else that you know authentically related about her, share this, and tell me how it shows her as a good example.

3. What are some of the benefits of knowing our Prophet, may Allaah's praise and salutations be upon him?

4. List five of the characteristics of the Prophet.

5. How can we implement some of these characteristics and make them a part of our character?

LESSON FIVE

> **The Principles of the Religion and its Fundamentals Consist of Two Matters:**
>
> *The First:* The command to worship Allaah alone, without associating any partners with Him, and being motivated by that, and inciting others towards it, and support and loyalty due to it, and to know that the one who leaves it has disbelieved.
>
> *The Second:* Warning away from *ash-shirk* (associating others along with Allaah in worship) in the worship of Allaah, and strength upon that, and enmity due to it, and knowing that the one who engages in it has disbelieved.

Terms from the *matn*, or text,:

asl:　　　　origin, root, principle, basis
ad-deen:　　religion, way of life
qaa'idah:　　fundamental, rule, principle
amraan:　　the dual of "*amr*", meaning matters, command, orders
'ibaadah:　　simply put, worship- all that Allaah is pleased with, done for the His pleasure
at-tahreed:　inciting, motivating, prompting, urging
al-mawaalah: support, loyalty, adherence
tark:　　　leave, quit, renounce, forsake
al-in`thaar:　warning
at-taghleedh: strength, thickening
al-mu'aadah: enmity, hostility, antagonism

Explanation:

This shows the well-known principle of *at-taqseem*, or division in knowledge based matters. For example, the scholars explain *at-tawheed* as being of three divisions. Likewise, with disbelief- there is disbelief which takes one outside of Islaam, and there is disbelief which does not take one outside of the religion. Or with innovation; again it is divided into different types, and the behavior and rulings concerning these is different depending upon the type. Here, Sheikh Muhammad ibn 'Abdul Wahaab, may Allaah have mercy upon him, has stated that there are two basic matters which make up the religion. Again, as I said before, he has made this division based upon the subject matter, and what he is presenting to the people.

The people of knowledge have explained that these two matters are related to general commanding of the good and forbidding the evil. All of mankind is commanded with these two matters. If a person engages in the matters that are commanded, then his faith will increase. And if he stays away from that which is prohibited, then his *eemaan* will increase also. The first matter is, even though here it is specifically related to belief and worship, considered commanding the good, the second likewise, is forbidding the evil.

Commanding the good in regard to belief and worship is comprised of two divisions:
1. *al-Ikhlaas*, or sincerity in worship of Allaah
2. Separation from *ash-shirk* and the people of *ash-shirk*

So let us look at the question of a man who does his obligatory acts, but leaves off of calling the people to *at-tawheed* and enjoining the good- has he disbelieved? The scholars agree that as long as the man affirms that commanding the good and forbidding the evil is of the obligatory acts, even if he does not engage in it, then he has not disbelieved- however, he has committed a major sin in his omission of acting upon an obligatory act.

If a person leaves worship of Allaah, has he disbelieved? This has to be divided and explained in a detailed manner. This will be discussed in more detail later in the series, so we will mention it only briefly here.

1. If he does not pronounce the *shahaadatain*, and he does not pray and leaves off the worship entirely, as well the worship of the heart, then this is disbelief.

2. If he does pronounce the *shahaadatain*, and does the worship of the heart, and he prays, then he is Muslim.

al-amr bi al-ma'roof wa an-nahi 'an al-munkar (commanding the good and forbidding the evil) has its basis in the Qur'aan and the Sunnah.

Allaah, the Most High, says, ﴾ *Let there arise out of you a group of people inviting to all that is good (Islaam), enjoining al-ma'roof (i.e. Islamic Monotheism and all that Islaam orders one to do) and forbidding al-munkar (polytheism and disbelief and all that Islaam has forbidden). And it is they who are the successful.* ﴿ –(Surat urat aal 'Imraan, Ayat 104)

And He, the Most High, says, ﴾ *You (true believers in Islamic Monotheism, and real followers of Prophet Muhammad] and his Sunnah) are the best of peoples ever raised up for mankind; you enjoin al-ma'roof and forbid al-munkar , and you believe in Allaah. And had the people of the scripture believed, it would have been better for them; among them are some who have Faith, but most of them are disobedient to Allaah and rebellious against Allaah's Command).* ﴿ –(Surat aal 'Imraan, Ayat 110) And Allaah, Glorified and Exalted is He, says, ﴾ *The believers, men and women, are auliyaa' (helpers, supporters, friends, protectors) of one another; they enjoin (on the people) al-ma'roof , and forbid (people) from al-munkar; they perform As-Salaat, and give the Zakaat, and obey Allaah and His*

Messenger . Allaah will have His Mercy on them. Surely, Allaah is All-Mighty, All-Wise. –(Surat at-Tawbah, Ayat 71)

It is reported on Abee Sa'eed al-Khudri, may Allaah be pleased with him, "I heard the Messenger of Allaah, may Allaah's praise and good mention be upon him, saying, *{The one who sees amongst you evil, should change it with his hand, and if he is unable to do that, then with his tongue. And if he is unable to do that, then with his heart (he should hate it in his heart), and that is the weakest of faith. }* (Collected by Muslim)

This hadeeth shows that commanding the good and forbidding the evil is part of *eemaan*, or faith, and also that *al-eemaan* is with the heart, the tongue, and the hand, alhamdulillah.

And, from a longer hadeeth found in *"Saheeh al-Bukhaari"*, Vol. 1, Book 10, No. 503, and from another chain in Vol. 2, Book 24, No. 516: Shaqiq narrated that he had heard Hudhaifah saying, *{ Once I was sitting with 'Umar and he said, 'Who amongst you remembers the statement of the Messenger of Allaah about the afflictions?' I said, 'I know it as the Prophet had said it.' 'Umar said, 'No doubt you are bold.' I said, 'The afflictions caused for a man by his wife, money, children and neighbor are expiated by his prayers, fasting, charity and by enjoining (what is good) and forbidding (what is evil).'}*

Sheikh al-Islaam ibn Taymiyyah, may Allaah have mercy upon him, said, *"Commanding the good and forbidding the evil is that with which Allaah revealed His books and sent His Messenger with, and it is part of the deen."* (From *"al-Amr bi al-Ma'roof wa an-Nahi 'an al-Munkar"*)

He, may Allaah have mercy upon him, also said, *'It is one of the most obligatory, most virtuous, and best acts."* (from *"Majmu' al-Fataawa"*)

Sheikh al-Islaam, may Allaah have mercy upon him, said, concerning its ruling, *"Commanding the good and forbidding the evil is not fard 'ayn, which means an obligation upon every Muslim; rather, it is fard kafiyyah, or a communal obligation, as proven by the Qur'aan."* (From *"Majmu' al Fatawa"*)

and he, may Allaah have mercy upon him, also said, *"This is a general obligation on every capable Muslim, is fard kafiyyah, and becomes fard 'ayn or a personal obligation for the capable person if no one else does it."* (From *"al-Hisbah"*)

Commanding the good and forbidding the evil has two *sharoot*, or conditions:

1. Capability of doing so

Sheikh al-Islaam ibn Taymiyyah, may Allaah have mercy upon him, said, *"Indeed capability is a condition for commanding good and forbidding evil. So its level of obligation on a particular person is in proportion to his capability, as Allaah, the*

*Most High, said, ⟨ **Have taqwa of Allaah as much as you are able.**⟩* –(Surat at-Taghaaboon, Ayat 16) (From *"Majmu' al Fatawa"*)

2. Security of the person who is doing so

Imaam Ahmad ibn Hanbal, may Allaah have mercy upon him, said, *"It is waajib on a person unless he becomes fearful; if he fears for himself, then he does not do it."* (From *"al-Amr bi al-Ma'roof wa an-nahi 'an al-Munkar"*)

Sheikh al-Islaam, Ibn Taymiyyah, may Allaah have mercy upon him, has listed some of the characteristics that one should have in commanding the good and forbidding the evil:

1. He must have the correct intention
2. He must do it upon knowledge and understanding
3. It should be done in accordance with *as-Sirat al-Mustaqim*, the Straight Path. He said that this means with:
   A. gentleness
   B. tolerance
   C. patience

Also, when commanding the good and forbidding the evil, one must weigh its possible benefits against its possible harms. For a very clear, excellent example of commanding the good and forbidding the evil, look to the athar of 'Amr ibn Salmah concerning Aboo Moosa al-Ash'aree and 'Abdullah ibn Mas'ood which was mentioned on page 46. Again, we see the importance of looking to the pious predecessors for examples to follow.

Concerning this, Ibn Taymiyyah, may Allaah have mercy upon him, said, *"Commanding a good should not result in the loss of a greater good, or in a greater evil (than what came before). And forbidding an evil should not result in a greater evil, or in the loss of a greater good (than what came before)."* (From *"al-Hisbah"*)

Ibn Qayyim al-Jawziyyah, who was a student of Ibn Taymiyyah, said, *"The Prophet, may Allaah's and good mention be upon him, made it obligatory for his Ummah to forbid evil so that the good loved by Allaah and His Messenger will come. So if one's act of forbidding evil will lead to that which is worse and more hated by Allaah and His Messenger, then it is not allowed to forbid it, even though Allaah hates it (that evil) and hates those who do it"* (From *"'Ilaam al-Muwaqi'in"*)

> The First: The command to worship Allaah Alone, without associating any partners with Him, and being motivated by that, and encouraging others to that and support and loyalty due to it, and to know that the one who leaves it has disbelieved.

Explanation: This can be broken down into four matters, comprising enjoining the good in matters of belief:

1. The command to worship Allaah alone
2. Urging others upon the good, by mentioning the rewards of doing it
3. Support and loyalty to the people of *at-tawheed* based upon your mutual belief
4. To know that the one who leaves it is a disbeliever

> The Second: Warning away from *ash-shirk* (associating others along with Allaah in worship) in the worship of Allaah, and strength upon that, and enmity due to it, and knowing that the one who engages in it has disbelieved.

This also comprises four matters related to forbidding the evil in matters of belief:

1. Warning away from *ash-shirk*
2. Being strong upon that
3. Enmity and hatred based upon it
4. Knowing that the one who commits *ash-shirk* has disbelieved

Key Terms in this Lesson

Define these terms:

asl:
qaa'idah:
at-tahreed:
al-mawaalah:
tark:
al-in`thaar:
at-taghleedh:
al-mu'aadah:
'ibaadah:

Lesson Questions:

Level 1: [required]

1. What are these two matters stated in the text referring to?
2. What is the meaning of *al-amr bi al-ma'roof wa an-nahi 'an al-munkar*?
3. What is its general ruling, according to Ibn Taymiyyaah?
4. Who was Ibn Qayyim al-Jawziyyah's most well known teacher?
5. List the two conditions mentioned by Ibn Taymiyyah for commanding the good and forbidding the evil?

Level 2: [supplementary]

1. Is a person who leaves off performing the obligatory acts of Islaam a disbeliever? Why or why not?
2. What characteristics did Sheikh al-Islaam Ibn Taymiyyah put forth for the one who commands the good and forbids the evil? Why do you think these are important?
3. Briefly explain the weighing of potential harm against potential good.
4. Give an example of when one SHOULD command the good and forbid the evil.
5. Give an example of when one SHOULD NOT command the good and forbid the evil.

QUIZ NUMBER ONE

This is a closed-book quiz. You cannot use your notes or the book to answer the questions. Please write neatly and answer each question as completely as you are able. Use as many sheets of notebook paper needed to answer the questions fully and legibly. Write your name and the quiz number, number each answer clearly.

1. Define these terms:

    al-ʿaqeedah:

    basmalah:

    at-tawheed:

    al-istislaam:

    al-inqiyaad:

    ash-shirk:

    al-walaa:

    al-baraa:

    asl:

    amr:

    qaaʾidah:

    al-ʿibaadah:

Questions:

1. Why is it important to study al-'aqeedah? What is the Islamic ruling on studying it?

2. Write a short paragraph about the life of Sheikh Muhammad ibn 'Abdul Wahaab, rahimahu Allaah.

3. What two conditions must be met for an act to count as a righteous action?

4. Give an example of someone trying to do a good deed, but whose action will not be accepted. Explain why her action will not be accepted. (Hint: Remember the six points needed for an act to conform to the shari'iah)

5. Explain how we can practice al-walaa and al-baraa in our everyday lives.

6. Explain how faith is an action of the heart, the tongue, and the limbs.

7. What is the ruling of beginning a book with the basmalah? What two examples are being followed by doing so?

8. List the five categories of actions, beginning with waajib, and list one thing that falls under each ruling.

9. What three fundamentals must each Muslim know and understand? Where does the Sheikh, rahimahu Allaah, find this list of three?

10. What are some of the benefits of knowing the names and attributes of Allaah?
11. Briefly explain the belief of ahl-as-Sunnah wa al-Jama'ah in regards to Allaah's names and attributes.

12. Tell me about our Prophet, may Allaah's praise and salutations be upon him, and try to mention all of the five things that Sheikh 'Utheimeen mentions are included in knowledge of the Prophet.

13. What are the two conditions for commanding the good and forbidding the evil?

14. Give an example wherein one should command the good and forbid the evil, and how she should do it. Then give an example of a time when one should remain silent.

LESSON SIX

> The Conditions of *ash-Shahadah* (*La ilaha ila Allaah*) None has the Right to be Worshipped but Allaah Alone

Explanation:

sharoot: This is the plural of *shart*. This generally means, condition, or conditions. The religious meaning is: That which if it is not present, the act is not valid, but its presence does not make the act obligatory. For example, the *wudoo*, or purification for prayer, is a condition of the prayer- without it the prayer is not valid. However, one can have *wudoo* and not have to make the prayer because they have it. So, these are the conditions that must be met in order for one's statement of *ash-shahadah* to be correct and accepted.

The verb, *shahadah*, has as one of its meanings to testify, or to bear witness. So we are testifying and bearing witness to the truth of these words, alhamdulillah. The specific religious meaning of the statement, "*ash-shahadah*" generally refers to these specific words: "*ash-shadu an la ilaaha ila Allaah, wa ash-shadu anna Muhammadan 'abduhu wa rasoolahu*", meaning, "I testify that there is no god worthy of worship in truth but Allaah, and I testify that Muhammad is His servant and Messenger." You will also find the term, "*ash-shahadah*" referring to the first part of this statement only, and "*ash-shahadatan*" meaning the entire statement.

la ilaha: the "*la*" here is known as the "*la naafiyyah lil-jins*". It acts like "*inna*" in that its *ism* is *mansoob* and its *khabr* is *marfoo'*. Thus, "*ilaha*" (god)has a *fathah* on it, as it is the *ism* of "*la*". Its *khabr*, however, is not present, and it is "*bi haq*", or "*haq*" or something similar to this, which means "in truth", or "in reality", or "the right".

"*ila Allaah*" is the *mustathna*- which simply means that it is removed from the above statement...so we say, "except Allaah" or "but Allaah"

So the correct translation and meaning of the words of *ash-shahadah*, is, "There is no god worthy of worship except Allaah." or, "There is no god that has the right to be worshipped except Allaah, alone." Or something with this meaning. And this is the statement of the *jamhoor*, or the majority of the scholars, past and present, alhamdulillah.

All of this is a demonstration of why it is important to learn your grammar! Many of the books translate the statement of *ash-shahadah* to mean, "There is no god but Allaah." This is wrong on a couple of levels. The first, is that there obviously are gods that are worshipped besides Allaah. There many evidences put forth in the Qur'aan and Sunnah which demonstrate this, mash'Allaah. Also, we witness it with our eyes and ears- think of the Christians, Hindus, or many of the traditional Native American religions, or even, from the past, the beliefs of the Greeks and Romans- they all worshipped other than Allaah alone. The second way that the translation is wrong, is shown in the grammatical analysis above, mash'Allaah. Thirdly, we look to the explanation of the *salaf* and the scholars to see the true meaning, alhamdulillah, with its correct explanation.

Sheikh 'Abdur Rahman ibn Hasn, the author of *"Fath al-Majeed"*, which is an explanation of *"Kitaab at-Tawheed"*, has an excellent explanation of the *shahadah* and some of its conditions, in reference to the following hadeeth:

The Prophet, may Allaah's praise and salutations be upon him, said, *{The one who testifies that there is no god worthy of worship except Allaah alone, without any partners along with Him, and that I am His slave and messenger, and that 'Isa was His slave and messenger and His word which He bestowed upon Maryam, and a spirit created by Him, and that Paradise is a fact, and the Hellfire is a fact, Allaah will allow him to enter into Paradise because of the deeds which he had done, even if those deeds are few." Junada, the subnarrator, added, "'Ubada (the companion who related this hadeeth, added, "Such a person can enter Paradise through any of its eight doors he likes."}* (Agreed upon)

The sheikh, may Allaah have mercy upon him, says,

"His, may Allaah's praise and salutations be upon him, saying, {The one who testifies that there is no god worthy of worship except Allaah alone...}; meaning, the one who states it, understanding its meaning, and acting upon that which it requires, both hidden and apparent. And undoubtedly contained in ash-shahadatain are knowledge, and certainty, and acting upon their meaning, as Allaah, the Most High, says,

◊ *So know that none has the right to be worshipped except Allaah alone...* ◊ – (Sura*t Muhammad, from Ayat 19)*

And His saying, ◊*...except for those who bear witness to the truth knowingly (i.e. believed in the Oneness of Allaah, and obeyed His Orders), and they know (the facts about the Oneness of Allaah).*◊ *–(Surat az-Zakhoof, from Ayat 86)*

As for saying it, without understanding its meaning, and without certainty, without acting upon that which is required by it: from separating oneself from ash-shirk, and sincerity of speech and action: speech of the heart and the tongue, and action of the heart and the limbs, then he is not successful, according to the majority of the scholars.

And al-Qurtubi says, in explanation of Saheeh Muslim: "Baab: It is not Sufficient to Merely Pronounce ash-Shahadatayn; Rather, it Necessitates Drawing upon the Heart": This explanation is a warning from the corruption that is put forth by the Murjiah, who are those who say that pronouncing ash-shahadatain is sufficient for faith. And the ahaadeeth in this chapter are a proof of its corruption...

And in this hadeeth is proof of this, and it is his, may Allaah's praise and salutations be upon him, saying, {The one who testifies...}. As ash-shahadah is not correct unless it is upon knowledge, certainty, sincerity, and truthfulness... (*end of quote from al-Qurtubi*)

And the meaning of "la ilaaha ila Allaah": Nothing is worshipped with truth except for Allaah...and the saying "alone" is a strengthening of "without any partners along with Him"- a strengthening of the negation. This is what al-Haafidh (ibn Katheer) states. As the Most High says,

❧ *And your God is One God (Allaah), La ilaaha ila Huwa (there is none who has the right to be worshipped but He), the Most Gracious, the Most Merciful.* ❧ *—(Surat al-Baqara, Verse 163)*

And He says, ❧ *And We did not send any Messenger before you (O Muhammad) but We revealed to him: La ilaaha ila Ana [none has the right to be worshipped but I (Allaah)], so worship Me (Alone and none else).* ❧ *—(Surat al-Anbiyyah, Ayat 25)*

And He says, ❧ *And to 'Aad (We sent) their brother Hud. He said: "O my people! Worship Allaah! You have no other God but Him. Will you not fear (Allaah)?* ❧ *—(Surat al-I'raaf, Ayat 65)…*

So that includes the negation of gods other than Allaah, and that is to be worshipped, and affirms Allaah alone, without associating any partners with Him. And the Qur'aan, from its start to its finish makes this clear, and establishes it, and guides to it.

(End of translation from *"Fath al-Majeed"*, as quoted in *"Fataawa al-A'imat an-Najdiyyaah"* Pages 156-158)

> The First: Knowledge, encompassing negation and verification

Explanation:

Question: What is *al-'ilm*, or knowledge?

Answer: There is more than one definition of this word.

1. It is that which Allaah says, and that which His Messenger, may Allaah's praise and salutations be upon him, said, on the understanding of *as-Saalif as-Saalih* (the pious predecessors)

2. It is to know Allaah with the evidences, and to know His Messenger with the evidences, and to know the religion of al-Islaam with the evidences.

3. It is the saying of Muhammad ibn 'Abdul Wahaab, may Allaah have mercy upon him- that it is to know Allaah, and His prophet, and the religion of Allaah with the evidences.

And all of these are correct, alhamdulillah, as they all have the same basic meaning. And the *'ilm* we are referring to here is the beneficial knowledge, and that which it is upon us to learn in order to be successful in this life, and the Hereafter.

As for **"Encompassing negation and verification"**: That is to say, that which is negated, (for example, *ash-shirk*) and that which is verified (for example, *at-tawheed*, or the worship of Allaah alone).

> The Second: Certainty, and knowledge is perfected through it, and it negates doubt and uncertainty

"Knowledge is perfected through it": meaning, the perfection of knowledge is knowledge of the meaning of *la ilaaha ila Allaah*

al-yaqeen: It is certainty. In the Arabic language, it means, repose, or tranquility, of the understanding along with the establishment of the commands. Meaning, there is no indecision or faltering.

"...and it negates doubt and uncertainty": This is an example of one of the methods that the scholars use to teach the people and clarify issues for them. The Sheikh, may Allaah have mercy upon him, is showing the meaning of the word "*yaqeen*" by presenting its opposites: "*ash-shak*" and "*ar-rayb*". I just want to mention that there are some differences in the meanings of these two words. I am not going to go into this in detail, mash'Allaah, because this is a beginning explanation- but know that *ash-shak*, that is, doubt, leads to *ar-rayb*, that is, uncertainty. *ar-rayb* is the true opposite of *al-yaqeen*.

> The Third: Sincerity, which negates *ash-Shirk*, which is associating others along with Allaah in worship

al-Ikhlaas encompasses sincerity and purity. So here we are discussing purity of all of our acts of worship for Allaah alone. That is to say, doing them sincerely for Allaah alone. Sheikh Muhammad ibn 'Abdul Wahaab, may Allaah have mercy upon him, says that this negates *ash-shirk*, and this is both minor and major *shirk*. For example, if you are doing all of your acts of worship only for Allaah, and not joining partners with Him, then this negates the major *shirk*. Likewise, if you are performing your acts of worship only for Allaah, and not to be seen by the people, then this negates the minor *shirk* of *ar-riyaa*, or showing off.

And Allaah knows best.

Key Terms in this Lesson

Define these terms:

ash-shahadah:
al-jamhoor:
al-yaqeen:
al-ikhlaas:

Lesson Questions:

Level 1: [required]

1. What is the meaning of *ash-shahadah*?
2. Why is it incorrect to translate it as "There is no god but Allaah"?
3. Who wrote "*Fath al-Majeed*"? What is it an explanation of?
4. What are the meanings of *al-'ilm* mentioned, and which is correct?
5. Discuss the meaning of *shart / sharoot*. Give an example other than the one I have given.

Level 2: [supplementary]

1. Why is it important to know the *sharoot* of an action before doing it?
2. Is it enough that a person says *ash-shahadah*? Why or why not?
3. What is meant by the Prophet's, may Allaah's praise and salutations be upon him, saying, *{ The one who testifies…}*?
4. Why does the Sheikh mention the opposite of many of the conditions?
5. A young man prays to Allaah because his father tells him to. He has no knowledge of Allaah, he just thinks it is a good thing to pray. He makes sure his friends see him. Based upon what was presented, do you think his prayer will be accepted? (and only Allaah knows if it will, in truth, be accepted)

LESSON SEVEN

> The Fourth: Truthfulness, which negates insincerity

First of all, we are going to continue briefly discussing these conditions with a little explanation, so that, insh'Allaah, you understand each of them fully. In the next class, insh'Allaah, we will discuss the proofs for each of them.

Explanation:

as-sidq: truthfulness, sincerity, honesty

al-kadhab: deceit, deception, lying, insincerity, falsehood

And this truthfulness also negates *an-nifaaq*, or hypocrisy. If we say that we believe that there is no god worthy of worship except Allaah alone, having no partners, and that Muhammad is His slave and Messenger, with knowledge and understanding, and we truly believe this, then this cancels out hypocrisy on our part. If, however, we say it, but don't totally believe it, or say it because others are saying it, then this opens the door to hypocrisy, may Allaah protect us all from that. And we have many narrations from the Companions and the righteous people who came after them, showing that they feared hypocrisy in themselves. As Sheikh Muhammad ibn 'Abdul Wahaab al-Wasaabi, may Allaah preserve him, said, it is the true believer who examines himself and fears hypocrisy for himself; the hypocrite is comfortable with his position, and doesn't trouble himself over it. (This is taken from an audio tape on the dangers of seclusion with the opposite sex and free mixing)

Narrated Abu Moosaa, that the Prophet, may Allaah's praise and salutations be upon him, said, {*The example of a believer who recites the Qur'aan and acts on it, is like a citron which tastes nice and smells nice. And the example of a believer who does not recite the Qur'aan but acts on it, is like a date which tastes good but has no smell. And the example of a hypocrite who recites the Qur'aan is like a Raihana (sweet basil) which smells good but tastes bitter And the example of a hypocrite who does not recite the Qur'aan is like a colocynth which tastes bitter and has a bad smell. }* ("Saheeh al-Bukhaari")

Ka'b, may Allaah be pleased with him, said that the Prophet, may Allaah's praise and salutations be upon him, said, { *The example of a believer is that of a fresh tender plant, which the wind bends at times and some other time it makes it straight. And the example of a hypocrite is that of a pine tree which keeps straight till once it is uprooted suddenly.}* ("Saheeh al-Bukhaari")

Narrated Abi Waih, that Hudhaifah bin al-Yaman, may Allaah be pleased with him, said, { *The hypocrites of today are worse than those of the lifetime of the Prophet, because in those days they used to do evil deeds secretly but today they do such deeds openly. }* ("Saheeh al-Bukhaari")

So we see the importance of truthfulness in our statement of *ash-shahadah*, as it is a protection for us against hypocrisy. And we will discuss this at greater length in a later lesson, insh'Allaah. May Allaah make us from among the truthful ones.

> The Fifth: Love for the statement, and that which it signifies, and contentment with that

Explanation:

al-muhabbah: love, attachment, inclination

as-suroor: contentment, joy, delight, pleasure

As the Sheikh, may Allaah have mercy upon him, said, this love includes the meaning of the statement, as well as all that it comprises, from beliefs and action. If we love someone we strive to please them and to make them happy- if this is true for one of the creation, then how much more so for the Creator?!?! We should be striving to please Allaah in all that we do, as well as striving to know more about His names and attributes so that we grow in love of Him through appreciation of all that He does for us, insh'Allaah.

And alhamdulillah, *as-suroor*, or contentment and pleasure in this, is truly a great blessing that we must be extremely thankful for.

'Amr bin Taghlib, may Allaah be pleased with him, said, *{ Some property or something was brought to the Messenger of Allaah and he distributed it. He gave to some men and ignored the others. Later he received news that he was being criticized by those whom he had ignored. So he glorified and praised Allaah and said, "Amma ba'du. By Allaah, I may give to a man and ignore another, although the one whom I ignore is more beloved to me than the one whom I give. But I give to some people as I feel that they have no patience and no contentment in their hearts and I leave those who are patient and self-contented with the goodness and wealth which Allaah has put into their hearts and 'Amr bin Taghlib is one of them." 'Amr added, By Allaah! Those words of the Messenger of Allaah are more beloved to me than the best red camels.}* ("*Saheeh al-Bukhaari*")

Abu Huraira, may Allaah be pleased with him, narrated that the Prophet, may Allaah's praise and salutations be upon him, said, *{ Being rich does not mean having a great amount of property. Rather, richness is self-contentment. }* ("*Saheeh al-Bukhaari*")

> The Sixth: Compliance with all that is required by them, and that is, the obligatory acts, sincerely for Allaah alone, seeking His pleasure

Explanation:

al-inqiyaad: compliance, submission, yielding, obedience
We must act upon all that *ash-shahadah* contains and implies. This is the action, which comes after knowledge. Specifically, we must perform the acts that are obligatory upon us in Islaam, with *al-ikhlaas*, or purity of intention that we do that act solely for Allaah, to gain His pleasure.

> The Seventh: Acceptance, which negates rejection

Explanation:

al-qabool: acceptance, assent. willingness, approval, agreement

ar-rad: rejection, returning, turning away, repelling, refusing

We willingly accept these words and all that they contain and imply, as they are all from that which Allaah, the Most High, revealed for us to follow. We do not reject anything that Allaah, the Most High, sent down to his Prophet, may Allaah's praise and salutations be upon him. This means total acceptance, with heart and mind and limbs. This is in opposition to following of our desires, and rejecting something because it does not go along with what we think or what we wish.

An example of this is Hassan Turabi, who said, in opposition to the authentic hadeeth in which we are told to dunk the fly that falls in our drink, in order to release the antidote for the poison of the fly, "I would rather follow the words of a disbelieving doctor!" He said that the words of a *kaafir* held more truth and weight than the words of the Messenger of Allaah! This is a rejection of that which the Prophet, may Allaah's praise and salutations be upon him, said, in favor of intellect.

Another example of this is the mixing of married people with their in-laws. This has become commonplace today, mash'Allaah. Yet, the Messenger of Allaah, may Allaah's praise and salutations be upon him, said, in an authentic hadeeth, *"The in-laws are death"!* But the people choose to ignore this strong warning from the Prophet, may Allaah's praise and salutations be upon him, to follow their own desires. May Allaah protect us from that.

Here I would like to mention to you one additional condition that some scholars, including ibn Qayyim al-Jawziyyah, place on *ash-shahadah* as well, insh'Allaah, along with its proof.

8. Disbelief in *at-taaghoot* (basically, anything that is worshipped other than Allaah)

And the proof of this is the saying of Allaah, the Most High, ❴*Whoever disbelieves in taaghoot and believes in Allaah, then he has grasped the most trustworthy handhold that will never break. And Allaah is All-Hearer, All-Knower.*❵ —(Surat al-Baqarah, from Ayat 256)

One of the techniques used by the people of knowledge throughout the ages is to remember things through poetry. There is one that is used to remember the conditions of *la ilaaha ila Allaah*:

محبة وإنقياد والقبول لها   علم يقين وإخلاص وصدقك مع

And to remember the additional condition, some have added to this:

سوى الإله من الأنداد قد ألها   وزيد ثامنها الكفران منك.بما

> The Evidences of these Conditions from the Book of Allaah, the Most High, and from the Sunnah of the Messenger of Allaah, may Allaah's praise and salutations be upon him

al-adilah: plural of *ad-daleel*: proofs, evidences

We see here the Sheikh following that which he said before; that we must have knowledge of our Lord, and our religion, and our Prophet, based upon PROOF. We see that the people of innovation come up with their innovation, and then search for proofs to support them in their deviance. The people of the Sunnah, however, look to the evidences that are there, to see the principles that they are proofs for. In other words, the principles are clear in the Qur'aan and Sunnah already, along with their proofs- we do not first have the idea, and then look for evidences that can be interpreted or twisted to support that idea, as the people of innovation do. We see that many of the people today follow their desires in this, forming an idea from themselves (or from the *Shaytaan*!) and then looking through the Qur'aan and the *ahadeeth* to support that deviation that they wish to act upon or propagate. This is very common amongst those people who try to change Islaam to make it more palatable for the disbelievers…for example, Aminah Wadud, may Allaah guide her, who has written a book on women in the Qur'aan, full of false statements and conjecture from her own self. Sadly, I have seen this in the Arabic as well, with approval of al-Azhar University. She said that she cannot "intellectually accept" certain rulings from the Qur'aan, and said, "The Qur'aan gives me the means to say "no" to the Qur'aan". So, she simply used the Qur'aan, which is the speech of Allaah, not created, to try to propagate what one translator called her own western, Afrocentric, feminist "version" of Islaam. (This information is from the introduction of the translation of "Noble Women Scholars of Hadeeth") May Allaah guide her, and protect the Muslims from her false ideas and misconceptions and the evil of others like her.

And these first seven conditions are those which are the most famous from the books of the scholars, may Allaah have mercy upon them.

NOTES

91

Key Terms in this Lesson

Define these terms:

as-sidq:

al-kadhab:

an-nifaaq:

al-muhabbah:

as-suroor:

al-inqiyaad:

al-qabool:

ar-rad:

al-adilah:

at-taaghoot:

Lesson Questions:

Level 1: [required]

1. How does truthfulness negate hypocrisy?

2. How does love for Allaah help us to worship Him better?

3. *al-inqiyaad* was mentioned in a previous lesson. What are the two conditions we mentioned before for an action to be accepted?

4. What condition do some of the scholars add to the ones that Sheikh Muhammad ibn 'Abdul Wahhab listed in "*al-Waajibaat*"? What is its proof?

Level 2: [supplementary]

1. How is truthfulness the opposite of hypocrisy?

2. Why is contentment with that which Allaah has commanded and decreed for us such a blessing?

3. How do the Muslims who adhere to the sunnah differ with those who are upon a way of innovation, in how they deal with evidence?

4. Give an example of someone rejecting something from the Qur'aan and Sunnah.

LESSON EIGHT

From the Proofs for Knowledge:

His, the Most High's, saying, ❴ *So know (Oh Muhammad) that la ilaha ila allaah (none has the right to be worshipped but Allaah)* ❵ –(Surat Muhammad, from Ayat 19)

And His saying, ❴*...except for those who bear witness to the truth knowingly (i.e. believed in the Oneness of Allaah, and obeyed His Orders and they know (the facts about the Oneness of Allaah)...* ❵ –(Surat az-Zakhroof, from Ayat 86). Meaning, with *"la ilaha ila Allaah"*. ❴*...and they know (the facts about the Oneness of Allaah)* ❵ –(Surat az-Zakhroof, from Ayat 86) (know) with their hearts, that which they say with their tongues.

And from the Sunnah: The hadeeth found in *"as-Saheeh"* on 'Uthmaan, may Allaah be pleased with him, wherein he said, Allaah's Messenger, may Allaah's praise and salutations be upon him, said, { *He who died, knowing with certainty that there is none worthy of worship except for Allaah, entered Paradise.*} ("Saheeh Muslim", No. 26)

Explanation: What is meant here by *al-ilm*, is that which increases us in obedience to Allaah, Glorified and Exalted, and His Messenger, may Allaah's praise and salutations be upon him, as well as that which increases us in fear and reverence for Allaah, the Most High. And it is the true, authentic, knowledge, with the meaning and significance of the *shahadatan* and that which both of them make obligatory from action.

The opposite of *al-ilm*, is *al-jahl*, or ignorance. And ignorance is that which has occurred among those who associated others with Allaah in this *Ummah* (nation) in contradicting its meaning, such that they did not even understand the meaning of "god", or one that is worshipped. And this is the significance of negation and affirmation. And their turning away from that which is intended by the meaning of this statement, and their contradiction of this meaning, as is indicated by their saying in the Qur'aan:

❴ *Has he made the aalihah (gods) (all) into One Ilaah (God – Allaah). Verily, this is a curious thing!* ❵ –(Surah Saad, Ayat 5)

and they say, ❴ *And the leaders among them went about (saying): "Go on, and remain constant to your aalihah (gods)! Verily, this is a thing designed (against you)!* ❵ –(Surah Saad, Ayat 6)

From the Proofs for Certainty:

His, the Most High's, saying, ❖ **Only those are the believers who have believed in Allaah and His Messenger, and afterward doubt not but strive with their wealth and their lives for the Cause of Allaah. Those! They are the truthful.** ❖ –(Surat al-Hujuraat, Ayat 15)

And it is a condition of truthfulness, their belief in Allaah and His Messenger, may Allaah's praise and salutations be upon him, making it a reality without any skepticism; that is to say, without doubting. As for the one who doubts, then he is from the hypocrites.

And from the Sunnah: The hadeeth found in *"as-Saheeh"* from Abee Hurairah, may Allaah be pleased with him, that he said, { The Messenger of Allaah, may Allaah's praise and salutations be upon him, said, *'I bear testimony to the fact that there is none worthy of worship except Allaah, and I am the Messenger of Allaah. The servant who would meet Allaah without entertaining any doubt about these two would enter heaven.'*} (*"Saheeh Muslim"*, No. 27)

And in another narration, { *The servant who would meet Allaah without any doubt about these two statements (the shahadatan), would never be kept from Paradise.'*} (*"Saheeh Muslim"*, No. 28)

And on Abee Hurairah also, from a long hadeeth, { *The one who you meet behind this garden, who bears witness that there is none worthy of worship but Allaah, and his heart is firm upon that, then give him glad tidings of Paradise.*} (*"Saheeh Muslim"*, No. 31)

Explanation: The opposite of this is doubt, and uncertainty.

And the meaning of this condition is that the one who fulfills the *shahadatayn*, it is necessary for him to be certain in his heart, and to believe truly in that which he says, which is that Allaah, the Most High, is the only God worthy of worship, and to verify the Prophethood of Muhammad, may Allaah's praise and salutations be upon him, and to know with certainty that anything that is worshipped besides Allaah is false, in any aspect of worship, and that anyone who calls to a prophet after Muhammad, may Allaah's praise and salutations be upon him, is false. As the one who doubts concerning the truth of its meaning, or is uncertain about the falseness of worshiping other than Allaah, will not be successful through these two sayings (*ash-shahadatan*).

And there is no doubt that the one who is certain of the meaning of *ash-shahadatayn*, that his limbs must then proceed in worship of the Lord, alone, and will go forth in obedience to the Messenger, may Allaah's praise and salutations be upon him.

From the Proofs of Sincerity:

The saying of the Most High, ﴾ ***Surely, the religion (i.e. the worship and the obedience) is for Allaah only...*** ﴿ –(Surat az-Zamr, from Ayat 3)

And His saying, Glorified is He, ﴾ ***And they were commanded not, but that they should worship Allaah, and worship none but Him Alone (abstaining from ascribing partners to Him)...*** ﴿ –(Surat al-Bayyinah, from Ayat 5)

And from the Sunnah, the hadeeth found in as-Saheeh on the authority of Abee Hurairah, may Allaah be pleased with him, on the Prophet, may Allaah's praise and salutations be upon him, { *The most pleased of the people with my intercession is the one who said la ilaha ila Allaah sincerely from his heart (or his self)* } ("Saheeh al-Bukhaari", No.99)

And in the Saheeh, on the authority of 'Utbaan ibn Maalik, may Allaah be pleased with him, from the Prophet, may Allaah's praise and salutations be upon him, that he said, { *Verily Allaah has made the Fire forbidden for the one who said, la ilaha ila Allaah, seeking by that the Face of Allaah, the Glorified, the Most Exalted.* } ("Saheeh al-Bukhaari", No. 425, "Saheeh Muslim", No. 33)

And from an-Nasaa'i, in his book, *"al-Yawm wa al-Layl"*, from a hadeeth of two men of the Companions, from the Prophet, may Allaah's praise and salutations be upon him, that he said, { *The one who says, 'There is none worthy of worship except Allaah Alone, without associating any partners with Him, to Him is the dominion over everything, and to Him is due all praise, and He has power over all things', and his heart is sincere upon it, and his tongue is truthful in saying it, except that Allaah will split the heavens open for him, until he sees the ones who say it from the people of the Earth. And the right of the servant is that Allaah looks upon him to grant him his request.* } (This is a weak narration. See *"Da'if at-Targheeb"*, No.932)

Explanation: The meaning of *al-ikhlaas* is that all acts of worship are done for Allaah, alone, without directing anything from them to other than Allaah, neither any angel brought near nor any prophet sent as a messenger. Likewise, *al-ikhlaas* in the following of Muhammad, may Allaah's praise and salutations be upon him, with limiting oneself to his Sunnah, and his rulings, and leaving innovation and those things in which there is differing; and likewise to leave the litigation by that which was put down by mankind of legislation and customs which they have invented, and they clash with the Islamic legislation. As the one who is pleased with them, or judges by them, is not from the people of sincerity. (We will learn more of this later in the course, insh'Allaah)

From the Proofs of Truthfulness:

The saying of The Most High,

❦ *Alif-Laam-Meem.*[These letters are one of the miracles of the Qur'aan, and none but Allaah (Alone) knows their meanings.]

Do people think that they will be left alone because they say: "We believe," and will not be tested?

And We indeed tested those who were before them. And Allaah will certainly make (it) known (the truth of) those who are true, and will certainly make (it) known (the falsehood of) those who are liars, (although Allaah knows all that before putting them to test).❧ —(Surat al-'Ankaboot, Ayat 1-3)

And the saying of The Most High,

❦ *And of mankind, there are some (hypocrites) who say: "We believe in Allaah and the Last Day," while in fact they believe not.*

They (think to) deceive Allaah and those who believe, while they only deceive themselves, and perceive (it) not!

In their hearts is a disease (of doubt and hypocrisy) and Allaah has increased their disease. A painful torment is theirs because they used to tell lies.❧ — (Surat al-Baqarah, Ayats 8-10)

And from the Sunnah: that which is found in the two Saheehs, on the authority of Mu'aadh ibn Jabal, may Allaah be pleased with him, that the Prophet, may Allaah's praise and salutations be upon him, said, *{ There is no one who testifies that there is none worthy of worship except Allaah, and that Muhammad is His servant and Messenger, truthfully from his heart, except that Allaah makes the Fire forbidden for him.}* (al-Bukhaari, No. 128, and Muslim, No.32)

The opposite of truthfulness is falsehood. As for the one who says it with his tongue, while being untruthful concerning its meaning and significance in his heart, then it will not bring him success, as Allaah says about the hypocrites, that they say,

❦… ***"We bear witness that you are indeed the Messenger of Allaah." Allaah knows that you are indeed His Messenger, and Allaah bears witness that the hypocrites***

*

are liars indeed. –(Surah al-Munaafiqoon, From Ayat 1)

And they are liars, as Allaah says,

And of mankind, there are some (hypocrites) who say: "We believe in Allaah and the Last Day," while in fact they believe not. –(Surat al-Baqara, Ayat 8)

So we must strive to gain knowledge of our way of life, our religion, our beliefs, and all that Islaam encompasses, with the hope that this knowledge will lead to certainty, which leads to truthfulness, and will increase us in faith, insh'Allaah.

Key Terms in this Lesson

Define these terms:

al-ikhlaas:

al-yaqeen:

al-jahl:

Lesson Questions:

Level 1: [required]

1. What sort of knowledge is being referred to in the first condition?

2. What are some of the fruits of *al-yaqeen?*

3. What is the meaning of *al-ikhlaas?*

4. What do you call a person who claims to be Muslim, but is not truthful in this statement?

Level 2: [supplementary]

1. How were the people at the time of the Prophet, may Allaah's praise and good mention be upon him, ignorant?

2. Why will a person who has doubts in his heart concerning the *shahadah* not be successful?

3. How is following the Sunnah a matter of *al-ikhlaas*?

4. After marrying a Muslim man, a woman takes her *shahadah*. She does it because she thinks it would be best for their children to be raised in one faith, and she thinks that there is a lot of good to be found in Islaam in a general sense. She does not know much about the belief system, but she knows there is no drinking or adultery, so that is good. Do you think her *shahadah* will be correct? Why or why not? (and only Allaah knows if it would, indeed, be correct)

LESSON NINE

From the Proofs of Love:

The saying of the Most High, ❨ *And of mankind are some who take (for worship) others besides Allaah as rivals (to Allaah). They love them as they love Allaah. But those who believe, love Allaah more (than anything else).* ❩ –(Surat al-Baqarah, from Ayat 165)

And His saying, ❨ *O you who believe! Whoever from among you turns back from his religion (Islaam), Allaah will bring a people whom He will love and they will love Him; humble towards the believers, stern towards the disbelievers, fighting in the way of Allaah, and never fear the blame of the blamers.* ❩ –(Surat al-Maa'idah, from Ayat 54)

And from the Sunnah: That which is found in the Saheeh, on the authority of Anas ibn Maalik, may Allaah's praise and good mention be upon him, that he said, "Allaah's Messenger, may Allaah's praise and salutations be upon him, said:

{ *Whoever possesses the following three qualities will have the sweetness (delight) of faith:*

1. The one to whom Allaah and His Messenger becomes dearer than anything else.

2. Who loves a person and he loves him only for Allaah's sake.

3. Who hates to revert to disbelief as he hates to be thrown into the fire.' }

(Found in the two Saheehs: al-Bukhaari, No. 16, and Muslim, No. 43)

Explanation: And this love negates its opposite, which is dislike and hatred. It is obligatory upon the servant to love Allaah and to love His Messenger, may Allaah's praise and salutations be upon him, and to love all of that which has been made obligatory from actions and deeds, as well as love for His supporters and those who are obedient to Him. In addition, one must love Islaam and all that it encompasses of actions of the heart, tongue, and limbs. The effects of this love, when it is sound and true, are evident on the body. So the servant who is truthful, who obeys Allaah and follows His Messenger, may Allaah's praise and salutations be upon him, and who worships Allaah as He has the right to be worshipped, and who takes pleasure in his obedience, and who hurries to all that pleases his Lord from sayings and actions… and he is seen to guard against sin and wrongdoing and to remove himself from it, and he detests and hates the people of wrongdoing- and this is whether the one who commits the sin is one of those who is beloved to him and customarily pleasant- through his knowledge that the Hellfire is surrounded by desires, and the Heaven is surrounded by that which is disliked- so when he is like that, then he is truthful, and is one who has the love (that is discussed here). And Dhu-Noon al-Misree was asked about this, may Allaah have mercy upon him. He was asked, "When do I love my Lord?" He said, "If what He hates is more bitter to you than *as-sabr*." (and *as-sabr* is an extremely bitter plant- the aloe).

And Allaah has made it a condition that one loves to follow the Prophet, may Allaah's praise and salutations be upon him, in His, the Most High's, saying, ❧ **Say (O Muhammad to mankind): "If you (really) love Allaah, then follow me. Allaah will love you and forgive you your sins. And Allaah is Oft-Forgiving, Most Merciful.** ❧ –(Surat aal-'Imraan, Ayat 31)

From the Proofs of Compliance:

The saying of The Most High is a proof for it: ❧ *And turn in repentance and in obedience with true Faith (Islamic Monotheism) to your Lord and submit to Him (in Islaam) before the torment comes upon you, (and) then you will not be helped.* ❧ –(Surat az-Zumar, from Ayat 54)

And His saying, ❧ *And who can be better in religion than one who submits his face (himself) to Allaah (i.e. follows Allaah's religion of Islamic Monotheism); and he is a Muhsin (a good-doer)* ❧ –(Surat an-Nisaa', from Ayat 125)

And His saying, ❧ *And whosoever submits his face (himself) to Allaah, while he is a Muhsin (good-doer, i.e. performs good deeds totally for Allaah's sake without any show-off or to gain praise or fame and does them in accordance with the Sunnah of Allaah's Messenger Muhammad), then he has grasped the most trustworthy handhold [la ilaha ila llaah (none has the right to be worshipped but Allaah)].* ❧ –(Surat Luqmaan, from Ayat 22) Meaning, to the statement, *"la ilaha ila Allaah"*.

And His, The Most High, saying, ❧ *But no, by your Lord, they can have no Faith, until they make you (O Muhammad) judge in all disputes between them, and find in themselves no resistance against your decisions, and accept (them) with full submission.* ❧ –(Surat an-Nisaa', Ayat 65)

And from the Sunnah, his, may Allaah's praise and salutations be upon him, saying, { One of you does not believe until his desires come after that which I have come with. } (This hadeeth is weak, see verification of *"al-Mushkaat"*, No. 167)

And this is from the completeness of compliance, and its purpose.

Explanation: As to the difference between *al-inqiyaad* (compliance) and *al-qabool* (acceptance):

al-inqiyaad: it is following with actions

al-qabool: demonstrating the truth of the meaning of that through speech. (And this is with the acceptance of the heart, as well)

And both of them make following Allaah and His Messenger, may Allaah's praise and salutations be upon him, obligatory. However, *al-inqiyaad* is submission and yielding or compliance and not leaving off something from the rulings of Allaah.

And from the conditions of sound faith is that one submits totally to the rulings of Allaah; meaning, they submit to and comply with that which has been revealed from their Lord.

Explanation:

So there is the one who knows the meaning of the *shahadatayn*, and is certain of its significance; however, he rejects them because of pride or envy; and this was the state of some of the Jews and Christians, as they bore witness that there is no god worthy of worship except Allaah alone, and they knew Muhammad, may Allaah's praise and salutations be upon him, like they knew their own sons, and with that, they did not accept him.
 Allaah says,

❀ *Many of the people of the Scripture wish that they could turn you away as disbelievers after you have believed, out of envy from their own selves, even after the truth (that Muhammad is Allaah's Messenger) has become manifest to them.*❀
–(Surat al-Baqarah, Ayat 109)

And likewise, the ones who associate others with Allaah (*al-mushrikoon),* understood the meaning of *la ilaaha ila Allaah,* and the truthfulness of Muhammad, may Allaah's praise and salutations be upon him, but they were too proud to accept him, as Allaah, the Most High, says,

❀*...it is not you that they deny, but it is the Verses of Allaah that the polytheists and wrong doers deny.*❀ –(Surat al-An'aam, from Ayat 33)

Some final words from Sheikh 'Abd-ul-Lateef ibn 'Abd-ur-Rahman, may Allaah have mercy upon him, from *"Fatawa al-A'imatu an-Najdiyyah",* Volume 3, Pages 19-20:

"And it is an error of many of those who associate others with Allaah in this age, that anyone (from the scholars, especially) who says that a person who says ash-shahadah has disbelieved (through some action or saying of his) then that person is from al-Khawarij. (This is not true). Rather, the pronouncing of ash-shahadatayn is not something that makes disbelief prohibited for that person- except for the one who understands the meaning of the two statements (I testify that there is no god worthy of worship except Allaah alone, and I testify that Muhammad is His slave and Messenger), and acts upon all that they signify, and performs acts of worship solely for Allaah and does not associate others with Him- this is when ash-shahadatan is of benefit to him.

As for the one who pronounces them, and yet there does not come from him compliance with all that they signify; rather, he associates others with Allaah, and takes mediation and intercession from other than Allaah, and seeks from them that which none has the ability to control other than Allaah, and attempts to draw close to them through sacrifice, and acts toward them as the people of ignorance did from those who associate others with Allaah- then ash-shahadatan will not benefit him; rather, he is a liar in his shahadah, as Allaah says,

❀ **When the hypocrites come to you (O Muhammad) they say: "We bear witness that you are indeed the Messenger of Allaah." Allaah knows that you are indeed His Messenger, and Allaah bears witness that the hypocrites are liars indeed."** ❀
—(Surat al-Munaafiqoon, Ayat 1)

And the meaning of testifying that there is no god worthy of worship except Allaah, is to worship Allaah, and to leave off of worshiping anything other than Him; as the one who is arrogant concerning His worship, and does not worship Him, then he is not from those who testify that there is no god worthy of worship except Allaah. And the one who worships Him and worships along with Him other than Him, then he is not from those who testify that there is no god worthy of worship except Allaah." (End of translation)

A reminder- as we learned before, it is not for us to say whether or not one has disbelieved- it is for the people of knowledge. But we need to understand clearly the line between belief and disbelief, for our own selves, as Muslim men and women, students, wives, mothers, sisters, husbands, fathers, brothers, teachers- it is vital that we understand this and guard ourselves and those we love as best we can- through teaching them, as well as implementing what we learn in our own lives.

So, may Allaah bless you all, we MUST understand the conditions of our *shahadah*, and learn about this amazing and complete way of life that we have been gifted with- the religion of Islaam, and we must act upon it, making it a reality in our lives, as this is the way to success in this life and the Hereafter. And Allaah knows best.

NOTE: A more detailed explanation of the proofs for the conditions of ash-shahadah by Sheikh 'Ubaid al-Jaabiree, may Allaah preserve him, is available as a free ebook at study.taalib.com, alhamdulillah.

Key Terms in this Lesson

Define these terms:

al-inqiyaad:

al-qabool:

Lesson Questions:

Level 1: [required]

1. What is the love that is spoken of in this condition? What does it include?
2. What is the proof that following the Prophet, may Allaah's praise and salutations be upon him, is part of this love?
3. Explain the difference between *al-inqiyaad* and *al-qabool*?

Level 2: [supplementary]

1. How do we show love for Allaah by following His Messenger, may Allaah's praise and salutations be upon him?
2. Give an example of *al-inqiyaad*. Give an example of *al-qabool*.
3. Explain how pride and envy leads to disbelief. Give examples of this.
4. How can someone who verbally states *ash-shahadah* still be a disbeliever? Who has the right to make the statement that one has disbelieved?

LESSON TEN

> **From the Things which Nullify Islaam**
>
> Know that there are ten things which nullify Islaam:

Explanation: Here, Sheikh Muhammad ibn 'Abdul Wahaab, may Allaah have mercy upon him, mentions ten things that nullify one's Islaam. In some of the manuscripts, it says, "From the Things...". This is the most correct, as the things that can nullify Islaam are many. These are just some of them, and they are all common ones that mankind fall easily into. And Allaah knows best.

nawaaqid: plural of "*naaqid*": and its religious meaning is, "Departing or deviating from the Legislation to other than it."

Again, I want to stress that it is not you and I who are the judges of whether or not one has left Islaam!! This is for the people of knowledge, only, alhamdulillah. These things that are mentioned as nullifying Islaam are for our knowledge, to assist us in safeguarding ourselves from their evil, as well as teaching our children, family, and Muslim brothers and sisters, insh'Allaah. Sadly, the *takfeeri minhaj* is widespread in the world today, and we see the trials that it causes when we look at the misguidance and evil that has been propagated by *al-Qaa'idah* and other astray organizations. May Allaah protect us from that and guide the Muslims to the Straight Path.

> *The First:* Associating others in the worship of Allaah, the Most High.
>
> Allaah, the Most High, says, ❦ *Verily, Allaah forgives not that partners should be set up with Him (in worship), but He forgives except that (anything else) to whom He wills...* ❧ –(Surat an-Nisaa, from Ayat 48)
>
> And He says, ❦ *Verily, whosoever sets up partners (in worship) with Allaah, then Allaah has forbidden Paradise to him, and the Fire will be his abode. And for the polytheists and wrong doers there are no helpers.* ❧ –(Surat al-Maa'idah, from Ayat 72)
>
> And from this is sacrificing to other than Allaah, such as the one who sacrifices to the *jinn*, or to the graves.

Explanation: *ash-shirk*, or associating others along with Allaah in worship, is generally divided into two levels: the greater or major *shirk* (*shirk akbar*) and lesser or minor *shirk* (*shirk asghar*). The one that takes one out of Islaam, the one mentioned here, is the greater *shirk*, and it is the greatest of the great sins. We will, insh'Allaah, be going into these in greater depth later on in the course, insh'Allaah.

Allaah, the Most High, says, ◈ *Verily, Allaah forgives not that partners should be set up with Him (in worship), but He forgives except that (anything else) to whom He wills...*◈-(**Surat an-Nisaa, from Ayat 48**)

This is if a person dies upon associating others with Allaah. Otherwise, Allaah's mercy is complete and perfect, and if one makes proper *tawbah*, or repentance, while he is alive, he will be forgiven, and Allaah knows best.

From the punishments for the one who associates others with Allaah, stated in this verse from Surat al-Maaidah:

1. He is forbidden from entering *al-Jannah*

2. That is forbidden for him forever

3. He is of the *dhaalimoon* (the wrongdoers)

4. There are no helpers for him

One can fall into *shirk* through belief, speech, actions, and intentions. An example of *shirk* in speech is if one were to say, "If Allaah and His Messenger will it to be." An example of *shirk* in actions is making prostration to an idol, or to a person who we think has some sort of power. And the example of *shirk* of intention is when we perform an act of worship without *al-ikhlaas*, or purity of intention, for Allaah alone. Sheikh 'Abdul Lateef ibn 'Abdur Rahman, may Allaah have mercy upon him, says of this last type of *shirk*, *"As for shirk of purpose and intention, then that is the sea which has no shore, and few are those who escape from it. As the one who desires by his actions other than the face of Allaah, the Most High, or intends something for a reason other than drawing nearer to Allaah, and seeks a portion from it, then he has committed shirk in purpose and intention."* (From *"Minhaj at-Ta'sees wa at-Taqdees"*, as quoted in, *"Fataawa al-A'imatu an-Najdiyyah"*, Vol. 2, Page 20) May Allaah protect us from falling into that sea.

The Sheikh, may Allaah have mercy upon him, goes on to say, *"The reason for ash-shirk is having the bad suspicion of Allaah, and His absolute perfection; and that is the greatest of sins to Allaah, Glorified is He. When we clarify this, we have spoken of a great principle which uncovers the secret of the matter. And it is that the greatest sin to Allaah is having the bad suspicion of Him."* The Sheikh, may Allaah have mercy upon him, goes on to say that this is because when one has this bad suspicion of Allaah, he has said that Allaah is not perfect in His names and attributes, and that He has some deficiency. And this is truly an evil thing. Conversely, it has also been said by one of the Salaf that *at-tawakkul*, or having reliance upon Allaah, is having the good suspicion of Him.

So this means in our everyday lives, depending and relying upon Allaah, the Most High, in all matters. We do not want to be like the people who, when calamity befalls them, they shake their fists at the sky and say, "Why me???" and lose their faith in Allaah. We must strive to always have the good suspicion of Allaah, that all that He has planned for us, and had happen to us, has a purpose, and that purpose is for our ultimate good. If we look at hardships as tests, we strive to get through them in the best possible manner, and are capable of success, insh'Allaah.

> *The Second:* One who sets up between himself and Allaah intermediaries, and supplicates to them and asks them for intercession and relies upon them: all of this is disbelief (*kafara*)

Explanation: *wasaa'it*: the plural of *waseetah*. It means, intermediary, or intermediaries. Here, Sheikh Muhammad ibn 'Abdul Wahaab, may Allaah have mercy upon him, is discussing when one sets up intermediaries between himself and Allaah, the Most High.

There are two types of *waseetah*:

1. Legislated *waseetah*
2. *Waseetah* that involves associating others with Allaah

The legislated *waseetah:* This includes the prophets, the scholars, and the pious people, who are intermediaries in that they are the ones who carry the knowledge to us. The proof of this is Allaah, the Most High, saying,

❰ *Messengers as bearers of good news as well as of warning in order that mankind should have no plea against Allaah after the (coming of) Messengers. And Allaah is Ever All-Powerful, All-Wise.* ❱ –(Surat an-Nisaa', Ayat 165)

The *waseetah* that involves associating others with Allaah: This is making someone other than Allaah, an intermediary between a person and his Lord. An example would be going to someone else to supplicate to Allaah for you, because you think you have too many sins, and Allaah would not answer your supplication. This is making the Creator like the created, and is forbidden in Islaam. For example, if you wanted a favor from the king, or president of the country, you would have to go through other people to get to him. You would not be able to go to him directly. This is not true of Allaah, the Most High, who listens to our supplications and answers them, alhamdulilaahi Rabbil 'Aalameen. Allaah says of this,

NOTES

❦ *And they worship besides Allaah things that harm them not, nor profit them, and they say: "These are our intercessors with Allaah." Say: "Do you inform Allaah of that which He knows not in the heavens and on the earth?" Glorified and Exalted is He above all that which they associate as partners (with Him)!*❧
–(Surat Yoonus, Ayat 18)

Insh'Allaah this will be discussed in much greater depth and clarified later in the series, in the study of "*Qawaa'id al-Arbaa*". The very basic explanation which is presented here is, insh'Allaah, sufficient for one to gain a general understanding of this belief.

Sheikh Muhammad ibn 'Abdul Wahaab al-Wasaabee, may Allaah preserve him, says, in *"al-Qawl ul-Mufeed"*, that the second thing which negates Islaam is hypocrisy, as here, the one who places intermediaries between himself and Allaah has entered into the first of the things that negate Islaam, and that is *shirk*- so this would fall into the first category. And Allaah knows best.

> *The Third:* The one who does not say that the ones who associate others along with Allaah in worship are disbelievers, or has doubt as to their disbelief, or who says that their way is correct, has himself disbelieved.

Explanation: This belief goes against that which Allaah has told us repeatedly in the Qur'aan. It is common in this age for the modernist Muslims to try to gloss over this, to deny it or explain it away, to make Islaam seem more to the liking of the disbelievers. In so doing, they have clearly disbelieved in that which Allaah, Glorified and Exalted is He, has informed us. And this, in turn, can lead one out of Islaam. May Allaah protect us from that.

And two of the sons of Sheikh Muhammad ibn 'Abdul Wahaab, Sheikh Husayn and Sheikh 'Abdullaah, may Allaah have mercy upon them all, were asked about a man who enters Islaam and loves it, yet does not have enmity for the disbelievers, or say that they are disbelievers. They said,

"The man is not a Muslim, unless he understands and submits with at-tawheed, and acts upon his love, and knows that that which the Messenger, may Allaah's praise and good mention be upon him, related is the truth, and obeys him in leaving that which he prohibited, and following that which he commanded, and believes in him and that which he came with. As the one who says, "I am not an enemy of the mushrikeen (the ones who associate other with Allaah in worship)", or, "I have enmity for them, but they are not disbelievers,"…then he is not Muslim. Rather, he is of the ones whom Allaah says of them,

❦ *Verily, those who disbelieve in Allaah and His Messengers and wish to make*

111

distinction between Allaah and His Messengers, saying, "We believe in some but reject others," and wish to adopt a way in between. They are in truth disbelievers. ◈ *–(Surat an-Nisaa', From Ayats 150-151)*

And Allaah, Glorified and Exalted is He, has made it obligatory to have enmity for those who associate partners with Him…and to affirm that they are disbelievers, as He says,

◈ **You will not find any people who believe in Allaah and the Last Day, making friendship with those who oppose Allaah and His Messenger , even though they were their fathers or their sons or their brothers or their kindred.** ◈ *–(Surat al-Mujaadilah, From Ayat 22)*

◈ **O you who believe! Take not My enemies and your enemies (i.e. disbelievers and polytheists) as friends, showing affection towards them, while they have disbelieved in what has come to you of the truth, and have driven out the Messenger and yourselves because you believe in Allaah, your Lord! If you have come forth to strive in My Cause and to seek My Good Pleasure, (then take not these disbelievers and polytheists, as your friends). You show friendship to them in secret, while I am All-Aware of what you conceal and what you reveal. And whosoever of you does that, then indeed he has gone (far) astray from the Straight Path.** ◈ *–(Surat al-Mumtahinah, Ayat 1)"* (End of translation from *"Fataawa al-A'imatu an-Najdiyyah*, Vol. 3)

> *The Fourth:* The one who believes that other than the guidance of the Prophet, may Allaah's praise and good mention be upon him, is more complete than his guidance, or that rulings other than his are better than his rulings, such as the one who places the judgments of the *tawagheet* (anything that is worshipped other than Allaah) before his (the Prophet's) rulings- than he is a disbeliever.

Explanation:
hadee: guidance
hukm: rulings, legislation

This is the one who believes that any form of guidance other than that which Allaah sent Muhammad, may Allaah's praise and salutations be upon him, with, is better than his, may Allaah's praise and salutations be upon him, guidance. An example of this today are those people who claim that democracy is better than the system of ruling that the Messenger of Allaah put in place, and that the Western legal system is more complete and perfect than that which he, may Allaah's praise and salutations be upon him, was sent with. Allaah says in the Qur'aan,

‹This day, I have perfected your religion for you, completed My favor upon you, and have chosen for you Islaam as your religion. But as for him who is forced by severe hunger, with no inclination to sin (such can eat these above mentioned meats), then surely, Allaah is Oft-Forgiving, Most Merciful. › –(Surat al-Maa'idah, from Ayat 3)

This includes also that which we mentioned previously, of the one who takes the ideas put forth in modern science over that which the Prophet, may Allaah's praise and salutations, came with. And Allaah knows best.

So we must know and affirm that we have been blessed with a complete religion, a complete way of life- again, the map has been placed before us, with the key being in following the guidance put forth in the Qur'aan and Sunnah, as understood and practiced by the pious predecessors, the *salaf as-saalih*, may Allaah have mercy upon them all. Alhamdulillah, learning the correct *'aqeedah* can put us firmly on the path of following this guidance, and increase us in love of Allaah, His Messenger, may Allaah's praise and salutations be upon him, and this beautiful deen of ours…may Allaah increase us in faith and righteous action, and make us strong on His Straight Path.

The Fifth: The one who hates something which the Messenger, may Allaah's praise and good mention be upon him, came with, even if he acts upon it, has disbelieved.

Explanation: *abghad:* to hate, to detest, to dislike, to loathe: This is something that resides in the heart, even if one acts upon the act that is hated, and it can nullify one's Islaam.

This is a mistake that we must be very careful to avoid, as many of the Muslims fall into it. They think that doing an act is enough, even if they dislike it. For example, a woman who wears the *hijaab*, but does not like it, is in danger of this *naaqid* of Islaam if her hatred of it leads her to hate the fact that Allaah has legislated it for her. Another, that is prevalent amongst the women, is a dislike of polygeny for our husbands. This is often simply an irrational dislike, based upon our own pride and our own desires, mash'Allaah. Yet, it IS a legislated act, and by hating it, it may lead to something that will make our Islaam invalid. Alhamdulillah, all that Allaah has legislated He did so with wisdom, and justice, and knowledge- when we hate something that He has made obligatory or permissible for us, then we are calling into question the perfection of Allaah in these attributes and in His judgment and that which He has written for us. This is very dangerous, and can lead to more sin and wrongdoing.

We have to supplicate to Allaah, to make us strong in our love for Him, His Messenger, and His religion, and to protect us from falling into this common mistake. And according to Sheikh al-Islaam ibn Taymiyyah and others, it is better to do the act than abandon it, and to ask for Allaah to remove any dislike we may have for it. By looking at the wisdom behind the act, it can also help us to grow in love and acceptance of it. For example, with polygeny, sisters need to look at it as a test, and as a way to revive a Sunnah that has been abandoned by many of the people today, especially the modernists, who apologize for it and claim that it is no longer a valid act in Islaam. Again, the one who enters into polygeny with honor and grace, can know that she is doing an act that will make her more beloved to her husband, and more beloved to Allaah, insh'Allaah, and can use it as a way to get closer to Allaah, and to build her faith through extra acts of worship and seeking knowledge. So we must ask Allaah for assistance and success, and have *tawakkul,* or reliance upon Him. And Allaah knows best.

There are two categories of *al-baghd*, or hatred:

1. Natural hatred or dislike
2. Intellectual dislike of what has been legislated for us by Allaah and His Messenger, may Allaah's praise and salutations be upon him

The first hatred is that which occurs naturally. There is the fear, though, that one may let this hatred lead to the second type of hatred, which is not permissible. For example, it is natural to hate the idea of being killed. However, when one goes on the legislated *jihaad*, and fights in the way of Allaah, it is very possible that he may be killed. He still has to go on the legislated *jihaad*, for the sake of Allaah, knowing that there is a great reward for the one who dies as a martyr. He must fight to overcome this natural hatred, and have trust in Allaah, rather than fall into something that may nullify his Islaam and make his acts lost for him.

The second category of *al-baghd* is that which is one of the things that nullify Islaam, which we have already discussed.

And we ask Allaah for success in rectifying our affairs.

115

Key Terms in this Lesson

Define these terms:

naaqid/nawaaqid:
waseetah/ wasaa'it:
hadee:
al-bughd:

Lesson Questions:

Level 1: [required]

1. Does all *shirk* take us outside of Islaam? Explain your answer.

2. List four of the punishments for *ash-shirk* mentioned in the *ayat*.

3. Explain the two types of *al-waseetah* discussed in the lesson.

4. What is the proof from the Qur'aan that the disbelievers will not be successful in the Hereafter?

5. Give two of your own examples of following guidance other than the guidance of Muhammad, may Allaah's praise and salutations be upon him.

6. What are the two types of hatred? Which one nullifies one's Islaam?

Level 2: [supplementary]

1. Why do we need to be aware of those things which nullify one's Islaam?

2. Allaah states that He will forgive any sin other than *ash-shirk*. Does that mean that if one commits any *shirk*, and repents from that, that he will not be forgiven? Why or why not?

3. Give an example of *ash-shirk* in speech, and one in action, and one in intention.

4. How is the *waseetah* that includes associating other with Allaah, likening the Creator to the created?

5. Explain how committing *shirk* is having the bad suspicion of Allaah? And having *tawakkul* is having the good suspicion of Allaah?

6. As long as we act upon Allaah's legislation, we are successful. Is this true? Why or why not?

LESSON ELEVEN

NOTES

The Sixth: The one who ridicules something from the religion of the Messenger, may Allaah's praise and good mention be upon him, or the reward or punishment of Allaah concerning it, has disbelieved.

And the proof is the saying of Allaah, the Most High, ◈ *If you ask them (about this), they declare: "We were only talking idly and joking." Say: "Was it Allaah and His Ayat (proofs, evidences, verses, lessons, signs, revelations, etc.) and His Messenger that you were mocking?"*

Make no excuse; you disbelieved after you had believed. ◈ —(Surat at-Tawbah, Ayats 65-66)

Explanation: *al-istihzaa':* the religious meaning of this is the disdaining, mocking, ridiculing, and deriding of something that is legislated in Islaam, making clear supposed defects or deficiencies, in order to make others laugh, or to make fun of it. And this can be by making fun of it in word, action, or word and action.

al-istihzaa' can be divided into two categories:

1. explicit (*sareeh*)
2. not explicit (*ghairu sareeh*)

The first category is open, clear ridiculing of something from the Qur'aan or Sunnah. An example of this is the hadeeth of 'Abdullah ibn 'Umar, which reveals the reason for the revelation of the above verse. He said,

{ *During the battle of Tabook, a man was sitting in a gathering and said, 'I have never seen any like these reciters of ours! They have the hungriest stomachs, the most lying tongues, and are cowards in battle.' A man in the masjid said, 'You lie. You are a hypocrite, and I will surely inform the Messenger of Allaah, may Allaah's praise and good mention be upon him.' This statement was conveyed to the Messenger of Allaah, may Allaah's praise and salutations be upon him, and also a part of the Qur'aan revealed about it."* 'Abdullah ibn 'Umar said, *"I have seen that man afterwards holding onto the shoulders of the Messenger's camel while stones were falling on him, declaring, 'Oh Messenger of Allaah! We were only engaged in idle talk and jesting, while the Messenger of Allaah was reciting, ◈ Was it at Allaah, and His Ayat and His Messenger that you were mocking...◈ "* }(at-Tabari, see *"Tafseer ibn Katheer"*)

An example of the second category would be throwing a copy of the Qur'aan (*mus-haf*), whether intentionally or unintentionally (for example, tossing it on the bed when you are done using it). In either category of *istihzaa'*, the intention is not what is important for the deed to be considered serious, as we see from the hadeeth above. The man did not intend to commit hypocrisy, he was only trying to make his friends laugh.

Sheikh Fauzaan, may Allaah preserve him, says of *al-istihzaa'*:

"It is obligatory upon the Muslim to have honor and reverence for the Book of Allaah, and the Sunnah of His Messenger, and the scholars of the Muslims, and to know the ruling of al-istihzaa' of the mention of Allaah, or the Qur'aan, or the Messenger, in order that the Muslim beware of that. As the one who derides, ridicules, or mocks the mention of Allaah, or al-Qur'aan, or the Messenger, or something from the Sunnah- he has disbelieved in Allaah, Exalted and Glorified is He, through his demeaning of the Lordship and the Message. And that is contrary to at-tawheed, and it is disbelief according to the agreement of the people of knowledge."

The Sheikh goes on to discuss the two verses above and the hadeeth that we have mentioned as the reason for the revelation of the verses. He then goes on to say,

"...So these two great verses, along with the reason of their revelation, present the clear proof of the disbelief of the one who ridicules Allaah, or His Messenger, or the verses of Allaah, or the Sunnah of the Messenger of Allaah, or the companions of the Messenger of Allaah- because it is deriding the Lordship and the message, even if one does not intend truly to demean it.

And from this chapter is the ridiculing of knowledge and its people, and the lack of honoring them…even if we do not intend ridiculing and lying, but are just playing around- and this playing around is the opposite of seriousness or earnestness-then Allaah has informed them on the tongue of His Messenger, may Allaah's praise and salutations be upon him, that their excuse for this does not suffice with Allaah anything, and that they have disbelieved after their believing by this…" (From *"al-Irshaad ila Tasheeh al-'Itqaad"*, Pages 91-99, as quoted in, *"Fataawa al-A'imatu an-Najdiyyah"*, Volume 4, Pages 266-267)

This is a very serious offence, and again, it is one that is taken lightly nowadays. People who do not believe that the *hijaab* is obligatory upon the women deride the ones who wear it, calling them ghosts, and ninjas, among other things. People also often ridicule the beard, which is obligatory for the men, or they make fun of the men who follow the Sunnah and wear their pants above their ankles. As for the second category of *istihzaa'*, then how often is it that we see people finish reviewing from the Qur'aan and then they drop it onto the ground next to them? Mash'Allaah sisters, we must be on our guard against the grave offense of *istihzaa'*, and warn our Muslim brothers and sisters about it as well, insh'Allaah.

> *The Seventh*: Magic, and from it is *as-sarf* and *al-'atf*, as the one who performs it, or is pleased with it has disbelieved.
>
> And the proof is the saying of Allaah, the Most High, ◈*...but they could not thus harm anyone except by Allaah's Leave. And they learn that which harms them and profits them not...*◈ –(Surat al-Baqarah, from Ayat 102)

Explanation: This *ayat* itself is not a complete proof that magic is from those things that nullify one's Islaam. Some of the publications of the text include the section of this verse which DOES contain the proof of this:

◈*...but neither of these two (angels) taught anyone (such things) till they had said, "We are for a trial, so disbelieve not (by learning this magic from us)."*◈ –(Surat al-Baqarah, from Ayat 102)

as-sihr: There are several definitions of this, perhaps that which is most clear is that of Ibn Qudaamah, may Allaah have mercy upon him. He said that it is the use of spells, charms, and the tying of knots, in order to influence the body and the heart; as it causes illness, ineffectiveness, and differences between the husband and wife and takes one of the spouses from his or her companion.

Some examples of this could be if someone suddenly, without warning, loses his senses, or becomes incredibly angry with his wife for no reason, or a man loves a strange woman with a very strong love without any reason. As one of the signs of magic is that one changes from one condition to another suddenly, without apparent reason- according to the wishes of the one who has caused the magic.

as-sarf: this is a category of magic in which one changes a person from love to hatred of another person

al-'atf: this is a category of magic in which one suddenly desires that which he did not desire before

Question: Is magic a reality, or not?

Answer: There is magic that is a reality, and there is magic that is illusion

The magic that is a reality is mentioned in the verse:

◈ *And from the evil of those who practice witchcraft when they blow in the knots*◈ –(Surat al-Falaq, Ayat 4)

The magic that is an illusion is mentioned in the verse wherein Moosaa confronts the magicians of Firaun:

◈*(Moosaa said), 'Nay, throw you (first)!' Then behold! Their ropes and their sticks, by their magic, appeared to him as though they moved fast.*◈ –(Surat Taa Haa, Ayat 66)

Sheikh Saalih Fauzaan, may Allaah preserve him, mentions two directions from which magic enters in to *ash-shirk* in his work, *"al-Irshaad ila Tasheeh al-'Itqaad"*:

1. *That which has in it making use of ash-shayateen, the devils, and attachment to them. And perhaps coming near to them through that which they love, in order that they carry out his service*

2. *That which contains claiming knowledge of the unseen, and claiming a partnership with Allaah in that, and this is disbelief and straying from the Straight Path. The Most High says,*

   ◌ ***And indeed they knew that the buyers of it (magic) would have no share in the Hereafter.*** ◌ –(Surat al-Baqarah, from Ayat 102) (End of translation from *"Fataawa al-A'imatu an-Najdiyyah"*, Volume 2, Pages 106-107)

Sheikh Fauzaan further says, in *"Fataawa al-'Aqeedah"*, pages 20:

"Magic is forbidden, and it is disbelief- learning it, and teaching it. (Here he quotes the verses mentioned above) *It is not permissible to utilize magic to fulfill any requirements- because it is forbidden, and it is disbelief. And that which is forbidden and disbelief is not permissible for the Muslim to use; rather, it is obligatory for him to leave it and annihilate it, and it is obligatory to kill the magician and release the Muslims from his evil."* (Collected from *"al-Muntaqa, min Fataawa Fadeelatu ash-Sheikh Saalih al-Fauzaan"*, Volume 1, Page 118)

Protection from Magic

Ibn Qayyim al-Jawziyyah, may Allaah have mercy upon him, says in *"at-Tibb an-Nabawi"*:

"Among the strongest and most beneficial of treatments for magic are the divine medicines; rather, they are the medicines beneficial for it by their essence. Magic is from the influence of the evil, lower spirits. Their influence will be repelled by that which opposes and resists them: by invocation of the name of Allaah (adh-dhikr), recitation of the Qur'aanic verses and supplications which cancel the action and effect of the spirits. The stronger and more sincere these supplications are, the more comprehensive and absolute is the protection they render. This is analogous to the meeting of two armies: each one has its troops and its weaponry, and whichever overcomes the other conquers it and takes control. Thus, when the heart is filled with Allaah, immersed in the remembrance of Him, through a daily portion (wird) of devotions, supplications, invocations, and taking refuge, and wherein the heart truly matches the tongue- this would be one of the most powerful means to prevent the attack of magic, and among the mightiest treatments for it once it has struck." (From *"Saheeh at-Tibb an-Nabawi"*, Pages 192-193)

Sheikh Muqbil, may Allaah have mercy upon him, said, as collected in *"Fataawa al-Maara'at al-Muslimah"*:

…then the most beneficial cure for it is to attach your heart to Allaah, Glorified is He, and the Most High; as Allaah holds the forelock of the Shaytaan in His hand, as He, the Most High, says,

❨ **There is not a moving (living) creature but He has the grasp of its forelock** ❩ –(Surah Hood, From Ayat 56) *And ash-Shaytaan has no power to change or strength, except by Allaah, the Most High. So I advise you to attach your heart to Allaah, the Most High, and to know that this Shaytaan is vile and lowly. So adhere to remembrance of Allaah, and to the performance of worship of Allaah, the Most Glorified, the Most Exalted. Then hope and expect that Allaah will remove it from you, and you are not in need of this one or that one.*

As strength in al-'aqeedah, and trust in Allaah, the Most Glorified, the Most Exalted, and adherence to the remembrance of Allaah, the remembrances of the morning and the evening, and acting upon that which you have learned from knowledge, such as adherence to the Sunnah, and performance of the prayers in their times- these are what anger the Shaytaan. And the Lord, the Most Glorified, says in His Noble Book, ❨ **ever feeble indeed is the plot of Shaytaan.**❩ *–(Surat an-Nisaa', from Ayat 76)…*

And be patient, as if you are on the good, it is necessary for you to be patient…"

(End of translation from Sheikh Muqbil, may Allaah have mercy upon him.)

There are also legislated readings that one can do over oneself, or have another read over him. Insh'Allaah they will be discussed later on in this series, in the explanation of *"Kitaab at-Tawheed"*.

> *The Eighth:* Assisting those who associate others in worship with Allaah, and supporting them against the Muslims.
>
> The proof is the saying of the Most High, ❨ *And if any amongst you takes them (the Jews and Christians) as Auliyaa' (friends, helpers, protectors), then surely, he is one of them. Verily, Allaah guides not those people who are the polytheists and wrong doers and unjust.* ❩ –(Surat al-Maa'idah, from Ayat 51)

Explanation: *al-mudhaahirah*: in the Arabic language, this means to help and protect. So, here we are speaking of helping those who associate others in worship with Allaah, supporting them against the Muslims, and drawing close to them, and having love for them, and helping them in that which they are upon. This can be with money, or with self, with ideas and opinions, and intimacy with them.

And this does not mean, as some misguided people say, that we fight against them or kill them. It means that we hate their sin of associating others with Allaah, and therefore we cannot love them totally either. We will still have the natural love for our relatives who are disbelievers, but we must always remember that they are committing the gravest of sins, and limit our interactions with them accordingly, insh'Allaah. It is permissible to love our relatives due to their ties with us, but it is not permissible to love them due to their religion. This includes not visiting them or congratulating them on their holidays, such as birthdays and Christmas. On the other hand, we should foster close relationships with the Muslims, particularly those who help us along the path to good, and encourage us in obedience and worship of Allaah. And when we deal with the disbelievers, we deal with them in a just and fair manner. A great deal of calling to Islaam is in that which is apparent of our speech, actions, and character. So you treat them well, and insh'Allaah Allaah will open up their hearts to Islaam.

Sheikh Saaleh Fauzaan, may Allaah preserve him, wrote:

"This, and before we finish with this summarized explanation of the principles of the Islamic beliefs, we mention that it is beloved that every Muslim who embraces this belief supports the people of it (the Muslims) and has enmity for its enemies. So he loves the people of at-tawheed and sincerity and supports them, and he hates the people who associate others with Allaah and is an enemy of them.

And that is from the religion of Ibraaheem and those who were with him, who we are commanded to follow the example of, when He, Glorified and Exalted is He, says,

❨ **Indeed there has been an excellent example for you in Ibraaheem and those with him, when they said to their people: "Verily, we are free from you and whatever you worship besides Allaah, we have rejected you, and there has appeared between us and you, hostility and hatred for ever until you believe in Allaah Alone," – except the saying of Ibraaheem to his father: "Verily, I will ask forgiveness (from Allaah) for you, but I have no power to do anything for you before Allaah." "Our Lord! In You (Alone) we put our trust, and to You (Alone) we turn in repentance, and to You (Alone) is (our) final Return** ❩ –(Surat al-Mumtahanah, Ayat 4)

It is from the religion of Muhammad, may Allaah's praise and salutations be upon him, as Allaah, the Most High, says:

❖ *O you who believe! Take not the Jews and the Christians as auliyaa' (friends, protectors, helpers), they are but auliyaa' of each other. And if any amongst you takes them as auliyaa', then surely, he is one of them. Verily, Allaah guides not those people who are the polytheists and wrong doers and unjust.* ❖ –(Surat al-Maa'idah, Ayat 51)

And this is a prohibition of supporting the People of the Book specifically. Allaah says, concerning the prohibition of supporting the disbelievers in general,

❖ *Oh you who believe! Take not My enemies and your enemies (i.e. disbelievers and polytheists) as friends, showing affection towards them...* ❖ –(Surat al-Mumtahanah, From Ayat 1)"

He goes on to say, may Allaah preserve him, *"Many of the people are ignorant of this great principle, until we hear some of those who are affiliated with knowledge and calling to Allaah in Arab broadcasting, saying of the Christians, "Indeed they are our brothers!" And what a grave statement this is!"*

Sheikh Fauzaan lists several aspects of supporting the disbelievers which we must avoid, along with examples and proofs for them. Among them are:

1. Resembling them in their clothing and their speech and other than these two things
2. Living in their countries, and leaving off moving from them to the land of the Muslims in order to establish the religion
3. Travelling to their lands as tourists, or for one's own pleasure
4. Assisting and helping them against the Muslims, and praising them and defending them- and this is from those things that nullify one's Islaam
5. Asking for their assistance, and relying upon them
6. Praising them, and commending their civilization, and admiring their mannerisms and expertise
7. To name our children with their names
8. Asking for forgiveness and mercy for them
9. Using their calendar instead of the Muslim calendar
10. Participating with them in their holidays and helping them to prepare for them

(End of section taken from *"Fataawa al-A'imatu an-Najdiyyaah"*, Volume 2, Pages 431-435)

Key Terms in this Lesson

Define these terms:

al-istihzaa':

as-sihr:

al-mudhaahirah:

Lesson Questions:

Level 1: [required]

1. List the two categories of *al-istihzaa'*, and give an example of each.
2. Is *sihr*, or magic, real, or is it an illusion? Explain your answer with proofs.
3. What are the two ways that magic enters into associating others with Allaah?
4. What are two proofs from the Qur'aan that we must show enmity to the disbelievers?
5. Is it permissible to send our mothers a card on Mother's Day to show her how much we love her? Explain.

Level 2: [supplementary]

1. A brother jokingly says that he must have really tough knees from prostrating all day. He says this, not meaning to show disdain for the prayer. Is this *istihzaa'*? Why or why not?
2. Give two examples of *as-sihr*.
3. How can we protect ourselves from magic? Should we be afraid of it?
4. How should we act towards the disbelievers who do not harm us or stop us from worship?
5. Choose five of the ways in which one falls into showing support for the disbelievers, and give an example for each of them.

LESSON TWELVE

The Ninth: The one who believes that some of the people are able to be exempt from the legislation of Muhammad, may Allaah's praise and good mention be upon him, just as al-Khidr made it possible to leave the legislation of Moosaa, may Allaah's praise be upon him- as he is a disbeliever.

Explanation:

The story of Moosaa, *aleihi as-salaam*, and al-Khidr is found in Surat al-Kahf, Ayats 60-82. It is also found in the Sunnah of the Messenger of Allaah, may Allaah's praise and salutations be upon him, such as in the hadeeth of Saa'eed bin Jubair found in *"Saheeh al-Bukhaari"*:

{ I said to Ibn Abbas, "Nauf Al-Bukah claims that Moosaa, the companion of Al-Khidr was not Moosaa (the prophet) of the children of Israa'eel, but some other Moosaa." Ibn 'Abbas said, "Allaah's enemy (i.e. Nauf) has told a lie. Ubay bin Ka'b told us that the Prophet said,

'Once Moosaa stood up and addressed Bani Israa'eel. He was asked who was the most learned man amongst the people. He said, 'I.' Allaah admonished him as he did not attribute absolute knowledge to Him. So, Allaah said to him, 'Yes, at the junction of the two seas there is a Slave of Mine who is more learned than you.' Moosaa said, 'O my Lord! How can I meet him?' Allaah said, 'Take a fish and put it in a large basket and you will find him at the place where you will lose the fish.' Moosaa took a fish and put it in a basket and proceeded along with his (servant) boy, Yusha 'bin Nun, till they reached the rock where they laid their heads (i.e. lay down). Moosaa slept, and the fish, moving out of the basket, fell into the sea. It took its way into the sea (straight) as in a tunnel. Allaah stopped the flow of water over the fish and it became like an arch (the Prophet pointed out this arch with his hands).

They travelled the rest of the night, and the next day Moosaa said to his boy (servant), 'Give us our food, for indeed, we have suffered much fatigue in this journey of ours.' Moosaa did not feel tired till he crossed that place which Allaah had ordered him to seek after. His boy (servant) said to him, 'Do you know that when we were sitting near that rock, I forgot the fish, and none but Shaytaan caused me to forget to tell (you) about it, and it took its course into the sea in an amazing way?.' So there was a path for the fish and that astonished them. Moosaa said, 'That was what we were seeking after.' So, both of them retraced their footsteps till they reached the rock.

There they saw a man lying covered with a garment. Moosaa greeted him and he replied saying, 'How do people greet each other in your land?' Moosaa said, 'I am Moosaa.' The man asked, 'Moosaa of Bani Israa'eel?' Moosaa said, 'Yes, I have come to you so that you may teach me from those things which Allaah has taught you.' He said, 'O Moosaa! I have some of the Knowledge of Allaah which Allaah has taught me, and which you do not know, while you have some of the Knowledge of Allaah which Allaah has taught you and which I do not know.' Moosaa asked, 'May I follow you?' He said, 'But you will not be able to remain patient with me for how can you be patient about things which you will not be able to understand?' (Moosaa said, 'You will find me, if Allaah so wills, truly patient, and I will not disobey you in aught.')

So, both of them set out walking along the sea-shore, a boat passed by them and they asked the crew of the boat to take them on board. The crew recognized Al-Khidr and so they took them on board without fare. When they were on board the boat, a sparrow came and stood on the edge of the boat and dipped its beak once or twice into the sea. Al-Khidr said to Moosaa, 'O Moosaa! My knowledge and your knowledge have not decreased Allaah's Knowledge except as much as this sparrow has decreased the water of the sea with its beak.' Then suddenly Al-Khidr took an adze and plucked a plank, and Moosaa did not notice it till he had plucked a plank with the adze. Moosaa said to him, 'What have you done? They took us on board charging us nothing; yet you I have intentionally made a hole in their boat so as to drown its passengers. Verily, you have done a dreadful thing.' Al-Khidr replied, 'Did I not tell you that you would not be able to remain patient with me?' Moosaa replied, 'Do not blame me for what I have forgotten, and do not be hard upon me for my fault.' So the first excuse of Moosaa was that he had forgotten. When they had left the sea, they passed by a boy playing with other boys.

Al-Khidr took hold of the boys head and plucked it with his hand like this. (Sufyaan, the sub narrator pointed with his fingertips as if he was plucking some fruit.) Moosaa said to him, "Have you killed an innocent person who has not killed any person? You have really done a horrible thing." Al-Khidr said, "Did I not tell you that you could not remain patient with me?' Moosaa said "If I ask you about anything after this, don't accompany me. You have received an excuse from me.'

Then both of them went on till they came to some people of a village, and they asked its inhabitant for wood but they refused to entertain them as guests. Then they saw therein a wall which was just going to collapse (and Al Khidr repaired it just by touching it with his hands). (Sufyaan, the sub-narrator, pointed with his hands, illustrating how Al-Khidr passed his hands over the wall upwards.) Moosaa said, "These are the people whom we have called on, but they neither gave us food, nor entertained us as guests, yet you have repaired their wall. If you had wished, you could have taken wages for it." Al-Khidr said, "This is the parting between you and me, and I shall tell you the explanation of those things on which you could not remain patient."

The Prophet added, "We wished that Moosaa could have remained patient by virtue of which Allaah might have told us more about their story. (Sufyaan the sub-narrator said that the Prophet said, "May Allaah bestow His Mercy on Moosaa! If he had remained patient, we would have been told further about their case.") }

Allaah informs us of how he explained his actions in the Qur'aan:

◌ As for the ship, it belonged to poor people working in the sea. So, I wished to make a defective damage in it, as there was a king behind them who seized every ship by force. And as for the boy, his parents were believers, and we feared lest he should oppress them by rebellion and disbelief. "So we intended that their Lord should change him for them for one better in righteousness and nearer to mercy. And as for the wall, it belonged to two orphan boys in the town; and there was under it a treasure belonging to them; and their father was a righteous man, and your Lord intended that they should attain their age of full strength and take out their treasure as a mercy from your Lord. And I did them not of my own

129

accord. That is the interpretation of those (things) over which you could not hold patience. –(Surat al-Kahf, Ayats 79-82)

Some of the Sufees are among those who use this story for an excuse to leave the legislation of Muhammad, may Allaah's praise and good mention be upon him. They believe that there are three categories of legislation:

1. The legislation for the common people- and they have to fast and pray and such as that
2. The legislation for the higher religious class- and there is no problem if they leave a legislated act
3. The legislation of the religious elite- it is not upon them to pray or fast and such, as they are like al-Khidr

And this is not true, as al-Khidr was sent to a specific people before Moosaa, *aleihi salaam*, and before the Prophet, may Allaah's praise and salutations be upon him, and he was upon that which Allaah taught him, which was different from that which Allaah taught Moosaa.

And a proof from the Sunnah that the legislation of Muhammad is the final legislation to be revealed, is the hadeeth of Nawaas, which Sheikh al-Albaani, may Allaah have mercy upon him, said was *hasan*, in which the Prophet, may Allaah's praise and salutations be upon him states that at the end of time 'Eesaa, *aleihi salaam*, will descend and judge by the *Shari'ah* of Muhammad, may Allaah's praise and good mention be upon him. (See *"al-Urwah"*). This is also in the hadeeth of Abu Hurairah, may Allaah be pleased with him, found in *"Saheeh Muslim"*:

{The Messenger of Allaah observed: What would you do when the son of Maryam would descend amongst you and would lead you as one amongst you ? Ibn Abi Dhi'b on the authority of Abu Hurairah narrated: Your leader amongst you. Ibn Abi Dhi'b said: Do you know what the words: "He would lead as one amongst you" mean? I said: Explain these to me. He said: He would lead you according to the Book of your Lord (Glorified is He and Most Exalted) and the Sunnah of your Prophet.}

And from the Qur'aan; Allaah, the Most High, says,

This day I have completed your religion for you, and perfected My blessings upon you, and am pleased with Islaam as your religion. –(Surat al-Maa'idah, Ayat 3)

The Messenger of Allaah, may Allaah's praise and salutations be upon him, was sent to all of mankind, the *jinn*, and the men. So it is clear that no one is exempt from his final legislation. This is established in the Qur'aan, the Sunnah of the Prophet, may Allaah's praise and salutations be upon him, and by the agreement of the scholars.

A Proof from the Qur'aan
Allaah, the Most High, says in His book,

❴ *Say, (Oh Muhammad), to all of the people, "I am the Messenger of Allaah to you all.* ❵ –(Surat al-A'raaf, From Ayat 158)

A Proof from the Sunnah
The hadeeth of Jaabir ibn 'Abdullah, may Allaah be pleased with him, which is found in both *"Saheeh al-Bukhaari"* and *"Saheeh Muslim"*. As part of a longer hadeeth, it says that the Prophet, may Allaah's praise and salutations be upon him, said, *{Every Prophet used to be sent to his nation only but I have been sent to all mankind.}*

The Agreement of the Scholars
This is what Sheikh al-Islaam ibn Taymiyyah, may Allaah have mercy upon him, says in *"al-Fataawa"* and *"al-Furqaan"*

Question: Was al-Khidr a prophet?

Answer: "There are five opinions concerning this:

1. He was a prophet- and this is the saying al the majority of the scholars of hadeeth
2. He was not a prophet, he was a *walee* (a holy person)- and this is the saying of some of the Sufees
3. He was not just a prophet, he was also a messenger- and this is the saying of ibn Jawzee
4. He was an angel from amongst the angels- and this is the saying of al-Khataabee
5. He was none of these things- we do not know what he was

And the first opinion is that which is correct, and Allaah knows best."

> *The Tenth*: Abandoning the religion of Allaah, the Most High; not learning about it or acting upon it.
>
> The proof is the saying of Allaah, the Most High, ⸢ *And who does more wrong than he who is reminded of the Ayat (proofs, evidences, verses, lessons, signs, revelations, etc.) of his Lord, then turns aside from them? Verily, We shall exact retribution from the criminals, disbelievers, polytheists, sinners.*⸥ — (Surat as-Sajdah, Ayat 22)

Explanation: *al-i'raad*: the religious meaning of this, as stated by ibn Qayyim, may Allaah have mercy upon him is:

"As for the disbelief of abandonment, by which it is abandoned by one's hearing and one's heart- that the Messenger of Allaah, may Allaah's praise and good mention be upon him- one does not necessarily verify his truthfulness, nor say that he was a liar, nor does he support him or attack him, and he does not pursue or endeavor to perform that which he came with at all."

There are two categories of *al-i'raad*:

1. That which is disbelief (which Ibn Qayyim mentioned in his definition)
2. That which is not disbelief (this is when one commits a prohibited act, but not with considering that that which is prohibited is permissible- or abandons an obligatory act, but with not believing that it is permissible to abandon the act (without making *al-istihlaal al-qalbiyyah*)

al-istihlaal is of two categories as well:

1. *Qalbiyyan*, or with the heart
2. *Fi'liyyan*, or through the actions

As for the first category, then an example of this is when one believes the alcohol is permissible, even though he does not drink it- this is disbelief

As for the second category, then an example of this is when one drinks alcohol, but he does NOT believe that it is permissible. And this is a sin, but is not disbelief.

And any abandoning of that which the Messenger of Allaah, may Allaah's praise and salutations be upon him, came with, has effects in both this life and the Hereafter, and we must guard ourselves against this, may Allaah grant us success in this life and the Hereafter.

And there is no difference in any of these things which nullify Islaam between the one who is joking, or the one who is in earnest, and the one who is afraid-except for the one who is forced. And all of them are from the greatest of the grave things, and of the most prevalent matters. So it is necessary that the Muslim be cautious of them, and be afraid of them for himself, and we ask Allaah's protection from anything that will bring about His wrath and the torment of His punishment.

Explanation: The person who performs these actions which nullify one's Islaam is not considered a disbeliever until after the conditions are fulfilled, and all that which prevented him from being called a disbeliever have been removed.

And these things, which prevent one who performs these actions from being a disbeliever are:

1. Being forced
2. Incorrect understanding
3. Ignorance
4. Mistake
5. Forgetting

Each of these has an explanation, and/or conditions which must be met, but that is beyond the scope of this discussion, and will be clarified later in the series, insh'Allaah.

And the conditions which must be fulfilled are:

1. That it is established in the texts (the Qur'aan and the Sunnah) that this act is disbelief
2. The proofs of the person's disbelief must be used in the correct manner and context
3. That which stood between him and disbelief must be discounted

An example of the second condition is the narration of 'Ali ibn Abi Taalib, may Allaah be pleased with him. At the time of the fighting between Mu'awiyyah and 'Ali, 'Ali and Mu'awiyah tried to come to a compromise, so they would have peace between them. The Khawaarij rejected the validity of this, saying, "There is no judgment except from Allaah." 'Ali, may Allaah be pleased with him, said, *"A word of truth, used for falsehood."*

Again, I want to stress to you that it not our place to judge someone's belief or disbelief. This is a matter that lies with the scholars of *ahl-as-Sunnah*. However, it is important that we understand the subject for our own selves, and Allaah knows best.

Imaam as-Saboonee, may Allaah have mercy upon him, said, in his book, "*'Itiqaad as-Salaf wa Ashaab al-Hadeeth*" Pages 65-67, concerning this issue:

"*Ahl-as-Sunnah believe that if a believer commits sins, however small or large they may be, he does not become a disbeliever. If he leaves this world without making repentance from them and he dies upon at-tawheed and al-ikhlaas, then his affair is entirely up to Allaah, the Most Mighty, the Most Majestic. If He wills, then He may forgive him and enter him into Paradise on the Day of Judgment, safe and sound without being affected by the Fire and without being punished for his performance of the sins.*

He will be brought on the Day of Judgment with his sins and misdeeds. If Allaah wills, He will punish him for a period in the Fire. If He punishes him, he will not however remain in the Fire forever. Rather, he will eventually be freed and removed from it, to the place of tranquility and content...

The final outcome for all of the believers is Paradise, as they were created for it and it was created for them, as a Mercy and a Blessing from Allaah."

He, may Allaah have mercy upon him, says later in the same book,

"*The People of Hadeeth believe and testify that the end of the slave is unknown. No one knows what his end shall be. They do not pass judgment on a specific person that he will be from the People of Paradise or from the People of Hell, because that is something that is hidden from them. They do not know in which state a person will die, whether it is upon Islaam or disbelief, so due to this fact they say, "Indeed we are Believers, if Allaah wills." That is, from those Believers who will have a good end, if Allaah wills.*"

And concerning ruling upon one who died upon belief or disbelief, he says,

"*And the People of Hadeeth witness for the ones who die upon al-Islaam that their end will be Paradise even if their fate was written by Allaah that they will be punished with the Fire for a period, as a result of their sins which they committed and did not repent from. They will eventually enter Paradise and no one from amongst the Muslims will remain in Hell eternally. This is a great blessing and favor from Allaah. If one dies upon disbelief, and Allaah's protection is sought from this, he will be thrown into the Fire and he will not be saved from it, and he will remain there forever.*" (From Page 73)

Key Terms in this Lesson

Define these terms:

al-i'raad:

al-istihlaal:

Lesson Questions:

Level 1: [required]

1. What are the proofs that the legislation of Muhammad is the final legislation?
2. What was al-Khidr?
3. List and explain the two types of *al-i'raad*.
4. What conditions must be fulfilled before a person can be considered a disbeliever?

Level 2: [supplementary]

1. How do some of the Sufees use the story of Moosaa and al-Khidr to justify some of them leaving the Islamic legislation? Is this correct? Explain.
2. Why must all of mankind, the *jinn* and the men, adhere to the legislation that the Messenger of Allaah, may Allaah's praise and salutations be upon him, came with?
3. List and explain the two types of *al-istihlaal*. Give an example of each.
4. What are those things which prevent a person who has committed an act of disbelief, from falling into disbelief.
5. We see that a person among us commits at least one of these things which nullify Islaam. We don't think that she is being forced or is ignorant...do we say that she is a disbeliever and separate from her? What would you do if this was one of your friends?

QUIZ NUMBER TWO

This is a closed-book quiz. You cannot use your notes or the book to answer the questions. Please write neatly and answer each question as completely as you are able. Use as many sheets of notebook paper needed to answer the questions fully and legibly. Write your name and the quiz number, number each answer clearly.

1. Define these terms:

   shart / sharoot:

   shahadah:

   at-taaghoot:

   al-'ilm:

   al-yaqeen:

   al-Ikhlaas:

   as-sidq:

   al-muhabbah:

   al-inqiyaad:

   al-qabool:

   ad-daleel / al-adilah:

   naaqid / nawaaqid:

   waseetah / wasaa'it:

   hadee:

   hukm:

   al-istihzaa':

   al-i'raad

1. List the conditions of *ash-shahadah* and their opposites (in Arabic or English).

2. Which condition or conditions of *ash-shahadah* negate hypocrisy?

3. How can love of Allaah bring about contentment in our hearts?.

4. What is the eighth condition, as mentioned by Ibn Qayyim?

5. How do *Ahl-as-Sunnah wa al-Jama'ah* understand and use the evidences? How does this differ from the people of innovations and desires?

6. What sort of knowledge is intended in the first condition? What is its opposite?

7. Explain how certainty leads to worshipping Allaah with our tongues and limbs.

8. Explain the saying of Dhu Noon al-Misree, when he was asked about when one loves Allaah: "If what He hates is more bitter to you than *as-sabr*."

9. What are the two categories of *ash-shirk*? Give an example of each. Which is the one mentioned here?

10. What are the two types of *al-waseetah*? How could this be considered *ash-shirk*?

11. How do we implement this *ayat* of Allaah in our lives: ❝ *You will not find any people who believe in Allaah and the Last Day, making friendship with those who oppose Allaah and His Messenger , even though they were their fathers or their sons or their brothers or their kindred.* ❞ –(Surat al-Mujaadilah, From Ayat 22)

12. What is the problem with accepting that which has been proven scientifically over something which comes in the Qur'aan and the Sunnah?

13. How can natural hatred lead to that hatred which may nullify one's Islaam?

14. Explain how *al-istihzaa* can be intended, or not intended. Is there a difference in their rulings?

15. What is *as-sihr*? Is it real, or illusion? How can we protect or cure ourselves from it?

16. List five of the ways that Sheikh Fauzaan mentioned as being examples of supporting the disbelievers.

17. How do some of the Sufees use the story of al-Khidr to allow them to leave off practicing that which was legislated by Allaah and His Messenger? Why is this incorrect?

18. What is the difference between abandoning an act, and it is a sin, and abandoning an act and it is disbelief?

19. What are the three conditions that the scholars use when determining if one of these *nawaaqid* of Islaam has, in reality, nullified someone's Islaam?

LESSON THIRTEEN

> At-Tawheed is of Three Categories

Explanation: Sheikh Sulaymaan ibn 'Abdullah ibn Muhammad ibn 'Abdul Wahaab, may Allaah have mercy upon them all, said, as quoted in "*Fataawa al-A'imat an-Najdiyyah*", page 121:

"*At-tawheed: it is the verbal noun of wahhada, yuwahhida, tawheedan; meaning, linquistically, he unified something and made it one.*

The religion of Islaam is designated by at-tawheed, because it is based upon the fact that Allaah is One, matchless in His dominion and His actions, with no partners ascribed to Him. He is Unique in His nature and His attributes, and none is equal to Him. He is alone in His status as God, and the worship of Him, and nothing is equal to Him.

The tawheed which the prophets and messengers came with from Allaah, is divided into these three categories, and they are inseparable; each category from them cannot be separated from the others. So the one who fulfills one of the categories, but does not fulfill the others-and what is that except that he does not achieve by it the desired perfection.

If desired, it may also be said, at-tawheed is of two types: tawheed al-ma'rifa wa al-ithbaat (comprehending and affirming), and this is tawheed ar-ruboobiyyah and tawheed al-asmaa wa as-sifaat, and tawheed at-talib wa al-qisd, (seeking and intention) which is tawheed al-uloohiyyah and 'abaadah. And this is mentioned by Sheikh al-Islaam, and ibn Qayyim, and in meaning it is mentioned by other than them." (End of translation)

Sheikh 'Abdul 'Azeez ibn 'Abdullah Ibn Baaz, may Allaah have mercy upon him, says, after mentioning first the division of *at-tawheed* into three divisions, and then the division into two divisions,

"*This is at-tawheed of comprehension and affirmation: To believe, and affirm that Allaah, Glorified is He, is Alone in His Lordship, He is Alone in His names and attributes and He is Alone in His planning for His slave, and He is the Creator of them, and the One Who Provides for them. And He is attributed with the perfect attributes and He is far above deficiency and defect. There are no partners along with Him in that, and nothing which resembles Him, and there is no equal to Him, Glorified and Exalted is He.*

And the second division: tawheed of seeking and intention: It is to single out Allaah, Glorified is He, in your intentions, and your seeking and your prayer, and your fast, and all of your acts of worship; seeking nothing by it except His Face, Glorified and Exalted is He. And likewise your charity, and all of your actions which you seek closeness to Him through them, having no goal except His face, Glorified and Exalted is He. So do not supplicate except to Him, and do not make a vow except by Him, and do not seek to draw near with pious acts except to Him, Glorified is He, and do not seek healing of illness and help from the enemies except from Him. Single Him out alone in all of that." (From "*Risaail fee at-Tawheed*", Pages 49-50)

Ibn Qayyim, may Allaah have mercy upon him, said, in "*Madaarij as-Saalikeen*", Vol. 3, from pages 449-450):

"*And most of the chapters of the Qur'aan- rather, every chapter of the Qur'aan- contains in it one of these two divisions of at-tawheed. Rather, we make a comprehensive statement: Indeed every verse in the Qur'aan includes within it at-tawheed, bearing witness to it, calling to it…*" (End of translation- he, may Allaah have mercy upon him, goes on to inform how different types of verses fit into each category of *at-tawheed*)

Sheikh Muhammad ibn 'Abdul Wahaab, may Allaah have mercy upon him, said, concerning *at-tawheed*,

"*There is no difference of opinion amongst the people in that at-tawheed necessarily occurs with the heart, which is the knowledge, and the tongue, which is the speech, and the action, which is compliance with the commands and the (leaving off of) forbidden things. So if one fails to perform anything from these, then the man is not a Muslim.*

If one affirms at-tawheed and then does not act upon it, then he is an obstinate disbeliever, such as Fir'awn and Iblees. And if he acts upon at-tawheed outwardly, but does not believe in it inwardly, then he is a clear hypocrite, the most evil of the disbelievers. And Allaah knows best." (From "*ad-Durur as-Sunniyyaah*" 2/124-125)

Sheikh Sulaymaan ibn 'Abdullah, may Allaah have mercy upon him, said,

"*Indeed the meaning of at-tawheed, and to bear witness that there is no god worthy of worship except Allaah: it is that one does not worship anything except Allaah, and that one does not believe that help or harm comes except from Allaah, and that one disbelieves in that which is worshipped besides Him, and that one frees himself from them and from whose who worship them.*" (From "*Tayseer al-'Azeez al-Hameed*", Page 102)

The First: Tawheed ar-Ruboobiyah (Tawheed in the Lordship of Allaah)

This is the one which the disbelievers at the time of the Messenger of Allaah, may Allaah's praise and good mention be upon him, affirmed, and yet it did not enter them into Islaam, and the Messenger of Allaah, may Allaah's praise and good mention be upon him, killed them, and made their blood and wealth permissible for the Muslims. It is the belief of Allaah by His actions.

The proof is the saying of the Most High, *Say (O Muhammad: "Who provides for you from the sky and the earth? Or who owns hearing and sight? And who brings out the living from the dead and brings out the dead from the living? And who disposes the affairs?" They will say: "Allaah." Say: "Will you not then be afraid of Allaah's punishment (for setting up rivals in worship with Allaah)?"* –(Surat Yoonus, Ayat 31) And there are many verses concerning this.

Explanation: Sheikh Sulaymaan ibn 'Abdullah ibn Muhammad ibn 'Abdul Wahaab said,

"This is accepting that Allaah, the Most High, is the Lord of everything, and its Master, and the One who created it, and the one who provides for it that which it needs, and the One who gives life and causes death, the One who allows any harm, and Who brings any benefit, the Sole Possessor of the ability to answer the supplications of the one in need. The command over all things is His, and in His hand is all good, He is the One with power over all things, and there are no partners with Him in that. And faith in al-qadr, or the Divine Decree, falls under this category.

This tawheed is not sufficient for the worshipper to attain Islaam. Rather, it is necessary that along with that comes the obligation of tawheed al-uloohiyah, or worship, because Allaah, the Most High, has narrated concerning the polytheists, that they affirm this tawheed to Allaah alone."

Sheikh 'Abdur Razzaaq ibn 'Abdul Muhsin al-'Ibaad al-Badr says, concerning this, after quoting the above verse from Surat al-Yunus, as well as several others with the same basic meaning,

"So they (the disbelievers) knew Allaah, and understood His Lordship, and His sovereignty, and His mastership, and along with that, and yet this acceptance was not sufficient for them and did not benefit them. And what is that except to their associating partners in tawheed of worship which is the meaning of "la ilaaha ila Allaah". And Allaah says, concerning them,

﴾ ***And most of them believe not in Allaah except that they attribute partners to Him*** ﴿ –(Surat Yoosuf, Ayat 106)

...and Mujaahid said, "Their faith in Allaah was their merely saying, "Allaah created us, and provides for us, and causes our deaths"; as this is faith along with associating others along with Him in worship." ("al-Mukhtasir al-Mufeed fee Bayaan Dalaa'il Aqsaam at-Tawheed", Page 10)

The Second: Tawheed'ul Uloohijah (Tawheed in worship)

It is that which conflict has occurred concerning it, in past ages and in modern times. It is the belief of Allaah by the actions of the worshipper, such as supplication, making a vow, slaughtering, hope, fear, reliance, desire, reverence, and turning to Allaah. Each category from these categories of worship is supported by proofs from the Qur'aan

---

Explanation: Sheikh Sulaymaan ibn 'Abdullah ibn Muhammad ibn 'Abdul Wahaab said, in the source mentioned above,

"This is built upon sincerity and purity in worshipping Allaah, the Most High, alone. This includes love, fear, hope, reliance, desire, reverence, supplication to Allaah alone; and purity in that all acts of worship, the outward and the inward, are done for Allaah, alone, without any partners along with Him, as nothing can be created or put in that place other than Him- not the angels drawn near, or the sent prophets, or other than them.

And this category of at-tawheed is the one which is contained in the saying of Allaah, Blessed is He, and Most High, ❦ **You alone do we worship, and You alone do we ask for help** ❧ *-(al-Faatihah, Ayat 5). And it is the first thing in the religion, and the last, the hidden and the apparent. It is the first thing that the messengers called to, and the last thing. It is the meaning of the words, "la ilaaha ila Allaah" (there is no god worthy of worship except Allaah). As He is the God to be worshipped with love, fear, with exaltation and glorification of Him, and with all of the aspects of worship. And the creation was created, and the messengers sent, and the books revealed, for the purpose of performing this aspect of at-tawheed. And the people are differentiated through it into Believers and disbelievers, and the happy people of Paradise, and the unhappy people of the Fire."*

Sheikh Sulaymaan goes on to say that following the Messenger of Allaah, may Allaah's praise and salutations be upon him, fits under this category of *at-tawheed*.

The Third: Tawheed adh-Dhaat wa al-Asmaa wa as-Sifaat (Tawheed in Allaah's being, His names and His attributes- and that they apply to Him Alone in perfection)

Allaah, the Most High, says, ❦ *Say: "He is Allaah, (the) One.*

Allaah-us-Samad [Allaah – the Self-Sufficient Master, Whom all creatures need, (He neither eats nor drinks)].

He begets not, nor was He begotten.

And there is none coequal or comparable to Him." ❧ –(Surat *al-ikhlaas*, Ayats 1-4)

And His, the Most High, saying, ❦ *And (all) the Most Beautiful Names belong to Allaah, so call on Him by them, and leave the company of those who belie or deny (or utter impious speech against) His Names. They will be requited for what they used to do.* ❧ –(Surat al-A'raaf, Ayat 180)

And He, the Most High says, ❦ *There is nothing like Him, and He is the All-Hearer, the All-Seer.* ❧ –(Surat ash-Shooraah, From Ayat 11)

Explanation: Sheikh 'Utheimeen, may Allaah have mercy upon him, says in his explanation of "*Usool ath-Thalaathah*",

"This is to affirm whatever names or attributes Allaah affirmed for Himself in His Book, or in the Sunnah of His Messenger, may Allaah's praise and salutations be upon him, in a manner which befits Him, without changing or distorting their wording or their meaning, without denial of them, without putting forth how they are, and without declaring them to be like the attributes of creation."

Ahl-as-Sunnah wa al-Jama'ah affirm that which Allaah and His Messenger, may Allaah praise and salutations be upon him, affirmed concerning the names and attributes of Allaah, without distortion, interpretation, or negation. They believe that these names are most excellent, and His attributes are perfect. They except them on their apparent meanings, and do not try to interpret them or look for some sort of other meaning for them beyond what has been revealed. They do not ask about the "how" of His names and attributes.

And we discussed this at length in Chapter 2, alhamdulillah. Insh'Allaah, return to that chapter and review that which was discussed concerning this category of *at-tawheed*.

Sheikh Sulaymaan ibn 'Abdullah ibn Muhammad ibn 'Abdul Wahaab said,

"And this is also not sufficient to attain Islaam. Rather, it is necessary to bring along with that the prerequisites of tawheed ar-ruboobiyyah and tawheed al-uloohiyyah. The disbelievers accept this category in form, though some of them reject some of that, either through ignorance or stubbornness."

So insh'Allaah, you understand the categories of *at-tawheed* and that which they encompass. Now what? It is obligatory for us to act upon our knowledge- so we act upon these categories by singling Allaah out with our worship, and knowing and understanding that which He does for us, and being grateful for that, and thanking and praising Him for that. We draw nearer to Him through worship, and through knowing and understanding His most perfect names and attributes. And, we follow the best of examples, the prophets and messengers, and call the people to it.

Sheikh Bin Baaz, may Allaah have mercy upon him, says concerning this,

"It is obligatory upon you, Oh Slave of Allaah: If you understand that which has been presented, that you expend every effort in explaining and clarifying this foundational principle, and to spread it amongst the people, and make it apparent to mankind, until he is educated from his ignorance, and until the one who associated partners with Him and differed with His command worships Allaah alone, and until you are, with that, following the messengers and proceeding upon their methodology in calling to Allaah, as they fulfilled the trust they carried. And there is for you like the rewards of the one who Allaah guides by your hand until the Day of Judgment. As Allaah, Glorified and Exalted, says,

Say (O Muhammad), "This is my way; I invite to Allaah with sure knowledge, I and whosoever follows me (also must invite others to Allaah). And Glorified and Exalted is Allaah (above all that they associate as partners with Him). And I am not of the mushrikeen (those who associate others with Allaah in worship). –(Surat Yoosuf, from Ayat 108)

And He, Glorified and Exalted is He, says,

Invite (mankind, O Muhammad) to the way of your Lord with wisdom (i.e. with the Divine Revelation and the Qur'aan) and fair preaching, and argue with them in a way that is better. –(Surat an-Nahl, from Ayat 125)

*And the Prophet, may Allaah's praise and salutations be upon him, said, in an authentic hadeeth, { **One who guides to that which is good has a reward similar to the one who performs (the good).}** (Saheeh Muslim, No.1893, from the hadeeth of Abi Mas'ood al-Ansaari)*

*And he, may Allaah's praise and salutations be upon him, said to 'Ali when he sent him to Khaybar, {...**for, by Allaah, if Allaah guides even one man through you, that is better for you than a red camel.** } (Saheeh al-Bukhaari, 2942, and Muslim, 2402, from the hadeeth of Sahl ibn Sa'd. And the red camel is from the most valuable of things)..."*

(End of translation from Sheikh Bin Baaz, may Allaah have mercy upon him, from "Risaail fee at-Tawheed", Pages 51-52)

Lesson Questions:

Level 1: [required]

1. Why is Islaam known by *at-tawheed*?
2. What are the three mentioned categories of *at-tawheed*? Write their names, English meanings, and give a brief description of each.
3. Why were the disbelievers not successful, even though they affirmed *tawheed ar-ruboobiyyah*?
4. How is it that *tawheed al-uloohiyyah* differentiates between the People of Paradise and the People of Hellfire?
5. How do we understand Allaah's names and attributes?

Level 2: [supplementary]

1. Ibn Taymiyyah and Ibn Qayyim divided *at-tawheed* into two categories. What are they? Where do the three categories of *at-tawheed* mentioned here fit into them?
2. How do we make *at-tawheed* a reality with our hearts, tongues and limbs?
3. The scholars have said that people commit *ash-shirk* through ignorance or through arrogance. Explain this as best as you are able, and give an example of each.
4. *Tawheed al-uloohiyyah* was mentioned as the meaning of *la ilaaha ila Allaah*. Explain this..
5. Is it sufficient for one to have any one of the categories of *at-tawheed* without the others? Why or why not?

LESSON FOURTEEN

> The Opposite of *at-Tawheed* (the worship of Allaah Alone) is *ash-Shirk* (associating others along with Him in worship)

Explanation: *ash-shirk*: Sheikh Saalih ibn Fauzaan al-Fauzaan, may Allaah preserve him, defines *ash-shirk* as:

"It is to divert something from the categories of worship to other then Allaah, such as supplication, sacrifice, swearing, and asking for help from other than Allaah in that which nothing has any power over except for Allaah." (From *"al-Irshaad ila Saheeh al-I'tiqaad wa ar-Rad 'ala ahl ash-Shirk wa al-Ilhaad"*, Page 43)

And Sheikh 'Abdul Lateef ibn 'Abdur Rahman, may Allaah have mercy upon them both, says,

"And ash-shirk is to make a partner to Allaah, the Most High, in that which He has the most right to from worship, both that which is hidden and that which is apparent, such as love and obedience, and glorification and fear, and hope and delegation, and reliance and devotion and obedience…and such as these, from the acts of worship." (From *"ad-Durur as-Sunniyyah"*, 12/205)

> It is of three categories: greater *shirk*, lesser *shirk*, and hidden *shirk*

Explanation: Again, there are other ways in which *ash-shirk* can be classified. For example, Sheikh al-Islaam ibn Taymiyyah and ibn Qayyim simply mention two categories of *ash-shirk*. Other scholars, such as Sheikh Muhammad ibn 'Abdul Wahhab in this instance, mention more. This is, as mentioned before, simply away by which the scholars break down a subject to make it easier for the ones they are teaching to understand.

The First Category from the Categories of ash-Shirk:

ash-Shirk al-Akbar- The Greater Shirk

Allaah, the Most Glorified, Most Exalted, says, ❧ *Verily, Allaah forgives not (the sin of) setting up partners (in worship) with Him, but He forgives whom He wills, sins other than that, and whoever sets up partners in worship with Allaah, has indeed strayed far away.* ❧ –(Surat an-Nisaa, Ayat 116)

And He, Glorified is He, says, ❧ *Surely, they have disbelieved who say: "Allaah is the Messiah (Jesus), son of Maryam (Mary)." But the Messiah said: "O Children of Israel! Worship Allaah, my Lord and your Lord." Verily, whosoever sets up partners (in worship) with Allaah, then Allaah has forbidden Paradise to him, and the Fire will be his abode. And for the polytheists and wrong doers there are no helpers.* ❧ –(Surat al-Maa'idah, Ayat 72)

And He, the Most High, says, ❧ *And We shall turn to whatever deeds they (disbelievers, polytheists, sinners) did, and We shall make such deeds as scattered floating particles of dust.* ❧ –(Surat al-Furqaan, Ayat 23)

And He, Glorified is He, says, ❧ *And indeed it has been revealed to you (O Muhammad),as it was to those (Allaah's Messengers) before you: "If you join others in worship with Allaah, (then) surely, (all) your deeds will be in vain, and you will certainly be among the losers.* ❧ –(Surat az-Zumar, Ayat 65)

And He, Glorified and Exalted, says, ❧ *But if they had joined in worship others with Allaah, all that they used to do would have been of no benefit to them.* ❧ –(Surat al-An'aam, from Ayat 88)

Explanation: So if one fasts, and prays, and does righteous deeds, then commits this greater *shirk*, even if only one time, and does not repent- then all of his good deeds will be on no benefit to him. As Allaah says in the verse above,

❧ *And indeed it has been revealed to you (O Muhammad),as it was to those (Allaah's Messengers) before you: "If you join others in worship with Allaah, (then) surely, (all) your deeds will be in vain, and you will certainly be among the losers.* ❧ –(Surat az-Zumar, Ayat 65)

The same is true of the one who has *al-ikhlaas* in times of danger and hardship, and then in times of ease directs some act of worship to other than Allaah. And remember that the verse above was directed to Muhammad, may Allaah's praise and salutations be upon him, who was the best of mankind, and then on to the rest of the people.

Again, you must remember that the punishment of the one who associates partners with Allaah being denied the forgiveness of Allaah – this is specific for the one who dies in this state. If a living person commits *shirk* and then repents from that, then Allaah is Oft Forgiving, Most Merciful.

The Greater Shirk is of Four Categories:

The First: Shirk of Supplication

The Proof is His, the Most High, saying, ﴾ *And when they embark on a ship, they invoke Allaah, making their Faith pure for Him only, but when He brings them safely to land, behold, they give a share of their worship to others.* ﴿ –(Surat al-'Ankiboot, Ayat 65)

Explanation: This is calling on other than Allaah when supplicating. This includes those people who call upon Allaah in times of hardship, but in times of ease supplicate to other than Him, as mentioned above.

Supplication is of two categories:

1. Supplication of worship (*du'a al-'ibaadah*)
2. Supplication concerning a matter, question, or problem (*du'a al-masa'lah*)

The difference between them is that the supplication concerning a matter contains a question, and *du'a* of worship includes all the categories of worship. For example, in the prayer, we supplicate, but not with asking a specific question.

And the verse mentioned above is a proof that the *shirk* of the early people was lesser than that of the people today, as Sheikh Muhammad ibn 'Abdul Wahaab, may Allaah have mercy upon him, mentions in *"al-Qawaa'id al-Arba"*…this is because they had *al-ikhlaas* in times of hardship- like when they are on the ship, as mentioned in the verse, and then went on to commit *ash-shirk* when they were in times of ease. The *mushrikeen* of later times, however, associate others with Allaah in times of both hardship and ease. And the *ikhlaas* of the early people did not benefit them, as was mentioned before- as long as *shirk* was mixed in at any time, then their acts were not correct and accepted.

And we will discuss supplication in greater detail in our discussion on *"Usool ath-Thalaathah"*, insh'Allaah.

The Second: Shirk of Intention, Desire, and Purpose

The proof is His, the Most High, saying, ❧ *Whosoever desires the life of the world and its glitter, to them We shall pay in full (the wages of) their deeds therein, and they will have no diminution therein.*

They are those for whom there is nothing in the Hereafter but Fire, and vain are the deeds they did therein. And of no effect is that which they used to do.❧
–(Surah Hood, Ayats 15-16)

Explanation: This verse is a general one on the subject. One that makes it more specific, and adds some clarity to the issue is Allaah, the Most High's, saying,

❧*Whoever desires the quick-passing (transitory enjoyment of this world), We readily grant him what We will for whom We like. Then, afterwards, We have appointed for him Hell; he will burn therein disgraced and rejected (far away from Allaah's Mercy).*❧ –(Surat al-Israa, Ayat 18)

As Allaah, Glorified is He, Most Exalted, gives to the disbelievers that which He wills in this world. They will desire something, and perhaps they will receive it, and perhaps Allaah will not give them that which they desire.

This type of *ash-shirk* shows us the reality of hypocrisy in belief. An example of this is the head of the hypocrites in al-Madinah at the time of the Prophet, may Allaah's praise and salutations be upon him. He had power and position before Islaam- then when the Prophet came to al-Madinah, he declared his Islaam, while remaining a disbeliever on the inside. This was in order that he be able to keep his power and position in what was now a city that was ruled by Islaam. He did the right thing, accepting Islaam, but his only reason for doing so, was for gain in this life- and so he gave away his Hereafter for the life of this passing world.

In our daily lives, we experience this when we begin a thing for the sake of Allaah, but other matters come into it that may corrupt or invalidate it. A person may memorize the Qur'aan so that he will be paid to teach it. Or one wears "fashionable" *hijaab* to show her figure, or her status. In this way intention may be somewhat for Allaah, or not at all for Allaah. The remedy for this is to increase in our supplications, and our asking for forgiveness, and to strive to rectify ourselves in all of our affairs, and to not open our hearts to *ash-Shaytaan*. If we ask ourselves before performing any act, *"Will this please Allaah or not?"* and *"Am I doing this act for Allaah alone?"*, then this is a step towards eradicating this type of *shirk*, and reducing the possibility of falling into it. It is also an important step towards making Allaah and our religion the center of our lives, as we think of what would please Him, rather than following our own desires. And Allaah knows best.

> *The Third: Shirk of Obedience*
>
> The proof is His, the Most High, saying, ❨*They (Jews and Christians) took their rabbis and their monks to be their lords besides Allaah (by obeying them in things that they made lawful or unlawful according to their own desires without being ordered by Allaah), and (they also took as their Lord) Messiah, son of Maryam, while they (Jews and Christians) were commanded to worship none but One Ilaah (God – Allaah), La ilaaha ila Huwa (none has the right to be worshipped but He). Glorified is He (far above is He) from having the partners they associate (with Him).*❩ –(Surat at-Tawbah, Ayat 31)
>
> And the explanation of it which has no ambiguity in it: Following the scholars and the worshippers in wrongdoing, not calling them their gods, as is explained by the Prophet, may Allaah's praise and good mention be upon him, to 'Adee ibn Haatim when he asked him when he said, "We did not worship them." He (the Prophet, may Allaah's praise and good mention be upon him, said, *{ Indeed your worship of them was your obeying them in wrongdoing.}* ("as-Saheehah", Number 3293)

Explanation: All of creation has been commanded to worship Allaah and none other than Him. As Allaah says,

❨ *I did not create jinn and mankind except to worship Me* ❩ –(Surat adh-Dhaariyaat, Ayat 56)

And part of this worship, as we have already learned, is in obedience to Him, and to that which He revealed to His last prophet and messenger, Muhammad, may Allaah's praise and salutations be upon him.

Concerning this subject, the Prophet, may Allaah's praise and salutations be upon him, said, *{ There is no obedience to anyone in sinning against Allaah. }* (by meaning, in al-Bukhaari and Muslim)

So if we are commanded to something by our parents, husbands, or the one who is in charge of our affairs, and this thing contradicts the command of Allaah and that which was brought by His Messenger, then we do not obey them in this thing. This falls under the above verse, ❨ *They took their rabbis and monks...*❩ We are told to ask the people of knowledge if we do not know something- and this means the true people of knowledge, not the astray callers and false scholars who will do nothing but lead us astray if we follow them in their misguidance.

At-Tirmidhi, may Allaah have mercy upon him, has declared the hadeeth mentioned here to be weak. However, Sheikh al-Albaani, may Allaah have mercy upon him, has declared it to be authentic in the above work. And Allaah knows best.

The Fourth: Shirk of Love

The proof is His, the Most High, saying, "❀ *And of mankind are some who take (for worship) others besides Allaah as rivals (to Allaah). They love them as they love Allaah.* ❀ –(Surat al-Baqara, from Ayat 165)

Explanation: An example of this is the *mushrikeen* of the tribe of Quraish. They loved Allaah, and they called upon Allaah. But *ash-Shaytaan* made beautiful for them the idea of worshipping and calling upon the idols, and they came to love them as they loved Allaah.

And love is an action of the heart. If this love is for Allaah, and because of Allaah, then insh'Allaah we will call upon Him for help, and have gratitude towards Him, and obey Him in all that He commands, and this will increase our faith and obedience to Him.

And love for that which is created, can start out as a good thing, and be turned into a bad thing. For example, a student naturally loves his teacher. He emulates him and learns from him. As long as the teacher is following Allaah and His Messenger, then that is fine, alhamdulillah, as long as it does not become excessive. It becomes excessive when the student believes that everything his sheikh says is correct, despite evidence. Or if he sees him do something that is in violation of Allaah's *Shari'ah*, and he follows him in this. May Allaah protect us from this.

Lesson Questions:

Level 1: [required]

1. What is the definition of *ash-shirk*?
2. What are the three categories listed here? Is this the only way one can classify *ash-shirk*?
3. What is the punishment of one who commits major *shirk*, and dies upon it?
4. What are the two classes of supplication? Give an example of each.
5. When is it permissible to disobey our husbands, parents, or those with power over us? Why?

Level 2: [supplementary]

1. The Quraish loved Allaah, and called upon him. Why were the ones who did not embrace Islaam, not successful?
2. Which type of major *shirk* is an example of hypocrisy in belief? Why?
3. Explain the *shirk* of intention. Give an example of it other than mine.
4. How did the Jews and Christians take their rabbis and monks as lords other than Allaah?
5. How could love for a person turn into the love that leads to *ash-shirk*?

LESSON FIFTEEN

> *The Second Category from the Categories of Shirk:*
>
> *ash-Shirk Asghar- the Lesser Shirk, and it is ar-riyaa'* (this is engaging in acts for the sake of the recognition by the people)
>
> *The proof is His, the Most High, saying,* ❝*...So whoever hopes for the Meeting with his Lord, let him work righteousness and associate none as a partner in the worship of his Lord.* ❞ –(Surat al-Kahf, from Ayat 110)

Explanation: *ar-riyaa*: The broader meaning of this is hypocrisy, duplicity, double-dealing. In this context, however, it is usually used specifically to mean to perform an act of worship for the notice and admiration of the people.

Sheikh 'Abdul 'Azeez bin Baaz, may Allaah have mercy upon him, said in *"Risaa'il fee at-Tawheed"*, Pages 19-20,

"And there is another category, that of ash-shirk al-asghar, the minor shirk. For example, ar-riyaah (showing off) and wanting to be well thought of in some of the actions or sayings. For example, a man says, "That which Allaah wills, and which so and so wills", and swearing by other than Allaah, such as swearing by honor and the Ka'bah and the Prophet, may Allaah's praise and salutations be upon him, and that which resembles this. As these things and that which resembles them from the lesser shirk- it is necessary that one guards against them.

The Prophet, may Allaah's praise and salutations be upon him, said, when a man said to him, { *That which Allaah wills, and you will"- he said, "Are you putting me together with Allaah? That which Allaah alone wills!* } (Collected by Ahmad, from the hadeeth of ibn Mas'ood, and Sheikh al-Albaani has declared it to be *hasan* in *"as-Saheeh"*) *And the Prophet, may Allaah's praise and salutations be upon him, said,* { *Do not say that which Allaah wills and which so and so wills. Rather, say, "That which Allaah wills and then so and so wills.* } (Collected in Abu Daawood, and Ahmad, from the hadeeth of Hudhaifah, and Sheikh al-Albaani has declared it to be authentic in *"Saheeh al-Jaami'"*)

And he, may Allaah's praise and salutations be upon him, said, {*Whoever has to swear an oath should swear by Allaah, or remain silent.*} (Agreed upon, from the hadeeth of Ibn 'Umar) *And he, may Allaah's praise and salutations be upon him, said,* {*Do not swear by your fathers or your mothers, or by those things which are worshipped other than Allaah. And do not swear by Allaah except that you are truthful.*} (Collected by Abu Daawood, and an-Nasaa'i, from the hadeeth of Abi Hurairah, and Sheikh al-Albaani has declared it authentic in *"Saheeh al-Jaami'"*) *And he, may Allaah's praise and salutations be upon him, said,* {*The one who swears by other than Allaah, has committed shirk.*} (Collected by Abu Daawud, and at-Tirmidhi from the hadeeth of

Ibn 'Umar, and Sheikh al-Albaani has declared it authentic in *"Saheeh al-Jaami'"*)
And other than these from the authentic hadeeth reported with this meaning.

And from that is his saying, may Allaah's praise and salutations be upon him, {**"That which I fear most for you is the minor shirk." He was asked about that, and he said, "ar-riyaa."**} (Collected by Ahmad, from the hadeeth of Mahmood ibn Labeed, and Sheikh al-Albaani has declared it authentic in *"Saheeh al-Jaami'"*)

And ar-riyaa can enter into the major shirk, if the person goes into the religion to show off, or hypocritically, and who manifests Islaam, but not upon faith, and not upon love. And by this he becomes a hypocritical disbeliever, of the greatest disbelief.

Likewise when one swears by other than Allaah, and by that glorifies and honors that which is being sworn by in the way that Allaah only is glorified, or believes that he knows the unseen, or makes correct that something should be worshipped other than Allaah, Glorified is He- he becomes by that one who associates others with Allaah, with the major shirk. As for when it comes off the tongue- the swearing by other than Allaah, such as the Ka'bah, and the prophet, and other than them, without this belief, then he has committed the minor shirk only." (End of translation from Sheikh Bin Baaz, may Allaah have mercy upon him)

So we see that the matters of minor *shirk* have much to do with our intention. We must strive to purify our intention in all that we do. We may start out an act intending it solely for Allaah, and then in the midst of the act our intention changes. We have to be diligent in steering it back to Allaah alone. The custom of the people of talking too much is one thing which leads to this veering off of correct intention. For example, a man lets it be known that he is taking ten classes- and this impresses the people much- but is he truly benefitting from them, or just sitting in them for another reason, such as having nothing else to do, or wanting the people to see him in these classes? Or a sister says to her friends, "I am really tired, from praying all night long." Now her act of worship, which may have been for Allaah alone in the beginning, runs the risk of becoming something done for the people, so they see how pious she is. Or letting it be known that one is fasting, without a reason for saying it to the people…and the examples could go on and on. We must look to the pious people for our examples, as one of the *salaf* said, *"We used to hide our good deeds, as we hid our bad deeds."* And this was out of fear of falling into this type of *shirk*.

Sheikh 'Abdur Rahman as-Sa'di, may Allaah have mercy upon him, said, in his explanation of *"Kitaab at-Tawheed"*:

"Among the worst behaviors that diminish sincerity is to perform acts just to be seen by people, for their praise, or to honor them, or doing deeds for the sake of worldly matters. This degrades sincerity and at-tawheed.

Some details concerning ar-riyaa:

If a worshipper does the deed with goal of having it be seen by the people, and he remains with this evil intention, then his deed is disgraced, and he commits minor shirk, and he runs the risk of it leading him into major shirk.

If the worshipper does a deed intending the Face of Allaah and with that, he is also intending it for the sight of the people- if he does not remove the riyaa from his deed, then the texts are clear that this deed is false.

When the worshipper does a deed for the Face of Allaah alone, but ar-riyaa comes to the surface for an instant during this deed; if he wards it off and purifies his sincerity for Allaah, then there is no harm in that deed. But if he settles for that, and becomes tranquil with it, then the value of the deed diminishes, resulting in a weakening of his faith in proportion to the amount of ar-riyaa that remained in his heart. Still, the deed remains for Allaah, but whatever portion of it he mixed up and was confused about is ar-riyaa.

ar-riyaa is a dangerous deed, which requires that the soul hasten to disciplining itself in sincerity, to wage war in defense against the destruction caused by ar-riyaa, to oppose its assault, seeking Allaah's help to defend against it, so that perhaps Allaah will purify the worshipper's faith and complete his tawheed.

As for deeds done merely for worldly reasons, or for the attainment of things in the world; then if the worshipper's intent is always for this goal, without having the objective of doing things for the Face of Allaah and the abode of the Hereafter, then there will be no reward for him in the Hereafter for these acts. Acts characterized in this manner will not be found in the heart of the believer, for the believer, even if his faith is weak, will certainly bring the goal of Allaah and the abode of the Hereafter to mind.

As for the one who does such acts for Allaah's Face, as well as for the sake of the world, these objectives being equal or approximately so, then these will, if he is a believer, diminish his faith, tawheed, and sincerity. His deeds will be diminished because he has forsaken complete sincerity in them." (End of translation from *"al-Qawl as-Sadeed fee Muqaasid at-Tawheed, Sharh 'Kitaab at-Tawheed'"*)

The punishment for major *shirk*, for the one who does not repent before his death, is that he leaves the religion, and will be punished in the Hellfire forever. As for minor *shirk*, then the Permanent Committee of Major Scholars in Saudi Arabia says,

"...So the minor shirk does not cause the one who falls into it to leave the religion of Islam; however, it is the most major of the major sins after the major shirk. Concerning that, Ibn Mas'ood said, "Because to swear by Allaah untruthfully is more beloved to me than that I should swear by other than Him truthfully." And concerning this, from its rulings, is that if the Muslim commits an act of minor shirk, then his relatives still inherit from him, and they inherit to the degree which has been brought forth and clarified by the Islamic legislation, and one prays upon him when he dies, and he is buried in the Muslim graveyard, and his sacrifice is eaten, and other examples like that from the rulings of Islaam. And he is not in the Hellfire forever, if he is put into it, like all of the people who commit the greater sins, according to ahl-as-sunnah wa ahl-al-jama', in contrast to (the beliefs of)al-Khawaarij and al-Mu'tazilah." (End of translation, as found in the book, *"Fatawa al-A'imat an-Najdiyyah", Page 48*)

The Third Category from the Categories of ash-Shirk

ash-Shirk khafee- the hidden shirk:

And the proof of it is the saying of the Messenger of Allaah, may Allaah's praise and good mention be upon him, { *Ash-Shirk in this Ummah (nation) is more hidden than the creeping black ant on a black piece of wood in the darkness of the night.}* ("*Musnad*" of Imaam Ahmad No. 18781)

And the expiation for it is his, may Allaah's praise and good mention be upon him, saying, { *Oh Allaah, indeed I ask You for protection from associating any partners along with You in worship, and I am aware of it, and I ask Your forgiveness for the sins which I am not aware of.* } ("*Saheeh al-Jaami*'" No.3731)

Explanation: *ash-shirk al-khafee* may be major *shirk*, or it may be minor *shirk*.

The opposite of hidden, is apparent (*al-jalee*). And that which is apparent is that which is seen from the people, whether major or minor *shirk*. An example of the apparent major *shirk*, is when one makes pilgrimage to the tomb of a righteous person and sacrifices at it. And an example of minor *shirk* which is apparent, is swearing by other than Allaah, without the intention of making that thing like Allaah.

Hidden *shirk*, or *ash-shirk al-khafee*, is that which is not seen by the people. It is a hidden, or not apparent. An example of the hidden major *shirk*, would be the belief that there are gods other than Allaah. An example of hidden minor *shirk*, is *ar-riyaa*. And this distinction and definition of *al-jalee* and *al-khafee* is that which is well known amongst the scholars.

Some concluding words from Sheikh Saalih Fauzaan al-Fauzaan, may Allaah preserve him,

"*Ash-shirk is the greatest of sins, because Allaah, the Most High has informed us that He does not forgive it from those who do not repent from it. Along with that, He, Glorified is He, has written mercy for Himself. And it is obligatory upon the worshipper to be strong in being on his guard against ash-shirk, and strong in his fear of ash-shirk- that this be of great importance to him. And that he should have (this caution and fear) in order that he understand ash-shirk in order to avoid it- because it is the most abominable of the abominable things, and the most oppressive oppression.*" (From "*Fataawa al-A'imat an-Najdiyyah*", Page 54)

Key Terms in this Lesson

Define these terms:

al-khafee:

al-jalee:

ar-riyaa:

Lesson Questions:

Level 1: [required]

1. List three examples of minor *shirk*.
2. When is swearing by other than Allaah minor *shirk*? When does it become major *shirk*?
3. How can *ar-riyaa* lead to major *shirk*?
4. What is the punishment of one who commits minor *shirk* and does not repent from it? How does this differ from the punishment for major *shirk*?

Level 2: [supplementary]

1. Give me two examples of *ar-riyaa* other than that which I have given you.
2. Is hidden *shirk* from the major or minor *shirk*? Explain, and give examples.
3. What is the state of one who begins an act solely for Allaah's sake, but somewhere in the act he falls into *ar-riyaa*? What affect can this have upon his faith?
4. What are some ways to guard ourselves against *ar-riyaa*?
5. Why is it important to be aware of the categories of *ash-shirk* and their rulings?

LESSON SIXTEEN

Kufr, (Disbelief) is of Two Types

Explanation: *al-kufr*: In the language of Arabic, it means, "enveloping" or "concealing"

The religious meaning, as stated by Ibn Taymiyyah, then mentioned by Sheikh Muqbil and Sheikh Fauzaan, and other than them, is that,

"It is the absence of faith in Allaah, and His Messenger, whether or not this is with denial, or not with denial. Rather, it is merely doubt and uncertainty or abandonment of this (faith), or envy, or pride, or following some of the desires that repel the following of the Messenger. And the kufr of denial is the greatest disbelief, and likewise the disbeliever and denier out of envy, along with certainty of the truth of the message." (*"Majmoo al-Fataawa"* of Sheikh al-Islaam ibn Taymiyyah, Vol. 12, Page 335)

The First Type: Disbelief which takes one out of the religion

And it is five categories:

Explanation: And this type of disbelief is the one which nullifies one's Islaam, as was mentioned under *al-i'raad* in the section on those things which nullify *al-Islaam* that we have already discussed in a previous chapter; if the items that stand between it and disbelief have been removed (such as ignorance, misunderstanding, mistake, etc) and the conditions have been fulfilled, then this type of disbelief takes one outside of Islaam. And this is a common failing amongst the people. In the morning they are believers in Allaah, attending classes, or going to the *masjid*, and then in the evening they fall into some aspect of disbelief, and they are not even aware of it. For example someone tells another person that something is *haraam*- and the person, says, "What's your proof that it is *haraam* and not merely disliked?" As he feels if it is merely disliked, then it is all right to enter into it- and it is his desires that lead him into this. So he enters into an argument, not knowing if what he is supporting is against that which is in the Qur'aan and the Sunnah. And wrongdoing builds upon and leads to more wrongdoing. Or again, falling into envy or pride, such as the People of the Book fell into envy and rejected the Message, and Fir'awn and Iblees fell into pride and rejected the Message. So we must increase in asking Allaah's forgiveness, and guard ourselves against this.

The First Category: Kufr of Falsehood and Denial

The proof is His, the Most High, saying, ◄ *And who does more wrong than he who invents a lie against Allaah or denies the truth (Muhammad and his doctrine of Islamic Monotheism and this Qur'aan), when it comes to him? Is there not a dwelling in Hell for the disbelievers (in the Oneness of Allaah and in His Messenger Muhammad)* ► –(Surat al-Ankaboot, Ayat 68)

Explanation: Allaah says, ◄ *And who does more wrong than he who invents a lie against Allaah or denies the truth when it comes to him?* ► The word in Arabic here is "أظلم" (adhlam) and this is known as an *ism tafdeel*, or a comparative or superlative adjective. Meaning, there are many injustices, but the one who falls into THIS injustice or wrongdoing, of creating a lie against Allaah- he has been the most unjust, or one of the most unjust, and done the greatest wrongdoing.

aftara: to create a lie, to slander, falsehood, defame

Examples of this type of disbelief, would be one who says that he has received revelation from Allaah, and he has not received revelation at all, such as the many false prophets who have appeared throughout the years since the Prophet, may Allaah's praise and salutations be upon him, was sent with the final message for mankind. As we know that there will be no prophets sent to mankind after Muhammad, may Allaah's praise and salutations be upon him. Or one who claims that he can do that which only Allaah can do, such as send down rain, or make it possible for a woman to have a baby, or bring the dead to life. Or the one who invents a lie against Allaah, perhaps by attributing to Him that which He has not attributed Himself with. There are also the *Shi'ah*, some of whom say that Allaah made a mistake, and sent the revelation to Muhammad, may Allaah's praise and salutations be upon him, rather than to 'Ali, who it was intended for. Another example would be one who denies the truth of Allaah's message, or a part of the truth, such as saying that the stories of the prophets are not true, they are only parables.

So we see the importance of having correct knowledge of Allaah, and His Book, and all that He sent down to His Messenger, Muhammad, may Allaah's praise and salutations be upon him, so that we may stay clear of this form of disbelief. This is also a reason to be sure that we are not saying anything about the religion that was not said by the people of knowledge before us, and why we must look to the scholars for guidance in our religion. And Allaah knows best.

> *The Second Category: Kufr of Rejection and Pride, along with Affirmation of the Truth*
>
> The proof is the saying of Allaah, the Most High, ◈ *And (remember) when We said to the angels: "Prostrate yourselves before Aadam." And they prostrated except Iblees, he refused and was proud and was one of the disbelievers (disobedient to Allaah).* ◈ –(Surat al-Baqarah, Ayat 34)

Explanation: *al-ibaa:* this is the word used both in the text and in the verse above to describe that which Iblees did- so in this context, it means rejection. So what is meant is, rejecting something out of pride.

al-kibr: pride, conceit

Qataadah said, concerning Allaah's statement, ◈ *And (remember) when We said to the angels: "Prostrate yourselves before Aadam"...* ◈ :

The obedience was for Allaah and the prostration was before Aadam. Allaah honored Aadam and commanded the angels to prostrate before him. ("Tafseer ibn Katheer", Vol. 1, Page 194)

Some of the people say that this was just a prostration of greeting. However, the correct opinion, that which is shared by ar-Raazi and others, is that this was a prostration showing honor, deference, and respect. Ibn Katheer says that this was a practice that was allowed for previous nations, but was repealed for ours. He uses as proof the hadeeth of Mu'aadh ibn Jabal, as found in *"Sunan at-Tirmidhi"*, and it is authentic: Mu'aadh said to the Messenger of Allaah, may Allaah's praise and salutations be upon him,

{I visited ash-Shaam and found that they used to prostrate before their priests and scholars. You, oh Messenger of Allaah, are more worthy of prostration." The Prophet, may Allaah's praise and salutations be upon him, said,
"No. If I were to command any human to prostrate before another human, I would command the wife to prostrate before her husband because of the enormity of his right over her.}

Concerning Allaah's statement, ◈ *And they prostrated except Iblees, he refused and was proud and was one of the disbelievers.* ◈ Ibn Katheer states,

Qataadah said...Iblees, the enemy of Allaah, envied Aadam because Allaah honored Aadam. He said, ◈ I was created from fire and he was created from clay. ◈ Therefore the first error ever committed was arrogance, for the enemy of Allaah was too arrogant to prostrate before Aadam. I, Ibn Katheer, say, the following is recorded in the Saheeh,
{ No person who has the weight of a mustard seed of arrogance in his heart shall enter

Paradise.} (Muslim, 93)

Iblees had disbelief, arrogance, and rebellion, all of which caused him to be expelled from the holy presence of Allaah, and His Mercy. (From "*Tafseer Ibn Katheer*", Page 195)

Iblees, who is of the *jinn*, knew the truth- he affirmed Allaah's Lordship. However, he was proud, thinking himself to be better than Aadam, and so he refused to obey Allaah out of this arrogance.

This is a trial we all face every day, as we increase in knowledge, or wealth, or children, or other than that. Along with this increase, can come an increase in pride. This can lead to many problems. For example, a brother studies in a center of learning for a short period of time, and then returns to his country. There, a person sees something that he is doing wrong, and gives him advice, based on the correct sources, and clarified by the people of knowledge. The brother says, "Who are you to give me advice? I have studied more than you!" When in truth, the advice was sound advice, based upon the Qur'aan and the Sunnah and the understanding of the Pious Predecessors and the scholars, and he knows this- so he is rejecting something from the religion, based upon his pride. Or perhaps a person may have a lot of money, or a good position somewhere, and so then cuts the ties of the womb with his poorer family members, out of pride- he is disobeying a command of Allaah out of his arrogance. Or a sister has been told she is beautiful, and wants the people to see it- so she uncovers her face in public, knowing that the evidences all indicate that to cover the face is obligatory for the woman. All of these things fall under the sin of rejecting something from Allaah, out of pride and arrogance.

The Third Category: Kufr of Doubt, and it is Kufr of Uncertainty

The proof is the saying of Allaah, the Most High, *And he went into his garden while in a state (of pride and disbelief), unjust to himself. He said: "I think not that this will ever perish.*

And I think not the Hour will ever come, and if indeed I am brought back to my Lord (on the Day of Resurrection), I surely shall find better than this when I return to Him."

His companion said to him during the talk with him: "Do you disbelieve in Him Who created you out of dust, then out of Nutfah (mixed drops of male and female sexual discharge), then fashioned you into a man?

But as for my part, (I believe) that He is Allaah, my Lord, and none shall I associate as partner with my Lord." –(Surat al-Kahf, Ayats 35-37)

Explanation: Before discussing how these *ayat* indicate the *kufr* of doubt and uncertainty, I would like to take a minute to point out how they also indicate the importance of having the good companion. The first man enters his garden, feeling prideful and pleased with himself, and says something that is clearly wrong from an Islamic standpoint. His companion does not keep silent; rather, he corrects the man's mistake, and clarifies that which he himself is upon. thereby commanding the good and forbidding the evil. Each of us needs to find companions like this to sit with, ones who will urge us towards the good, remind us of Allaah and His rights over us and His blessings to us, and who will warn us away from the evil, and remind us of the punishment that awaits the evil doers.

Concerning the *kufr* of doubt: In these verses, we are told of a man who enters his garden, thinking that the good that he sees in this garden came about due to his knowledge, or good works. He says, ❨ *I think not the Hour will ever come...*❩ meaning, the Last Hour, when the Day of Judgment is established. This is common-many of the people do not think that the Hour will come, when they will be held accountable for all of their beliefs, actions and statements on this Earth, or that the Hour is very far away- so they do not concern themselves with it, and do not fear Allaah as they should. And this can be removed through *al-yaqeen*, or certainty. If we have certainty in that which Allaah has said concerning the Last Hour, and the Resurrection, and the Judgment and all that these entail, then we should increase in fear of Allaah, and His punishment. Just as certainty in the opposite- the *Jennah*, and the reward for the believers, should lead us to good works and increase in worship so that we can be raised in its levels, insh'Allaah.

The man in the garden goes on to say, ❨*...and if indeed I am brought back to my Lord (on the Day of Resurrection), I surely shall find better than this when I return to Him* ❩; meaning, he thinks that he has good works, and that he will be rewarded with *Jennah* only due to his good works. And this is not the belief of *Ahl-as-Sunnah wa al-Jama'ah*. Imaam as-Saboonee, may Allaah have mercy upon him, says, regarding this,

The People of Hadeeth believe and testify that no one is entitled to Paradise, even if he has performed good deeds and his worship was the most sincere, or his obedience was the purest obedience, and his way was a pleasing one, unless Allaah favors him, thus granting it to him, through His Blessings and Graciousness. Since the good deeds which the person performed were not made easy for him, except by the facilitation of Allaah, Mighty is His Name. So if He had not made it easy for him, the person would not have been able to accomplish this deed and if He did not guide him to it he would never have accomplished it out of his own effort and exhortation. Allaah, the Mighty and Majestic says,

Had it not been for the Grace of Allaah and His mercy upon you, not one of you would have been purified. However, Allaah purifies whom He wills. –(Surat an-Noor, Ayat 21)

And He said, concerning the people of the Paradise,

And they say all praise is for Allaah, Who has guided us to this. Never could we have found guidance were it not that Allaah guided us. –(Surat al-A'raaf, Ayat 43) (From "'Aqeedat as-Salaf wa Ashaab al-Hadeeth", Pages 78-79)

So we see that we will not enter *Jennah* by our deeds alone; rather, we must depend on Allaah's Mercy to gain entrance. This does not mean that we do not strive to do good and worship Allaah in the best manner possible. This is a trick of the *Shaytaan*, one that the Christians have fallen entirely into. They believe that as long as you are baptized into Christianity, you are in their Heaven no matter what you do in this life- so they have no real reason to do good. The Jews also believe that just because they are Jews, they will enter their Heaven. However, the Muslim has the balanced and correct understanding. He knows that he will be judged for his good and bad deeds on the Day of Judgment, and that he will be rewarded for his good deeds and punished for his sins. He strives to gain knowledge to worship Allaah correctly, knowing that that knowledge will be a proof upon him on the Day of Judgment- if he believed in it, and acted upon it, then he will have the reward, and if he had the knowledge and did not act upon it, then it will be a proof against him. He knows all of this, and he knows, also, that ultimately his success lies with Allaah, who enabled him to gain the knowledge and to act upon it, through His Wisdom and Mercy. Allaah guides the people in the religion, alhamdulillah, and that which occurs to them occurs only through His permission.

Imaam as-Saboonee, may Allaah have mercy upon him, says, concerning Allaah's guidance and decree,

"The People of Hadeeth witness that Allaah, the Most High, gives guidance to His religion to whom He wills, and He misguides whom He wills away from His religion. There is no argument for the one who is misguided by Allaah, and he has no excuse.

Say, with Allaah is the perfect proof and argument. If He had willed, He would have guided you all. –(Surat al-An'aam, Ayat 149)

And if We had willed, We would have given every person guidance. But the Word of truth from Me is to fill Hellfire with the jinn and mankind all together. –(Surat as-Sajdah, Ayat 13)

◈ *Indeed I have created many for Hell from amongst the jinn and humans,* ◈ – (Surat al-A'araaf, Ayat 179)

So He, the One free from all deficiencies, created the creation without having need for them. He made them into two groups, one for the Paradise out of His favor, and one for the Hell out of His justice. He has made from them some misguided and some rightly guided, joyful and miserable. Some are near to His mercy and some far.
◈ *He cannot be questioned for what He does, but they will be questioned.* ◈ – (Surat al-Anbiyyah, Ayat 23)

◈ *Indeed the Creation and the Commandment is His. Blessed be Allaah, Lord of the Worlds* ◈ –(Surat al-A'araaf, Ayat 54)

…'Abdullah ibn Mas'ood said, { The Messenger of Allaah, may Allaah's praise and salutations be upon him, and he spoke the truth and his word was believed, said,

Indeed you are created from being collected in the womb of your mother for forty days in the form of a drop, Then it becomes a piece of congealed blood after a similar period. Then it becomes a lump of flesh after a similar period. Then Allaah sends to it an angel, with four things: his provision, his deeds, his period of life and whether he will be wretched or blessed. By Him in Whose Hand my soul is in, one of you will do the deeds of those who will go to Paradise, so that there will only be an arm span between him and it. Then what is decreed for him will overcome him, so that we will do the deeds of those who go to Hell, and then enter into it. Also one of you will do the deeds of those who will go to Hell, so that there will be only an arm span between him and it. Then what is decreed for him will overcome him, so that he will do the deeds of those who go to Paradise and then enter into it.} (Agreed upon)" (End of translation from *"Aqeedat as-Salaf wa Ashaab al-Hadeeth"*, Pages 8-9)

Again, the opposite of *ash-shak*, or doubt, is *al-yaqeen*, which we discussed under the conditions of *ash-shahadah*. We must strive to have certainty in our hearts about Allaah, and His religion, including the rewards and the punishments, and the Divine Decree, among other things. We must increase in remembrance of Allaah, and asking His forgiveness, and making *du'a* that our knowledge increase, along with our acting upon it, so that our scales will be heavy on the Day of Judgment, and that we increase in certainty in Allaah's Mercy and Justice, so that we can be of the people of Paradise, if Allaah so wills.

Key Terms in this Lesson

Define these terms:

al-kufr:
What it means in the language:
What the religious meaning is:
al-ibaa:
al-kibr:

Lesson Questions:

Level 1: [required]

1. What conditions cause *al-kufr* which take one out of Islaam?

2. What is the most unjust act a person can commit?

3. Who are two examples of disbelief out of arrogance that we know of from the Qur'aan? Explain.

4. What is the stance of *ahl-as-Sunnah wa ahl-al-Jama'ah* in regards to entrance to Paradise?

Level 2: [supplementary]

1. Give two examples other than those stated of someone inventing a lie against Allaah.

2. How can an increase in wealth or knowledge, lead to disbelief? How can we protect against this?

3. Knowing that we will only gain Paradise through the mercy of Allaah, do we still have to do good deeds? Explain.

4. How do we fight against the possibility of falling into the disbelief of doubt?

LESSON SEVENTEEN

> *The Fourth Category: Kufr of Abandonment*
>
> The proof is the saying of the Most High, ⟨ ***But those who disbelieve, turn away from that whereof they are warned.*** ⟩ –(Surat al-Ahqaaf, from Ayat 3)

Explanation: This is *al-i'raad*, which we discussed in the chapter on those things which nullify al-Islaam. This is abandoning something from that which Muhammad, may Allaah's praise and salutations be upon him, brought to us from Allaah, the Most High.

Again, for abandonment to fall into this category, one must make the *istihlaal al-qalbiyyah*, in which one abandons that which is obligatory with his heart, in his belief. This is in opposition to the one who does *istihlaal al-fi'liyyah*, in which he abandons acting upon that thing, but does not in his heart believe that the thing is not obligatory. The person in this case is committing a serious wrongdoing, but it is not one that directly takes him out of Islaam. However, we must be on our guard against this, as it is the case that one wrongdoing can easily lead to more wrongdoing, which could lead us into disbelief. May Allaah protect us all from that.

> *The Fifth Category: Kufr of Hypocrisy*
>
> The proof is His, the Most High, saying, ⟨ ***That is because they believed, and then disbelieved; therefore their hearts are sealed, so they understand not.*** ⟩ –(Surat al-Munaafiqoon, Ayat 3)

Explanation: This is an action of the heart, as well. It is important to remember that when we are discussing belief, it is known to us to be an action of the heart. This is different from what the Western idea of belief is. They connect belief to the intellect, and do not consider it an action. However, in Islaam, the things such as belief, love, and certainty that take place in the heart are indeed actions, and fall under the category that is meant when it is said that we must act upon our knowledge. We must foster these actions of the heart, just as we work to increase ourselves in good deeds with our limbs, perfecting our prayer, giving charity, and such as that.

As we learned before, the two conditions of *ash-shahadah* which negate *an-nifaaq*, (hypocrisy), are sincerity and truthfulness. This is because hypocrisy is by definition insincerity, and deceit, as one acts as though they are submitting to Allaah when in reality their hearts are not in a state of submission.

Allaah, the Most High, says, ◊ *That is because they believed...* ◊; meaning, with their tongues. And then He, Glorified and Exalted is He, says, ◊ *and then disbelieved* ◊ meaning, with their hearts. As their belief does not go past their lips, and join with their hearts- their hearts are not guided, nor did they experience the light of faith. And so no good will come to them through their sayings and their actions done under the guise of Islaam, as truly they are disbelievers. Allaah tells us that their hearts are sealed, so they do not understand. This is a very common illness, one that we must do all we can to be on our guard against- imagine the state of having one's heart sealed from Allaah and His guidance- what a terrible state that would be. This is the illness of hypocrisy, may Allaah protect us from this and make our hearts compliant.

Insh'Allaah, we will be going deeper into *an-nifaaq* in the next lesson, which deals with the different types of hypocrisy and what falls under them.

The Second Type from the Types of Disbelief: It is lesser disbelief, and it does not remove one from the religion, and it is the disbelief in Allaah's beneficence

The proof is the saying of Allaah, the Most High, ◊ *And Allaah puts forward the example of a township (Makkah), that dwelt secure and well-content; its provision coming to it in abundance from every place, but it (its people) denied the Favors of Allaah (with ungratefulness). So Allaah made it taste extreme of hunger (famine) and fear, because of that (evil, i.e. denying Prophet Muhammad) which they (its people) used to do.* ◊ –(Surat an-Nahl, Ayat 112)

Explanation: Ibn Katheer states,

This example refers to the people of Makkah, which had been secure, peaceful and stable, a secure sanctuary while men were being snatched away from everywhere outside of it. Whoever entered Makkah, he was safe, and he had no need to fear, as Allaah says,

◊ *And they say: "If we follow the guidance with you, we would be snatched away from our land." Have We not established for them a secure sanctuary (Makkah), to which are brought fruits of all kinds, a provision from Ourselves, but most of them know not."* ◊ –(Surat al-Qasas, Ayat 57)

Likewise, Allaah says here, ◈ *its provision coming to it in abundance* ◈ *meaning, with ease and plenty,* ◈ *from every place, but (its people) denied the favors of Allaah.* ◈ *meaning, they denied the blessings of Allaah towards them, the greatest of which was Muhammad, may Allaah's praise and salutations be upon him, being sent to them, as Allaah says,*

◈ **Have you not seen those who have changed the Blessings of Allaah into disbelief (by denying Prophet Muhammad and his Message of Islaam), and caused their people to dwell in the house of destruction? Hell, in which they will burn, – and what an evil place to settle in!** ◈ *–(Surat Ibraaheem, Ayats 28-29)*

Hence, Allaah replaced their former blessings with the opposite and said, ◈ **So Allaah made it taste extreme hunger and fear** ◈ *meaning, He inflicted it and made them taste of hunger after fruit of all kinds and provision in abundance from every place had been brought in to it. This was when they defied the Messenger of Allaah, may Allaah's praise and salutations be upon him, and insisted on opposing him, so he supplicated against them, asking Allaah to send them seven years like the seven years of Yoosuf, and they were stricken with a year in which everything that they had was destroyed, and they ate the hair of the camel mixed with its blood when it is slaughtered. "and fear" refers to the fact that their sense of security was replaced with fear of the Messenger of Allaah, may Allaah's praise and salutations be upon him, and his Companions after they had migrated to al-Madinah. They feared the power and the attack of his armies, and they started to lose and face the destruction of everything that had belonged to them, until Allaah made it possible for His Messenger, may Allaah's praise and salutations be upon him, to conquer Makkah. This happened because of their evil deeds, their wrongdoing, and their rejection of the Messenger, may Allaah's praise and salutations be upon him, that Allaah sent to them from amongst themselves....and this was the opinion of al-'Awfi and ibn 'Abbaas, Mujaahid, Qataadah, 'Abdur Rahman ibn Zayd ibn Aslam, and Maalik narrated it from az-Zuhri as well, may Allaah have mercy upon them all.* (From "Tafseer ibn Katheer", Vol. 5, Pages 533-536)

The people of Makkah were punished for denying the blessings of Allaah- but Allaah did not say that those who do this are disbelievers because of it. This differentiates this lesser disbelief from the major disbelief that takes one outside of Islaam.

It is important to remember that we must remember Allaah's blessings upon us in times of trial as well as in times of ease. The action of the heart we are discussing here is that of *ash-shukr*, which means, thankfulness and gratitude. In times of trial, we must have patience, and we must also try to foster gratitude within ourselves- gratitude that Allaah does provide for us, and watches over us, and has planned everything for a reason. You are never alone in your test, as Allaah is with you with His knowledge. In times of plenty we are tested because it is in these times that people tend to slack off a bit in worship, and take things for granted, and often fall into this lesser disbelief by feeling pleased with themselves for the condition they find themselves in, when indeed, it is Allaah who granted them these blessings.

So for example, a couple wants a baby. They try and try for years, and never have one. Then, after a number of years, they are gifted with a child through the Grace of Allaah. Instead of being grateful to Allaah, they give thanks to their fertility doctor, and are proud of themselves for what they have achieved after all those years. They do not thank Allaah, alone, for granting them that baby. Then, after three years, the child is killed in a car accident. What do these people do? Instead of thanking Allaah for every moment they had with that baby, they instead lose their faith, or blame Allaah for taking the baby from them. In this case, they disbelieved in Allaah's beneficence in times of ease, and His Mercy and Wisdom in times of hardship. And Allaah knows best.

A Summary of the Differences between the Major and Minor Disbelief

Sheikh Saalih ibn Fauzaan ibn 'Abdullaah al-Fauzaan, may Allaah preserve him, says, concerning this:

1. *The major kufr, or disbelief, causes one to leave the religion, and righteous works to be lost, while the minor kufr does not cause one to leave the religion, or the works to be lost; however it decreases their worth according to the extent of the disbelief, and it exposes the one who falls into it to the promised punishment.*

2. The major kufr causes the one who falls into it to enter into the Hellfire forever. As for the minor kufr, if the one who performs it enters into the Hellfire, he will not be in it forever. And Allaah may pardon the one who performs it, so that He will not enter him into the Hellfire at all.

3. The blood and wealth of the one who falls into major disbelief is permitted, while the minor kufr does not cause it to be permissible.

4. *The major kufr makes absolute enmity obligatory between the one who falls into it and the Believers, so that it is not permissible for the Believers to love him, or support him even if he is from the closest family. As for the minor disbelief, then it does not make forbidden support in all cases. Rather, the one who falls into it may be loved and supported for that which is with him of faith, and is hated and made an enemy for that which is with him of disobedience.*

(From *"Aqeedatu at-Tawheed"* by Sheikh Fauzaan, pages 103-104)

We must protect ourselves from both categories of disbelief, and increase in asking for forgiveness, and increase in supplication and in acts of worship, in order to guard against them. It is possible that the minor disbelief may develop into the major disbelief, as falling into wrongdoing often leads to falling into more wrongdoing. For example, one could not be grateful to Allaah for the blessings He has bestowed upon him, and take the credit for himself and become arrogant and turn away from the guidance of Allaah, thus falling into major disbelief.

We must also remember that any act of disobedience, large or small, is to be avoided at all costs, as we do not want to incur Allaah's anger or punishment. The scholars have made these divisions for clarity of understanding and explanation, not so that we feel that it is okay to fall into minor disbelief as long as we stay away from the major disbelief, or okay to commit minor *shirk* as long as we stay away from major *shirk*, or that we can commit small sins as long as we stay away from major sins. This is simply a trap of the *Shaytaan*. Every act that Allaah is not pleased with, is an act to be avoided, whether major or minor. And small things turn into big things through doing them often, or through leading one to that which is worse, and every wrongdoing has an effect, in this life and the Hereafter.

May Allaah increase us in love of Him, and fear of His punishment, and protect us from His anger.

Key Terms in this Lesson

Define these terms:

al-i'raad : (from a previous lesson!)
an-nifaaq: (from a previous lesson!)
ash-shukr:

Lesson Questions:

Level 1: [required]

1. Explain the *kufr* of abandonment, in the context of *istihlaal al-qalbiyyah,* and *istihlaal al-fi'liyyah.*
2. What is the effect of hypocrisy on the heart?
3. Whom is the *ayat* of Surat an-Nahl referring to? What blessings did they deny?
4. List and explain the differences between the major and minor disbelief.

Level 2: [supplementary]

1. Give an example of *kufr* of abandonment.
2. How is hypocrisy an action of the heart? What two other actions of the heart negate it? Explain.
3. Give your own example of disbelief in the blessings of Allaah in times of hardship and ease.
4. Is it okay for us to fall into minor disbelief since it won't take us out of Islaam? Explain.

LESSON EIGHTEEN

Categories of Hypocrisy

Explanation: Sheikh Saalih ibn Fauzaan ibn 'Abdullah al-Fauzaan, may Allaah preserve him, says concerning *an-nifaaq*, or hypocrisy:

"The literal, linguistic meaning of an-nifaaq: it is derived from the hole of al-yarbu', (a rodent like burrowing animal) from which he leaves his burrow. As if he is being chased from one, he flees to the other, and exits from it. And it is said, it is a tunnel, and it is a tunnel which he hides in. (taken from *"an-Nahiyyah"* of Ibn al-Atheer, 5/98, in meaning)

As for the meaning of an-nifaaq in religious legislation: To manifest Islaam and the good outwardly, but to harbor inside disbelief and evil. It is called that because one enters into the religion from one door, and exits from it by another door. And Allaah, the Most High, called attention to that with His saying,

❧ **Verily the hypocrites are the rebellious.** ❧ –(Surat at-Tawbah, Ayat 67*)*

That is to say, they are the ones who rebel against Islamic legislation.

And Allaah considers the hypocrites to be more evil than the disbelievers, as He says,

❧ **Verily the hypocrites are in the lowest level of the fire (ad-dirk al-asfal min an-naar)** ❧ –(Surat an-Nisaa, Ayat 145*)*

Allaah, the Most High, says,

❧ **The hypocrites (think) that they deceive Allaah when in fact it is Allaah who deceives them** ❧ –(Surat an-Nisaa, Ayat 142*)*

And He, the Most High, also says,

❧ **They (think) that they deceive Allaah and the believers, but they deceive only themselves; but they do not know. In their hearts is a disease, and Allaah has increased their disease to them; and for them is a grievous punishment because they lied.** ❧ –(Surat al-Baqara, Ayats 9-10*)"* (From *"Aqeedatu at-Tawheed",* Pages 105-106)

Hypocrisy existed at the time of the Prophet, may Allaah's praise and salutations be upon him, and exists today, mash'Allaah. The head of the hypocrites at the time of the Prophet, may Allaah's praise and salutations be upon him, was 'Abdullah ibn Ubay- he was a leader of the people in the time of ignorance, and after Islaam he wanted to keep his position; so, in front of the people he abandoned worshipping idols, and prayed with the Muslims- however these actions did not benefit him because in reality he simply concealed his disbelief and put on a veneer of Islaam.

Hypocrisy is of two categories: hypocrisy of belief, and hypocrisy of action

Explanation: Hypocrisy, like *ash-shirk* and *al-kufr* and other than them, is divided into two categories. One is that of belief of the heart, and the other, that of actions (including sayings) of the limbs. One is of a more severe degree than the other, but we must be on our guard against them both.

Hypocrisy of Belief

It is of six categories: The one who engages in them is from lowest depths of the Hellfire:

Explanation: Sheikh Fauzaan, may Allaah preserve him, says in the above mentioned work,

Hypocrisy is of two types:

1. Nifaaq al-'itiqaadee (Hypocrisy of belief)

"This is major hypocrisy, in which the one who falls into it manifests Islaam outwardly, and conceals disbelief. This is the category which causes one to leave the religion entirely, and condemns the one who falls into it to the lowest level of the Hellfire. Allaah has described its people as possessing all evil characteristics: such as disbelief, and lack of faith, and derision of the religion and its people, and mocking them, and inclining wholly toward the enemies of the religion, and sharing with them in their enmity towards Islaam. People such as this exist in every age, particularly when Islaam is strong, and they cannot resist it openly- so they publicly enter into it for the purpose of plotting against it and its people in private. And because they live with the Muslims, they want to ensure the safety of their blood and their wealth. A hypocrite manifests openly that he believes in Allaah, His angels, His books, His messengers, and the Last Day; while in fact, in private, he is far from believing in all that and denies it, and does not believe in Allaah. He does not believe that Allaah uttered speech which He revealed to a human, and then sent him as a messenger to mankind to guide them with the permission of Allaah, and to warn them against His punishment. Allaah has revealed those hypocrites, and exposed their secrets in the Noble Qur'aan, and unveiled to His slaves their states; all in order that they be on their guard against hypocrisy and its people.

Allaah, the Most High, mentions three categories of people in the beginning of Surat al-Baqara: the Believers, the disbelievers, and the hypocrites. He mentions the four Ayat concerning the Believers, and two Ayat concerning the disbelievers- and concerning the hypocrites, He revealed thirteen Ayat, due to their large number and the universality of affliction through them, and the severity of their trial upon Islaam and its people. As the affliction suffered by Islaam because of them is very severe, because they are counted as Muslims, and seem to be helpers and supports of Islaam, while in actuality they are enemies of it. They express their enmity to Islaam in every form, and the ignorant ones believe it to be knowledge and reform, when in reality it is ignorance and corruption." (Sheikh Fauzaan took this, by meaning, from Ibn Qayyim, in his clarification of the attributes of the hypocrites. It is translated from Sheikh Fauzaan's book, *"Aqeedatu at-Tawheed"*, Pages 106-107)

Allaah says concerning the punishment of the one who falls into the hypocrisy of belief:

◈ **Verily the hypocrites are in the lowest level of the fire (ad-dirk al-asfal min an-naar)** ◈ –(Surat an-Nisaa, Ayat 145)

What is intended by this, is that they have the most severe of punishments- and the "fire" mentioned here is the fire of *Jahannum*, in which it has been authentically related that it has seven levels- and the hypocrites are in the lowest level of these.

The First: Denial of the Messenger, may Allaah's praise and good mention be upon him

The Second: Denial of some of what the Messenger, may Allaah's praise and good mention be upon him, came with

The Third: Hatred of the Messenger, may Allaah's praise and good mention be upon him

The Fourth: Hatred of some of what the Messenger, may Allaah's praise and good mention be upon him, came with

The Fifth: Happiness with a lowering of the religion of the Messenger, may Allaah's praise and good mention be upon him

The Sixth: Dislike with the victory of the religion of the Messenger, may Allaah's praise and good mention be upon him

---

Explanation: Alhamdulillah each of these is basically self explanatory, so we will discuss them briefly.

The first is denial of the Messenger, may Allaah's praise and salutations be upon him.

This is to believe that he was not a messenger of Allaah, sent to all of mankind with the final revelation from Allaah.

Allaah, the Most High, says, concerning this,

❴Then if they deny you (O Muhammad) so were Messengers denied before you, who came with al-Baiyyinaat (clear signs, proofs, evidences) and the Scripture and the Book of Enlightenment ❵ –(Surat al-'Imraan, Ayat 184)

The second is denial of some of what the Messenger of Allaah, may Allaah's praise and salutations be upon him, came with. This is to deny some of the message or some of the Sunnah of the Prophet, may Allaah's praise and salutations be upon him. As the Sunnah is from Allaah, just as the Qur'aan is from Allaah, and we are commanded to follow it. Indeed, there is no way to obey Allaah without obeying and following the Messenger, as we are commanded in the Qur'aan with following him. Also, the wording in the text is *some* of what he came with- so this can include accepting part of the message, while denying other parts of it.

Allaah, the Most High, says, concerning following the Messenger,

❴And whatsoever the Messenger (Muhammad) gives you, take it; and whatsoever he forbids you, abstain (from it).❵ –(Surat al-Hashr, From Ayat 7)

And He, Glorified and Exalted is He, says,

❴ Say (O Muhammad to mankind): "If you (really) love Allaah, then follow me (i.e. accept Islaam, follow the Qur'aan and the Sunnah)❵ –(Surat al-'Imraan, from Ayat 31) And there are many more ayat in this.

The third is hatred of the Messenger, may Allaah's praise and salutations be upon him. A way to combat this is to read about his life, and about his personality and how he interacted with the people. Once we see his honesty, kindness, his mercy, his sense of humor, his honor, and all of the other things that we have been told about him from authentic sources, we can come to love him, and protect ourselves from this type of hypocrisy.

The fourth is hatred of some of what the Messenger, may Allaah's praise and salutations be upon him, came with. And in this we could include the hatred of polygyny, or *jihaad*, or *hijaab*, or other than them. Again, the text states, *some*, not all of that which he came. And this is as was mentioned before- hatred, even if you act upon it. If one finds hatred in one's heart over some part of the message, then he should still act upon it, making *du'a* that his heart become reconciled and he come to love and accept that thing.

The fifth is rejoicing over the decline of the religion of the Messenger, may Allaah's praise and salutations be upon him. This is feeling happiness over the Muslim's subjugation to the enemies of Islaam. An example of this could be being happy to see that the women are going to college, mixing with the men, and out in the work force instead of learning their religion, and marrying and raising a family and working in permissible way according to the conditions of the Qur'aan and Sunnah in order to benefit the Ummah. It could also be rejoicing over the Muslims in some country being oppressed by the disbelievers- for example what is happening in Afghanistan or Palestine, mash'Allaah. Or even the more subtle changes that are taking place in Saudi, with the allowing of women in government positions and opening a coeducational college- this should not make us happy- and we should increase in our *du'a* that Allaah guides the rulers to good.

The sixth is resenting the victory of the religion of the Prophet, may Allaah's praise and salutations be upon him. For example, seeing the spread of the *Salafi da'wah* in Yemen, and elsewhere, and all thanks is due to Allaah for that, and being resentful of it, as some of the common people are. They fear the rise of Islaam, as it threatens their wishes of following their desires and seeking the worldly pleasures. And yet, they would consider themselves Muslims, mash'Allaah. Another example would be disliking that the *hudood*, or Islamically legislated punishments, were put in place in a Muslim country.

These are the categories of the hypocrisy of belief. They take place in the heart, and, as the nature of hypocrisy is deceit, are not clearly evident from what a person manifests on the outside. We must guard ourselves from these beliefs, through increasing in asking forgiveness of Allaah, and supplicating to Him, and gaining knowledge of Allaah, our religion, and the Messenger of Allaah, may Allaah's praise and salutations be upon him.

Key Terms in this Lesson

Define these terms:

an-nifaaq:
Linguistically:
The religious meaning:

Lesson Questions:

Level 1: [required]

1. What are the proofs that hypocrisy is more evil than disbelief?
2. What is meant by Allaah's stating that the hypocrites are in the lowest level of the fire?
3. What are two proofs that we must follow the Messenger of Allaah?
4. Give an example of being happy over the lowering or decline of the religion, other than what I gave.
5. Give an example of resenting the victory of Islaam, other than what was mentioned.

Level 2: [supplementary]

1. There were no hypocrites in al-Madinah. Is this statement true? Explain your answer.
2. Why would anyone become a hypocrite?
3. Was Muhammad the only prophet who was denied? Give another example of this.
4. Is a person clearly a hypocrite if he acts upon that which he dislikes about the religion? Explain.
5. What are some ways to guard ourselves against hypocrisy of belief?

LESSON NINETEEN

> *Hypocrisy of Action*
>
> The hypocrisy of action is of five types:
>
> And the proof is the saying of the Messenger of Allaah, may Allaah's praise and good mention be upon him, The Prophet said, { *The signs of a hypocrite are three: Whenever he speaks, he tells a lie. Whenever he promises, he always breaks it (his promise). If you trust him, he proves to be dishonest. (If you keep something as a trust with him, he will not return it.) }* ("*Saheeh al-Bukhaari*", No. 33, and "*Saheeh Muslim*", No.59)
>
> And in another narration, *{... Whenever he makes a covenant, he proves treacherous and whenever he quarrels, he behaves in a very imprudent, evil and insulting manner.}* ("*Saheeh al-Bukhaari*",No. 34, "*Saheeh Muslim*", No. 58)

Explanation: The full texts of the two hadeeth are as follows:

Narrated 'Abdullah ibn'Amr, may Allaah be pleased with him, The Prophet, may Allaah's praise and salutations be upon him, said,

{ Whoever has the following four (characteristics) will be a pure hypocrite, and whoever has one of the following four characteristics will have one characteristic of hypocrisy unless and until he gives it up:

1. **Whenever he is entrusted, he betrays (proves dishonest and untrustworthy)**
2. **Whenever he speaks, he tells a lie**
3. **Whenever he makes a covenant, he proves treacherous**
4. **Whenever he quarrels, he behaves in a very imprudent (excessive), evil and insulting manner.}**

Narrated Abu Hurairah, may Allaah be pleased with him, The Prophet, may Allaah's praise and salutations be upon him, said,

{ The signs of a hypocrite are three:

1. **Whenever he speaks, he tells a lie**
2. **Whenever he promises, he always breaks it (his promise)**
3. **Whenever he is entrusted, he betrays (is dishonest, and untrustworthy- if you keep something as a trust with him, he will not return it).}**

And these two hadeeth are Agreed Upon, meaning, they are found in both "*Saheeh al-Bukhaari*" and "*Saheeh Muslim*".

Sheikh Muhammad ibn 'Abdul Wahaab says, in the text, "*And in another narration…*".

This is most often used for two hadeeths which share the same narrator. That is not the case here, however, as the Sheikh is referring to two hadeeth with different narrators.

The meaning of the first hadeeth, according to the majority of the scholars, is that these are all characteristics of the hypocrite, and the one who performs any of them is resembling the hypocrites in this characteristic, and behaving as they behave. And al-Khataabee, may Allaah have mercy upon him, states that its meaning is to warn the Muslim away from developing or making a habit of these five traits.

Sheikh Saalih ibn Fauzaan ibn 'Abdullah al-Fauzaan says, regarding this category of hypocrisy,

"The second category, and it is hypocrisy of action: it is to perform a deed from the acts of the hypocrites, while retaining eemaan, or faith, in the heart. This does not cause one to leave the religion; however it is a means which may lead to it. A person who falls into it, has both faith and hypocrisy in himself, and if it (the hypocrisy) grows, (and becomes prevalent) then because of it a person becomes a pure hypocrite...." (Translator's note: the Sheikh then brings the first hadeeth, on 'Abdullah ibn 'Amr, as a proof of this.) He goes on to say,

"...The one who combines these four traits, he has combined in himself evil, and all the traits of the hypocrites. But he who has one of them, then he possesses a trait of hypocrisy. A servant may combine traits of goodness and traits of evil, and characteristics of faith and characteristics of disbelief and hypocrisy. He is deserving of rewards or punishment in accordance with the traits which necessitate that (reward or punishment)

An example of that is one being lazy about attending the congregational prayer in the masjid (for the men), as this is an attribute of the hypocrites. Hypocrisy is evil, and very dangerous. The Companions were afraid of falling into it. Ibn Abee Malikah said, "I have met thirty Companions, of the Messenger , may Allaah's praise and salutations be upon him, all of whom feared hypocrisy for themselves." (End of translation from *"'Aqeedatu at-Tawheed"*, Page 108)

We must fear performing any of these five actions, as they may make an imprint upon our hearts, and may lead to hypocrisy of belief- and perhaps we will not even realize that we have fallen into it, may Allaah protect us from that.

And the hypocrites are somewhat like the Jews, in that they have the knowledge, but do not act upon it in reality. The Jews make their disobedience open, and the hypocrites keep it concealed, but it is the same disease. And we live in a time in which it is easy to be a hypocrite- even many of the Muslims who would consider themselves "religious" do not fulfill the obligatory acts, such as the congregational prayer for the men, or not resembling the disbelievers. It is easy for the ones who hold hypocrisy in their hearts to go along with what is considered almost normal now- for example, a man not attending the congregational prayers will most often not be censured for this act- indeed it goes almost unnoticed in society today! It is upon us to take great care, and pay attention to the state of our actions, and the state of our hearts, as wrongdoing most often leads to more wrongdoing.

We should not take sins lightly, as we do not know if Allaah will forgive us or not- we are dependent upon His Mercy, and upon His being Oft-Forgiving. So how many times must we ask for forgiveness for a sin, to have it be forgiven? We must increase in sincerity and in asking for forgiveness, and guard ourselves against smaller sins that build up, and may lead to that which is greater.

The first hadeeth above says, { ...*Whenever he is entrusted, he betrays (proves dishonest and untrustworthy)* }. And this is when he has no excuse. For example, if we lend a book to a sister, and she says she will return it the next day, and she does not return it because she is ill, for example- then she is not falling into this characteristic of hypocrisy because she has an excuse for not fulfilling the trust. And Allaah knows best.

Sheikh Fauzaan, may Allaah have mercy upon him, mentions the differences between major and minor hypocrisy:

1. Major hypocrisy causes one to leave the religion, while minor hypocrisy does not.

2. In major hypocrisy, there is a difference between that which is concealed and that which is made public, in belief. In minor hypocrisy, the difference between the inner and outer is a matter of actions, only, without belief.

3. Major hypocrisy cannot come from a believer, but minor hypocrisy can come from a believer.

4. A person who falls into major hypocrisy does not usually repent, and if he does repent, scholars differ in regards to the acceptance of his repentance with a judge. This differs from the minor hypocrisy- as the one who falls into it, and repents to Allaah, then Allaah will accept his repentance.

Sheikh al-Islaam, ibn Taymiyyah, may Allaah have mercy upon him, said,

Often a believer manifests a branch from the branches of hypocrisy, then Allaah forgives him this. And some of that which indicates hypocrisy may reach his heart, and Allaah protects him from it. The believer may be subjected to the whispers of ash-Shaytaan, and the whispers of disbelief, by which his heart becomes straitened. As one of the Companions said, { Oh Messenger of Allaah, one of us may find in his self that which it would be more beloved to him to fall from the sky to the earth than to speak them." He, may Allaah's praise and salutations be upon him, said, That is the pure eemaan (faith)} (Related in Imam Ahmad's "Musnad" and "Saheeh Muslim") *And in another version, when (the desire) to speak of these things becomes intense, say, { All praise is due to Allaah, who reduced the plot of ash-Shaytaan to mere whispering. } Meaning, these whisperings occur, along with intense hatred (of them), and repulsing them from the heart- this is an expression of pure eemaan."* (End of Sheikh Fauzaan's quote from Ibn Taymiyyah)

Sheikh Fauzaan goes on to say,

As for those who fall into major hypocrisy, then Allaah has said, concerning them.

They are deaf, dumb, and blind, so they return not (to the Right Path). –(Surat al-Baqarah, Ayat 18) *That is to say, (they do not return to Islaam) internally. And the Most High says, concerning them,*

See they not that they are put in trial once or twice every year (with different kinds of calamities, disease, famine)? Yet, they turn not in repentance, nor do they learn a lesson (from it). –(Surat at-Tawbah, Ayat 126)

Sheikh al-Islaam Ibn Taymiyyah, may Allaah have mercy upon him, said, "Scholars differ as to the acceptance of their public repentance, as it cannot be verified, even if they were to always manifest Islaam outwardly." (From *"'Aqeedatu at-Tawheed"*, by Sheikh Fauzaan, Pages 109-110)

So we see the grave state of the one who falls into hypocrisy- the lesser or the greater hypocrisy- as it may leave a mark upon the person's heart, and drive them permanently from Allaah's guidance and mercy. When the whisperings of *ash-Shaytaan* come to one of us, urging us to do one of those acts which is considered an act of hypocrisy, she must guard herself against this thing, again, by increasing in remembrance of Allaah, and supplication, and asking for Allaah's forgiveness. This is not a minor matter, it is a major matter, one that we must all be aware of and do our utmost to protect ourselves from. As was mentioned in a previous lesson, even the Companions of the Messenger of Allaah, may Allaah's praise and salutations be upon him, feared hypocrisy for themselves, and they were the best of generations!! So how about us, in this day- we feel comfortable with our condition, and don't call ourselves into account or take a constant tally of what we have done, and how we may stand before Allaah on that day when there are no helpers for us. May Allaah make us of those who call themselves to account, and who turn our faces to Allaah, and work to purify our hearts, our beliefs, and our actions.

Lesson Questions:

Level 1: [required]

1. What are the signs of the hypocrite, as mentioned in the two hadeeth?
2. How do we understand this, as explained by the scholars?
3. In what way do hypocrites resemble the Jews?
4. Why does Sheikh al-Islaam ibn Taymiyyah say that the public repentance of a hypocrite may not be accepted, according to some of the scholars?
5. What are the differences between the hypocrisy of belief and the hypocrisy of action? Why must we guard against them both?

Level 2: [supplementary]

1. If a person performs some of the actions of a hypocrite, is he a hypocrite?
2. How can these characteristics lead to hypocrisy of belief, which takes one out of Islaam?
3. You lend some money to Brother So and So. He is supposed to return it on Friday, but he does not. Should you immediately believe that he has one of these signs of hypocrisy? Explain.
4. Explain that which Sheikh Fauzaan said, "*Major hypocrisy cannot come from a believer, but minor hypocrisy can come from a believer.*"
5. Explain the statement of the Prophet, may Allaah's praise and salutations be upon him, { *That is the pure eemaan (faith)* }.

LESSON TWENTY

The Meaning of *at-Taaghoot* and the Foremost of its Categories

Know, may Allaah, the Most High have mercy upon you: Indeed the first thing that Allaah made obligatory upon the sons of Aadam was the disbelief in *at-taaghoot* and belief in Allaah.

The proof is the saying of the Most High, ❴ *And verily, We have sent among every Ummah (community, nation) a Messenger (proclaiming): "Worship Allaah (Alone), and avoid taaghoot (all false deities, i.e. do not worship anything besides Allaah).* ❵ –(Surat an-Nahl, from Ayat 36)

As for the description of disbelief in *at-taaghoot*: To believe that worship of anything other than Allaah is false, and to leave it, to dislike it, and to know that the ones who engage in it are disbelievers, and are enemies.

As for the meaning of belief in Allaah: To believe that Allaah is the only god worthy of worship, without anything other than Him being worthy of worship, and to make all acts of worship intended solely for Allaah alone, and to deny all that is worshipped other than Him, and to love the people of faith and devotion (*al-Ikhlaas*) and to have hatred for the people who associate others with Allaah and make them enemies.

This is the religion of Ibraaheem, and the one who turns away from it has shown himself to be devoid of good sense and judgment. And this is the example which Allaah informed us of in His saying, the Most High, ❴ *Indeed there has been an excellent example for you in Ibraaheem and those with him, when they said to their people: "Verily, we are free from you and whatever you worship besides Allaah, we have rejected you, and there has appeared between us and you, hostility and hatred for ever until you believe in Allaah Alone," – except the saying of Ibraaheem to his father: "Verily, I will ask forgiveness (from Allaah) for you, but I have no power to do anything for you before Allaah." "Our Lord! In You (Alone) we put our trust, and to You (Alone) we turn in repentance, and to You (Alone) is (our) final Return.* ❵ –(Surat al-Mumtahanah, Ayat 4)

And *at-taaghoot* is general: as everything which is worshipped other than Allaah, and is pleased with that worship, from that which is worshipped, followed, or obeyed with other than obedience to Allaah and His Messenger, may Allaah's praise and good mention be upon him; it is a *taaghoot*. And they are many, and the foremost of them are five:

Explanation: *at-taaghoot*: derived from *tughyaan*, which means to exceed the boundaries, as Allaah says, concerning the flood at the time of Nuh:

◆ *Verily, when the water rose beyond its limits, We carried you (mankind) in the floating [ship that was constructed by Nuh].* ◆ –(Surat al-Haaqqah, Ayat 11)

"*inna lama taagh al-maa'u*": "Verily when the water rose beyond its limits". This is an example of the linguistic meaning of *at-taaghoot*.

The religious meaning of *at-taaghoot* is explained very clearly above. In addition, Sheikh Sulaymaan ibn Sahmaan, may Allaah have mercy upon him, says, "*The best that has been said concerning this, is the saying of Ibn Qayyim, may Allaah have mercy upon him, when he says, ' at-taaghoot is anything, regarding which the servant exceeds the due limits, whether it is someone worshipped, obeyed, or followed.'* " (From "*Fataawa A'imatu an-Najdiyyah*", Vol. 1, Page 337)

Sheikh 'Utheimeen, may Allaah have mercy upon him, in his "*Sharh Usool ath-Thalaathah*", says,

"*What he means by someone "worshipped, obeyed, or followed", is other than the righteous and pious people. As for those who are righteous, then they are not taaghoot even if the evil ones that come after their deaths began to direct worship to them, or if they are followed or obeyed by the people. But the idols which are worshipped besides Allaah, they are the taaghoots; and the evil scholars- meaning, those who call to misguidance and disbelief, or call to innovation, or to making lawful that which Allaah has made unlawful, and or forbidding that which Allaah has made lawful, and those who present it as being acceptable to those in authority that they should abandon the Islamic legislation in favor of systems introduced from outside which are contrary to the religion of Islaam- then they are taaghoots because they have exceeded their limits. This is because the scholar's limit is that he should be one who follows that which the Prophet, may Allaah's praise and salutations be upon him, came with, as they are truly the inheritors of the prophets...*" (End of translation)

As for the "obeyed"- concerning the rulers, then Sheikh 'Utheimeen, may Allaah have mercy upon him, goes on to say that this "obey" does not refer to the rulers, as it is legislated and decreed that they be followed in that which is not contrary to the command of Allaah- we must hear and obey. This will be discussed further, insh'Allaah, in our study of "*'Usool ath-Thalaathah*". And Allaah knows best.

The First: ash-Shaytaan, the one who calls to the worship of other than Allaah

The proof is the saying of the Most High, ◆ *Did I not command you, O Children of Aadam, that you should not worship Shaytaan? Verily, he is a plain enemy to you.* ◆ –(Surah YaaSeen, Ayat 60)

Explanation: This includes *ash-shayaateen* in general, and specifically, their leader, Iblees, about whom Allaah stated,

❨ *And My curse is upon you until the Day of Resurrection.* ❩ –(Surah Saad, Ayat 78)

Concerning Iblees, Allaah says,

❨ *(Iblees) said: "Allow me respite till the Day they are raised up (i.e. the Day of Resurrection)."*

(Allaah) said: "You are of those respited."

(Iblees) said: "Because You have sent me astray, surely, I will lie in wait against them (human beings) on Your straight path.

Then I will come to them from before them and behind them, from their right and from their left, and You will not find most of them as thankful ones (i.e. they will not be dutiful to You). ❩ –(Surat al-A'raaf, Ayats 14-17)

And He, the Most High, says,

❨ *Allaah cursed him. And he [Shaytaan] said: "I will take an appointed portion of your slaves.*

Verily, I will mislead them, and surely, I will arouse in them false desires; and certainly, I will order them to slit the ears of cattle, and indeed I will order them to change the nature created by Allaah." And whoever takes Shaytaan as a protector or helper instead of Allaah, has surely suffered a manifest loss. ❩ –(Surat an-Nisaa, Ayats 118-119)

He is the leader of *ash-shayateen*, and they rush to do his bidding and please him. An authentic hadeeth, found in *"Saheeh Muslim"*, states on the authority of Jaabir:

The Messenger of Allaah, may Allaah's praise and salutations be upon him, said, { *Iblees places his throne upon water; he then sends detachments (to lead the people astray); the nearer to him in rank are those who are most notorious in creating dissension. One of them comes and says, 'I did so and so'. And he says, 'You have done nothing!' Then one amongst them comes and says, 'I did not spare so and so until I sowed the seed of discord between a husband and a wife.' The Shaytaan goes near him and says, 'You have done well!'" A'mash said: He then embraces him.}*

Their tricks are many, and insh'Allaah we will discuss them in more detail in a later book in the series, insh'Allaah, as well as the many protections that have been legislated for the believer to protect him or her from the plots and deceptions of *ash-shayateen*.

> *The Second: the unjust judge who alters the rulings of Allaah, the Most High*
>
> The proof is the saying of Allaah, the Most High, ◈ *Have you not seen those (hypocrites) who claim that they believe in that which has been sent down to you, and that which was sent down before you, and they wish to go for judgment (in their disputes) to the taaghoot (false judges) while they have been ordered to reject them. But Shaytaan wishes to lead them far astray.* ◈ –(Surat an-Nisaa, Ayat 60)

Explanation: Ibn Katheer, may Allaah have mercy upon him, says in his *Tafseer* concerning this verse:

"It was reported that the reason behind revealing this verse was that a man from the Ansaar and a Jew had a dispute, and the Jew said, "Let us refer to Muhammad to judge between us." However, the Muslim said, "Let us refer to Ka'b ibn al-Ashraf (who was a Jew) to judge between us." It was also reported that the verse was revealed about some hypocrites who pretended to be Muslims, yet sought to refer to the judgment of the time of ignorance. Other reasons were also reported behind the revelation of the verse. However, the verse has a general meaning, as it chastises all of those who refrain from referring to the Qur'aan and Sunnah for judgment and prefer the judgment of whatever they chose of falsehood."

And the Permanent Committee of Major Scholars said, when asked about the meaning of *at-taaghoot* in this verse:

"First: what is intended by at-taaghoot in the general sense: It is all that is worshipped other than Allaah unrestrictedly, in order to draw closer to it through prayer, fasting, making vows, sacrificing, or consulting or seeking refuge through it, in that which is from Allaah's affairs- in order to drive away that which is harmful, or to bring benefit, or to arbitrate or judge for him in the place of the Book of Allaah and the Sunnah of His Messenger, may Allaah's praise and salutations be upon him, and that which is like these.

And that which is intended by at-taaghoot in the verse: All that which turns away from the Book of Allaah and the Sunnah of the Prophet, may Allaah's praise and salutations be upon him, and turns to the one who rules upon the matter from: a system, a law, something put in place (by man), or tradition and that which has been passed on of custom, or the head of a tribe to decide between them with that, or by that which the leader of the society deems to be appropriate, or the soothsayer. And from that which clarifies this: Verily the system which is put in place in order to be used to judge by, which competes with the legislation of Allaah, enters into the meaning of at-taaghoot...(From "Fataawa al-Lajnat ad-Daa'ima lil Bahooth al-'Ilmiyyah wa al-Iftaa", Volume 1, Page 542, as quoted in "Fataawa al-A'imatu an-Najdiyyah", Volume 1, Page 332)

The scholars have stated that this is the person who changes the legislation of Allaah for other than that, believing that it is better than that which Allaah revealed. He said that in this category, the person makes *istihlaal* in which he makes that *halal* which Allaah has made *haram*, or makes *haram* that which Allaah has made permissible. He said that this is a matter of *kufr* (disbelief). And Allaah knows best.

The Third: The one who judges by other than that which Allaah revealed

The proof is the saying of Allaah, the Most High, ◊ *And whosoever does not judge by what Allaah has revealed, such are the Kaafiroon (disbelievers).* ◊ –(Surat al-Maa'idah, from Ayat 44)

Explanation: The difference between this category and the one just mentioned, is that here the person does not believe or say that that which he is judging by is better than Allaah's legislation. Rather, an example of this would be the judge who takes a bribe and rules in favor of the one who bribed him. Generally speaking, this is less than the other category- Ibn 'Umar and others said that it is an act of disbelief but it is not disbelief in and of itself. This is in refutation of the ones who say that the one who rules or judges unjustly is automatically a disbeliever, as the person could be committing this injustice without falling into disbelief- he is committing a grave sin which he must repent to Allaah for. And Allaah knows best.

The Fourth: The one who professes to have knowledge of the unseen other than Allaah

The proof is the saying of the Most High, ◊ *(He Alone is) the All-Knower of the Ghaib (Unseen), and He reveals to none His Ghaib (Unseen)."*

Except to a Messenger whom He has chosen (He informs him of the Unseen as much as He likes), and then He makes a band of watching guards (angels) to march before him and behind him, ◊ –(Surat al-Jin, Ayats 26-27)

And His, the Most High, saying, ◊ *And with Him are the keys of the Ghaib (all that is hidden), none knows them but He. And He knows whatever there is in the land and in the sea; not a leaf falls, but He knows it. There is not a grain in the darkness of the earth nor anything fresh or dry, but is written in a Clear Record.* ◊ –(Surat al-An'aam, Ayat 59)

Explanation: This includes anyone who says that he has knowledge of that which Allaah alone has knowledge of. This includes the ones who interpret omens, or predict the future, or claim to know something that is happening in another place- and this includes horoscopes, which most of you from the West will be familiar with, may Allaah protect us from the evil in all of these things and that which is like them. They are ascribing to themselves that which is only with Allaah, alone, and through this drawing the people into sin and transgression and possibly to disbelief.

The Fifth: The one who is worshipped other than Allaah and he is pleased with that worship

The proof is the saying of the Most High, ﴾ *And if any of them should say: "Verily, I am an ilaah (a god) besides Him (Allaah)," such a one We should recompense with Hell. Thus We recompense the polytheists and wrong-doers.* ﴿ –(Surat al-Anbiyaa, Ayat 59)

Explanation: This is anyone who the people worship, and he is pleased with their worship. As Sheikh 'Utheimeen, may Allaah have mercy upon him, said, in the previous quote,

"As for those who are righteous, then they are not taaghoot even if the evil ones that come after their deaths began to direct worship to them, of if they are followed or obeyed by the people. But the idols which are worshipped besides Allaah, they are the taaghoots; and the evil scholars…"

And there is a difference of opinion concerning this that we will discuss later in the series, *insh'Allaah.*

Note: Before going on, I would like to point out to you that the listing of *at-taaghoot* in *"'Usool ath-Thalaathah"* differs from this listing. Instead of the second one listed here, Sheikh Muhammad ibn 'Abdul Wahaab, may Allaah have mercy upon him, lists,

Whoever calls the people to worship of himself: And this is whoever calls the people to worship him, whether the people answer his call, or not- and this differentiates it from "the one who is worshipped other than Allaah and he is pleased with that", as the other is more general- he did not necessarily call the people to his worship, rather they began to worship him and he was pleased with that. And Allaah knows best.

And we will end with the words of Sheikh Muhammad ibn 'Abdul Wahaab, may Allaah have mercy upon him, himself, as he summarizes beautifully all that we have been discussing:

And know that mankind cannot become true Believers in Allaah without disbelieving in *at-taaghoot*.

The proof is the saying of the Most High, *﴾ There is no compulsion in religion. Verily, the Right Path has become distinct from the wrong path. Whoever disbelieves in taaghoot and believes in Allaah, then he has grasped the most trustworthy handhold that will never break. And Allaah is All-Hearer, All-Knower. ﴿* –(Surat al-Baqarah, Ayat 256)

ar-rushd (the right path): the religion of Muhammad, may Allaah's praise and good mention be upon him.

al-ghay (the wrong path): the religion of Abee Jahl

al-'urwat al-wuthqa: (the trustworthy handhold that will never break): to testify that there is none worthy of worship except for Allaah.

And this includes negation and affirmation. The negation of every category of worship to other than Allaah, the Most High, and affirmation of every aspect of worship, all of them, to Allaah alone, without associating any partners with Him.

All praise is due to Allaah, by whose blessing good deeds are completed.

Lesson Questions:

Level 1: [required]

1. What is the linguistic meaning of *at-taaghoot*?
2. How does Ibn Qayyim define *at-taaghoot*?
3. Who is the head of the *shayateen*? What is his goal in life?
4. What is another category of *at-taaghoot*, as stated in *"Usool ath-Thalaathah"*?
5. What is *al-ghaib*? Who has knowledge of it besides Allaah?

Level 2: [supplementary]

1. What does staying away from *at-taaghoot* encompass?
2. What does belief in Allaah encompass?
3. How is an evil scholar a *taaghoot*? What is the role of the righteous scholar?
4. What is the difference between the second and third categories of *at-taaghoot*?
5. What is *al-'urwat al-wuthqa:* (the trustworthy handhold that will never break)? What does it entail?

BENEFICIAL REMINDERS FROM OUR STUDY OF
al-Waajibaat

This is a brief listing of some of the important points that we have covered in these lessons. For in depth discussion of them, and their proofs, please refer back to the indicated lesson, insh'Allaah.

Lesson One

1. It is the belief of *Ahl-as-Sunnah wa al-Jama'ah* that the correct Islamic *aqeedah* is found in the Book of Allaah and in the authentic Sunnah of the Messenger of Allaah, may Allaah's praise and salutations be upon him, as understood by the Companions and the Pious Predecessors who came after him. These are the sources from which we understand our religion, and that which we base our beliefs and actions upon.

2. It is obligatory upon the Muslim to learn and understand the correct Islamic 'aqeedah, as well as that which is Islamically legislated.

3. It is then obligatory upon the Muslim to act upon what he knows, as speech and action follow from knowledge. Knowledge without action is not sufficient for the believer to be successful.

4. The scholars have explained that *al-aqeedah, al-eemaan* and *at-tawheed* are all the same thing in the general sense. They comprise belief in the heart, speech of the tongue, and action of the limbs.

5. The Muslims should follow the examples set by the prophets, Allaah's praise be upon them, as their calls were all to *at-tawheed*, to worshipping Allaah alone, without partners. Thus, we should do so as well, and inform others of the correct beliefs.

6. Allaah should be at the center of our existence. We should judge everything by the criteria of whether or not that thing is pleasing to Allaah or not.

7. It is vital that we read about and contemplate the lives of the Prophet, may Allaah's praise and salutations be upon him, and his Companions, may Allaah be pleased with them, and of the righteous people who have come after them through the ages. These are the people we should try to emulate in our everyday lives- they are the best examples for us, mash'Allaah.

8. Muhammad ibn 'Abdul Wahaab, may Allaah have mercy upon him, called to *at-tawheed*, and to a purification of the practice of the religion based upon the Book and the Sunnah and the understanding of the Pious Predecessors. He did not call to himself or his own ideology.

9. Allaah alone granted him the great success that he achieved in his lifetime.

10. All actions can be broken down into five categories: *waajib* (obligatory), *mustahab* (recommended), *mubah* (neutral), *makrooh* (disliked) and *haraam* (forbidden).

Lesson Two

1. It is *mustahab* to begin a book with the *basmalah*, as it is following that which Allaah does in the Qur'aan by beginning with Surat al-Faatihah, which in turn begins with the *basmalah*, and it was the practice of the Messenger of Allaah, may Allaah's praise and salutations be upon him, to begin his letters with it.

2. The scholars often classify things into a certain number of principles or categories in order to make the subject clearer and more understandable by his students. Thus, at different instances you may find a scholar saying that there are two categories of such and such, and at other times three categories of the same thing. As long as this is a knowledgeable, righteous scholar from *Ahl-as-Sunnah wa al-Jama'ah*, then this is acceptable, as it is based upon evidence. As for the evil scholars, they may lead the people astray through this.

3. In general, women are commanded with the same obligations as them men; however is specific areas, such as inheritance, *jihaad*, and rulings regarding the menses, they differ.

4. It is obligatory upon every Muslim to know his Lord, his Prophet, and his religion, all with the proofs. These are what he will be questioned upon when the angels come to him in his grave.

5. If it is said to you: Who is your Lord? Then say: My Lord is Allaah, who has nurtured me and all of the creation with His blessings and beneficence. He is the only One I worship, there is nothing worthy of being worshipped other than Him.

6. We learn about Allaah through His Book, and that which his Messenger Muhammad, may Allaah's praise and salutations be upon him, has related concerning him, as well as from His creation, and His signs, and through that which He has legislated upon us. And we understand these things on the basis of the understanding of the Companions and the Pious Predecessors.

7. *Ahl-as-Sunnah wa al-Jama'ah* affirm that which Allaah and His Messenger, may Allaah praise and salutations be upon him, affirmed concerning the names and attributes of Allaah, without distortion, interpretation, or negation. They believe that these names are most excellent, and His attributes are perfect. They accept them on their apparent meanings, and do not try to interpret them or look for some sort of other meaning for them beyond what has been revealed. They do not ask about the "how" of His names and attributes.

8. Some of the fruits of learning and using the names and attributes of Allaah, are, that this may lead to an increase of our love for Him, and our fear of Him, and increase our faith so that we will act in a more righteous manner, one that is more pleasing to him. Also, we are told to call upon Him with His most excellent names- we must learn them and understand them correctly in order to do this. Learning about His names and attributes increases us in understanding and implementation of *at-tawheed*, insh'Allaah.

Lesson 3

1. If it is said to you: What is your religion? Then say: My religion is al-Islaam, and it is to submit to Allaah Alone, with *at-tawheed*- joining none along with Him in worship, and complying with Him with obedience, and being free from associating others with Allaah and those who do so.

2. The concept of *al-walaa'* and *al-baraa'* is integral to Islaam. *al-walaa'* is to support and show allegiance- and this is for the Believers to show towards the Believers. *al-baraa'* is the opposite- it is enmity, separation, and disassociation- and this is for the Believers to show towards the disbelievers.

3. The one who submits herself totally to Allaah alone, and complies with that which He has commanded, is truly from the *ghuraba*- from the strangers…as to be led by one's desires is the norm.

4. The believer must yield obediently to Allaah, and be led by that which He has set forth in His book, and that which the Messenger of Allaah, may Allaah's praise and salutations be upon him and his family, was sent with and set forth for us as an example. It is not for the true believer to come up with his own path that he thinks will lead to goodness or salvation. Rather, he is to follow the guidance of Allaah in all matters. Islaam is a complete religion, alhamdulillah, a complete way of life, and we can find guidance for anything that occurs to us in life within it, alhamdulillah.

5. The scholars have said that an act of worship will only count as a righteous or accepted action when two conditions are fulfilled. They are:
   A. Purity of intention- it is being done for the pleasure of Allaah
   B. Following the Qur'aan and the Sunnah of the Messenger of Allaah, may Allaah's praise and good mention be upon him, in that act.

6. As for the following of the Qur'aan and Sunnah in that act, then six conditions must be met for that act to be in conformance with the *Shari'ah*:
    A. The action must be done for the correct reason.
    B. The action must be done with the correct type of material or accessory that is associated with that action.
    C. The amount of the action must be correct.
    D. The action must be done in the correct form or manner.
    E. The action must be done at the right time.
    F. The action must be done in the correct place.

7. The religion of Islaam is upon the heart with belief, with love and hatred (for the sake of Allaah). And it is upon the tongue by the pronunciation and leaving off speaking the speech of disbelief. And it is upon the limbs through performing the pillars of Islaam, and leaving the actions of disbelief. If one leaves one of these three, then he has committed disbelief (*kufr*) and apostated- and this is if he has abandoned it in his belief, and not just in his action.

8. The boundary between disbelief and Islaam is the pronunciation of the *shahaadatain* with truthfulness and sincerity while he makes that a reality in his life- then he is a Muslim, a true believer. As for the hypocrite, then he is not truthful, and is not sincere and he is not a believer. And likewise the one who pronounces them and enters into that which nullifies them from *ash-shirk*.

Lesson 4

1. If it is said to you: Who is your Prophet? Then say: Muhammad ibn 'Abdullah ibn 'Abdal-Mutalab ibn Haashim; and Haashim is from the tribe of Quraish, and Quraish is from the Arabs, and the Arabs are from the descendents of Ismaa'eel ibn Ibraaheem, upon them both, and upon our Prophet the best of praise and salutations.

2. Sheikh 'Utheimeen mentioned five matters that are connected with knowledge of the Prophet. It is important that you know these vital things about the Prophet, may Allaah's praise and salutations be upon him. They are:
    A. His lineage
    B. The age he attained, the place he was born, and where he migrated to
    C. Knowledge about his life as a Prophet
    D. Through what did he become a prophet and a messenger
    E. What was the message he was sent with, may Allaah's praise and salutations be upon him, and why was he sent?

3. Sheikh al-Islaam ibn Taymiyyah says, concerning the difference between a prophet and a messenger, that they both receive revelation, but that a prophet is one who teaches and spreads the *shar'iah* (legislation) of the prophet who came before him, while a messenger is given a new *shar'iah* to teach the people. So, all messengers are prophets as well, because they both receive revelation; but not every prophet is a messenger, as he is not given a new *shar'iah*. And Allaah knows best.

4. We must read about the life of the Prophet, may Allaah's praise and salutations be upon him, in order that we know about him- and this will, insh'Allaah, increase us in love and obedience to him and the Message with which he was sent. He is the best example for all of us to follow, alhamdulillah, and the way to do so is to know what he was like, and then emulate him and encourage our children to emulate him as well.

Lesson 5

1. The Principles of the Religion and its Fundamentals Consist of Two Matters:

   The First: The command to worship Allaah Alone, without associating any partners with Him, and being motivated by that and inciting others to it, and support and loyalty due to it, and to know that the one who leaves it has disbelieved.

   The Second: Warning away from *ash-shirk* (associating others along with Allaah in worship) in the worship of Allaah, and strength upon that, and enmity due to it, and knowing that the one who engages in it has disbelieved.

2. The Muslims have been enjoined to command the good and forbid the evil. It is a part of *al-eemaan,* or faith, which is belief, speech, and action. Sheikh al-Islaam ibn Taymiyyah said it is one of the most obligatory and virtuous and best acts.

3. There are two conditions for commanding the good and forbidding the evil:
   A. Capability of doing so
   B. Security of the person who is doing so

4. Sheikh al-Islaam, Ibn Taymiyyah, may Allaah have mercy upon him, has listed some of the characteristics that one should have in commanding the good and forbidding the evil: He must have the correct intention, he must do it upon knowledge and understanding, and it should be done in accordance with *as-Sirat al-Mustaqim*, the Straight Path. He said that this means with gentleness, tolerance, and patience.

5. Ibn Taymiyyah, may Allaah have mercy upon him, said, "Commanding a good should not result in the loss of a greater good, or in a greater evil (than that which came before). And forbidding an evil should not result in a greater evil, or in the loss of a greater good (than that which came before)."

6. Sheikh al-Islaam, ibn Taymiyyah, may Allaah have mercy upon him, has stated that commanding the good and forbidding the evil is *fard kafiyyah* upon the Muslims. That is to say, that it is not an individual obligation upon each and every Muslim, like the prayer; rather, as long as there are a sufficient number of people doing it, then it is not obligatory upon an individual to do it.

Lesson 6

1. The most correct translation and meaning of the words of *ash-shahadah*, is, "There is no god worthy of worship except Allaah." or, "There is no god that has the right to be worshipped except Allaah, alone." Or something with this meaning. And this is the statement of the *jamhoor*, or the majority of the scholars.

2. "The one who testifies that there is no god worthy of worship except Allaah alone"; means, the one who states it, understanding its meaning, and acting upon that which it requires, both hidden and apparent. And undoubtedly contained in *ash-shahadatain* are knowledge, and certainty, and acting upon their meaning.

3. The conditions of *ash-shahadah are*: knowledge, certainty, sincerity and purification of intention, truthfulness, love, compliance, acceptance, and rejection of *at-taaghoot*. One must know and understand each of these, and strive to implement them in the actions of their hearts, minds, tongues, and limbs.

As a poet said:

علم يقين وإخلاص وصدقك مع محبة وإنقياد والقبول له

4. The knowledge that is referred to in the conditions of *ash-shahadah*, is that which Allaah says, and that which His Messenger, may Allaah's praise and salutations be upon him, said, on the understanding of *as-Saalif as-Saalih* (the pious predecessors). It is knowledge of Allaah, and His prophet, and the religion of Islaam, with the proofs and evidences.

5. The *shahadah* contains negation (there are no gods worthy of worship) and affirmation (except Allaah alone)

Lesson 7

1. Truthfulness, (*as-sidq*), and purity of intention, (*al-ikhlaas*), are the conditions of *ash-shahadah* which negate *an-nifaaq*, (hypocrisy)- as hypocrisy is by definition deceit, and it entails doing actions outwardly which are not sincerely done for Allaah alone.

2. Love for Allaah opens up many pathways of good for us. It leads us to obey His Messenger, and to love that which He has sent down to us. It brings us to doing more good deeds, as we want to please the One whom we love, and it keeps us from doing bad deeds, as we do not want to do that which will displease the One we love. It leads to obeying the Messenger of Allaah, may Allaah's praise and salutations be upon him, as we know that Allaah is pleased with our following of His Messenger. It can lead to contentment in our hearts for that which has been decreed for us, and this is a great blessing.

3. Compliance, or *al-inqiyaad*, is the action which comes after the knowledge. We comply with that which Allaah has legislated for us.

4. Acceptance, or *al-qabool*, means that we accept all that the Messenger of Allaah, may Allaah's praise and salutations be upon him, was sent with. We accept it, even if we do not know the reason behind it, because it is revelation from Allaah- this is enough for us. We do not take the words of man, over that which Allaah revealed to us.

5. The importance of the proof and evidence to *Ahl-as-Sunnah wa al-Jama'ah*- this cannot be overstressed. And the people of the Sunnah look to the evidences that are found in the Qur'aan and the Sunnah in order to see the principles behind them which are evident in the sources themselves. They also base their understanding on that of the Pious Predecessors. The people of innovation and misguidance, however, most often come up with their own ideas, and then search through the Qur'aan and the Sunnah to find things that support what they have come up with, or which they can twist to make it seem like a support for it.

Lessons 8 and 9

Included in these two lessons are the proofs and evidences for the conditions of *ash-shahadah* that preceded. I recommend to all of you that you do your best to memorize these proofs, or at least one from each condition. There are many benefits in this. One of them is that with the increase in knowledge and understanding, *yaqeen*, or certainty, becomes firmly established in our hearts- we can see where each of these conditions comes from. It is also of benefit when giving da'wah or teaching others, including our children, about Islaam, as we can tell them exactly where what we are saying comes from- it does not come from ourselves, our own ideas and desires- rather, it comes from the Lord of the Worlds. Again, for a more detailed discussion of these conditions, see the self study course at **study.taalib.com**.

Lesson 10

1. Sheikh Muhammad ibn 'Abdul Wahaab here lists ten of the things which can nullify Islaam. There are more than this, but these are ones that it is common for the people to fall into, and which they must take care to avoid. They are: associating others in worship with Allaah, one who sets up between himself and Allaah intermediaries, and supplicates to them and asks them for intercession and relies upon them: all of this is disbelief, one who does not say that the ones who associate others along with Allaah in worship are disbelievers, or has doubt as to their disbelief, or who says that their way is correct, has himself disbelieved, one who believes that other than the guidance of the Prophet, may Allaah's praise and good mention be upon him, is more complete than his guidance, or that rulings other than his are better than his rulings, The one who hates something which the Messenger, may Allaah's praise and good mention be upon him, came with, even if he acts upon it, has disbelieved, one who ridicules something from the religion of the Messenger, may Allaah's praise and good mention be upon him, or the reward or punishment of Allaah concerning it, magic, and from it is *as-sarf* and *al-'atf*, as the one who performs it, or is pleased with it has disbelieved, Assisting those who associate others in worship with Allaah, and supporting them against the Muslims, The one who believes that some of the people are able to be exempt from the legislation of Muhammad, and abandoning the religion of Allaah, the Most High; not learning about it or acting upon it.

2. Allaah says, ❬*Verily, Allaah forgives not that partners should be set up with Him (in worship), but He forgives except that (anything else) to whom He wills...*❭ –(Surat an-Nisaa, from Ayat 48). And this is when a person dies upon while committing this *shirk*- otherwise, one must turn to Allaah in repentance and with hope for the Mercy and Forgiveness of Allaah, the Most High.

3. One can fall into associating others with Allaah in belief, speech, action, and intention.

4. Sheikh 'Abdul Lateef ibn 'Abdur Rahman, may Allaah have mercy upon him, says, *"The reason for ash-shirk is having the bad suspicion of Allaah, and His absolute perfection; and that is the greatest of sins to Allaah, Glorified is He. If we clarify this, we have spoken of a great principle which uncovers the secret of the matter. And it is that the greatest sin to Allaah is having the bad suspicion of Him."* And, conversely, one of the Salaf said that *at-tawakkal*, or placing one's trust in Allaah, is having the good suspicion of Him.

5. There are two types of *waseetah*, or placing intermediaries between the servant and Allaah. They are, that which is legislated, and *waseetah* that involves associating others with Allaah. The legislated *waseetah* includes the prophets, the scholars, and the pious people, who are generally intermediaries in that they are the ones who carry the knowledge to us. The *waseetah* that involves associating others with Allaah, is making someone other than Allaah, an intermediary between a person and his Lord.

6. Sheikh Muhammad ibn 'Abdul Wahaab al-Wasaabee, may Allaah preserve him, says, in *"al-Qawlu al-Mufeed"*, that the second thing which negates Islaam is hypocrisy, as here, the one who places intermediaries between himself and Allaah has entered into the first of the things that negate Islaam, and that is a type of *shirk*.

7. Allaah, the Most High, has made it obligatory upon us to believe that the ones who associate others along with Him in worship are disbelievers, and to have enmity for them. He says, *You will not find any people who believe in Allaah and the Last Day, making friendship with those who oppose Allaah and His Messenger , even though they were their fathers or their sons or their brothers or their kindred.* —(Surat al-Mujaadilah, From Ayat 22)

8. The one who believes that any form of guidance other than that which Allaah sent Muhammad, may Allaah's praise and salutations be upon him, with, is better than his, may Allaah's praise and salutations be upon him, guidance, has committed disbelief. By this, she believes that Allaah is not Perfect in His Wisdom and Guidance for us, or that the religion is somehow not complete- and this contradicts what Allaah tells us directly, *This day I have completed for you your religion...*

9. Likewise, hatred of that which Allaah has legislated or decreed for us, is questioning the Perfection of Allaah and that which he sent down to Muhammad, may Allaah's praise and salutations be upon him. All that He does for us is done with Knowledge, and Wisdom, and we have to foster thankfulness and patience in our hearts, and ask that Allaah remove any dislike or hatred from our hearts.

10. There are two categories of *al-baghd*, or hatred. They are natural hatred or dislike, and intellectual dislike of what has been legislated for us by Allaah and His Messenger, may Allaah's praise and salutations be upon him. The first hatred is that which occurs naturally. There is the fear, though, that one may let this hatred lead to the second type of hatred, which is not permissible. For example, it is natural to hate the idea of your husband caring for another woman. However, Allaah has made it permissible for a man to marry more than one wife. So, one must strive to understand the wisdom of this, and accept it, or it may become the impermissible hatred, where she hates the legislation of this itself. The second category of *al-baghd* is that which is one of the things that nullify Islaam.

Lesson 11

1. *Al-istihzaa':* the religious meaning of this is the disdaining, mocking, ridiculing, and deriding of something that is legislated in Islaam, making clear supposed defects or deficiencies, in order to make others laugh, or to make fun of it. And this can be by making fun of it in word, action, or word and action.

2. There are two types of *al-istihzaa.* The first is explicit, such as making a joke about some aspect of Islaam, or one of the righteous scholars. The second is not explicit, and it can include tossing the Qur'aan in a disrespectful manner.

3. Magic, or *as-sihr*, is the use of spells, charms, and the tying of knots, in order to influence the body and the heart; as it causes illness, ineffectiveness, and differences between the husband and wife and takes one of the spouses from his or her companion.

4. One sign of magic, is if one changes quickly from one state to another, without apparent reason. For example, a man suddenly cannot stand his wife, whereas before they were close companions. Or he falls ill in the street and he was a healthy person before that.

5. Some magic is reality, and some of it is illusion. There are examples of both in the Qur'aan.

6. It is forbidden to practice magic (indeed, the punishment for the one who practices it is death) and it is ALSO forbidden to ask someone else to do it for you, or even to be pleased with it.

7. There are many legislated ways to protect oneself from magic, some of which are very specific. Some of the more general ways are: to have *tawakkul* in Allaah, to increase in supplication and remembrance of Him, to attach one's heart to Allaah, and to recite Qur'aan and contemplate its verses. One must remember that Allaah holds the Shaytaan by the forelock- He has power and mastery over him, alhamdulillah.

8. We are forbidden to help those who associate others in worship with Allaah, or support them against the Muslims, or to draw close to them, and have love for them, or to help them in that which they are upon. This can be with money, or with self, with ideas and opinions, and intimacy with them. This does not mean, as some misguided people say, that we indiscriminately fight against them or kill them. It means that we hate their sin of associating others with Allaah, and therefore we cannot love them totally either.

9. Sheikh Fauzaan lists several aspects of supporting the disbelievers, along with examples and proofs for them. Among them are:

-Resembling them in their clothing and their speech and other than these
two things
-Living in their countries, and leaving off moving from them to the land of the Muslims
in order to establish the religion
-Travelling to their lands as tourists, or for one's own pleasure
-Assisting and helping them against the Muslims, and praising them and defending
them- and this is from those things that nullify one's Islaam
-Asking for their assistance, and relying upon them
-Praising them, and commending their civilization, and admiring their mannerisms and
expertise
-To name our children with their names
-Asking for forgiveness and mercy for them
-Using their calendar instead of the Muslim calendar
-Participating with them in their holidays and helping them to prepare for them

Lesson 12

1. Al-Khidr was sent to a specific people. The Messenger of Allaah, may Allaah's praise and salutations be upon him, was sent with the final revelation and legislation for all mankind until the Day of Judgment.

2. There are two categories of *al-'iraad*. The first, which is disbelief, is abandoning something from the religion with belief that it is not a part of the religion. The second, which is not disbelief, but which is still wrongdoing and sin, is to abandon acting upon something from the religion, but not in one's heart.

3. Under this heading, is what is known as *al-istihlaal*. *al-istihlaal* (to make something permissible which Allaah has made impermissible) has two categories as well. The first category is to make something permissible which Allaah has forbidden- and to believe in one's heart that that thing IS permissible. This is disbelief. The second is to perform a forbidden act, but to NOT believe that it is permissible. And this is wrongdoing and sin.

4. It is for the people of knowledge to say whether a person has disbelieved or not. It is not our place to make that judgment upon anyone. There are specific conditions that must be met before a person may be ruled a disbeliever. They are:
- That it is established in the texts (the Qur'aan and the Sunnah) that this act is disbelief
- The proofs of the person's disbelief must be used in the correct manner and context
- That which stood between him and disbelief must be discounted

And those things which stand between him and disbelief are:
- Being forced
- Incorrect understanding
- Ignorance
- Mistake
- Forgetting

5. *Ahl-as-Sunnah wa al-Jama'ah* do not make a person a disbeliever because he commits sins, as some of the people of innovation claim. Rather, he has his lifetime to turn to Allaah in repentance and ask His forgiveness; and if he dies upon *at-tawheed*, even with having been a sinner, then he has hope for Allaah's mercy and his eventual entrance into *Jennah*. The final end of a person is unknown to any but Allaah, the Most High.

Lesson 13

1. Islaam is known by *at-tawheed*, as it is based upon worshipping Allaah alone, without any partners with Him, and He is perfect and matchless and His names are the most excellent of names, and He is perfect in His attributes. There is nothing like Him and nothing equal to Him.

2. *At-tawheed* can be divided into three categories: *tawheed ar-ruboobiyyah, tawheed al-uloohiyyah*, and *tawheed al-asmaa wa as-sifaat*. It may also be divided into two categories, as in mentioned by Sheikh al-Islaam ibn Taymiyyaah and other than him: *tawheed al-ma'rifa wa al-ithbaat* (comprehending and affirming), and this is *tawheed ar-ruboobiyyah* and *tawheed al-asmaa wa as-sifaat*, and *tawheed at-talib wa al-qisd*, (seeking and intention) which is *tawheed al-uloohiyyah and 'abaadah*.

3. Ibn Qayyim, may Allaah have mercy upon him, states that every chapter and every verse of the Qur'aan contains in it something of one of these categories of *at-tawheed*.

4. There is no difference of opinion amongst the people in that *at-tawheed* necessarily occurs with the heart, which is the knowledge, and the tongue, which is the speech, and the action, which is compliance with the commands and the (leaving off of) forbidden things.

5. *Tawheed ar-ruboobiyyah* (*tawheed* in the Lordship of Allaah). And this is the one which the disbelievers at the time of the Messenger of Allaah, may Allaah's praise and good mention be upon him, affirmed, and yet it did not enter them into Islaam, and the Messenger of Allaah, may Allaah's praise and good mention be upon him, killed them, and made their blood and wealth permissible for the Muslims. It is the belief of Allaah by His actions. Belief in this alone, does not make one a believer- as it was the belief of the Quraysh, and it was the belief of Fir'awn and Iblees- and they were not made successful through it without the belief in the other categories of *at-tawheed*.

6. The Second: *tawheed al-uloohiyyah* (*tawheed* in worship): It is the belief of Allaah by the actions of the worshipper, such as supplication, making a vow, slaughtering, hope, fear, reliance, desire, reverence, and turning to Allaah.

7. *Tawheed al-uloohiyyah* truly separates the believers from the disbelievers. This is singling out Allaah alone for every act of worship, be it hidden or apparent, with sincerity and purity of intention.

8. *Tawheed adh-dhaat wa al-asmaa wa as-sifaat* is to affirm whatever names or attributes Allaah affirmed for Himself in His Book, or in the Sunnah of His Messenger, may Allaah's praise and salutations be upon him, in a manner which befits Him, without changing or distorting their wording or their meaning, without denial of them, without putting forth how they are, and without declaring them to be like the attributes of creation.

9. And it is not sufficient that a person fulfill just one of the categories of *at-tawheed*. Rather, she must have all of them, in order to be truly a believer. And again, she must act upon them with heart, tongue, and limbs.

10. Once you have knowledge, and practice *at-tawheed*, it is obligatory upon you that you expend every effort in explaining and clarifying this foundational principle, and to spread it amongst the people, and make it apparent to mankind. In that you are following the messengers and proceeding upon their methodology in calling to Allaah, as they fulfilled the trust they carried. And there is for you like the rewards of the one who Allaah guides by your hand until the Day of Judgment.

Lesson 14

1. *Ash-shirk* is the act of associating partners with Allaah, the Most High, in any act of worship, from the hidden or the apparent. It is to direct any portion of any act of worship, both hidden and apparent, to other than Allaah, Glorified and Exalted is He.

2. One of the ways the scholars have explained *ash-shirk*, is to divide it into three categories. The first is the major *shirk*. This is the one that takes one outside of Islaam, and there is no forgiveness for the one who commits it if he dies upon it. The second is the minor *shirk*, which does not take one outside of Islaam, but which is from the greatest of sins, and may lead to major *shirk*. The last category is the hidden *shirk*, which can be major (such as believing that something is worthy to be worshipped other than Allaah) or it may be minor (such as *ar-riyaa*, which is performing a religious act for the sight of the people rather than purely for Allaah, alone.) It is that *shirk* which cannot be plainly seen by the people, rather it is inside oneself.

3. The major, or greater *shirk*, is divided further into four categories:

   - *Shirk of supplication*- this is calling on other than Allaah when supplicating. This includes those people who call upon Allaah in times of hardship, but in times of ease supplicate to other than Him.
   - *Shirk of intention, desire, and purpose*- This is the reality of hypocrisy. It is the desire for the pleasures of this world, over the desire for that which Allaah has promised the Believers in the Hereafter. It is performing an act of worship not for Allaah alone- rather for some other benefit. Sheikh 'Abdul Lateef ibn 'Abdur Rahman, may Allaah have mercy upon him, says, "As for *shirk* of purpose and intention, then that is the sea which has no shore, and few are those who escape from it. As the one who desires by his actions other than the face of Allaah, the Most High, or intends something for a reason other than drawing nearer to Allaah, and seeks a portion from it, then he has committed *shirk* in purpose and intention"
   - *Shirk of obedience*- This is, as was explained in the authentic hadeeth, following someone by obeying them in wrongdoing, as the Christians and Jews do by obeying their priests and rabbis in opposition to that which Muhammad, may Allaah's praise and salutations be upon him, was sent with.
   - *Shirk of love*- This is to love other than Allaah as one loves Allaah. Such as the idol worshippers amongst the Quraysh. They loved Allaah, but they loved their idols along with Him.

Lesson 15

1. The second category from the categories of *ash-shirk*, is the minor *shirk*, or the lesser *shirk*. Performing this type of *shirk* does not cause one to leave the religion of Islaam. However, the one who does it is committing a grave sin, and must leave it and repent to Allaah.

2. The most common example of this type of *shirk* is *ar-riyaa*, and this is doing an act of worship, at least in part, to be seen by the people, instead of doing it solely for Allaah. And this is the minor *shirk* that Allaah's Messenger, may Allaah's praise and salutations be upon him, mentioned he was most afraid of for his people.

3. Also included in this category is swearing by other than Allaah- WITHOUT belief in one's heart for that which he has uttered with his tongue. If he believes in that which he is swearing by, such as the Ka'bah, then this is major *shirk*.

4. Also included in this is when one says, "If Allaah and so and so wills it." Again, without believing that so and so has the same power that Allaah has to make this thing happen. Rather, one should say, "If Allaah wills it, and *then* if so and so wills it", thus making a critical distinction between Allaah and the person mentioned.

5. *Ar-riyaah* can easily lead into major *shirk* of intention, purpose and desire, if one enters into the religion hypocritically, or performs his acts of worship solely for the people, and not for Allaah. So we must guard against ourselves strongly against *ar-riyaah*, and strive to purify our intentions for Allaah alone in every act of worship which we perform, and ask Allaah's forgiveness for both our apparent and our hidden sins.

6. Sheikh 'Abdur Rahmaan as-Sa'di, may Allaah have mercy upon him, said, concerning *ar-riyaa*, "…*if a worshipper does the deed with goal of having it be seen by the people, and he remains with this evil intention, then his deed is disgraced, and he commits minor shirk, and he runs the risk of it leading him into major shirk. If the worshipper does a deed intending the Face of Allaah and with that, he is also intending it for the sight of the people- if he does not remove the riyaa from his deed, then the texts are clear that this deed is false. When the worshipper does a deed for the Face of Allaah alone, but ar-riyaa comes to the surface for an instant during this deed; if he wards it off and purifies his sincerity for Allaah, then there is no harm in that deed. But if he settles for that, and becomes tranquil with it, then the value of the deed diminishes, resulting in a weakening of his faith in proportion to the amount of ar-riyaa that remained in his heart. Still, the deed remains for Allaah, but whatever portion of it he mixed up and was confused about is ar-riyaa.*"

Lessons 16 and 17

1. Sheikh al-Islaam ibn Taymiyyah, may Allaah have mercy upon him, defined *al-kufr* as: *"It is the absence of faith in Allaah, and His Messenger, whether or not this is with denial, or not with denial. Rather, it is merely doubt and uncertainty or abandonment of this (faith), or envy, or pride, or following some of the desires that repel the following of the Messenger. And the kufr of denial is the greatest disbelief, and likewise the disbeliever and denier out of envy, along with certainty of the truth of the message."*

2. *Kufr*, or disbelief, is divided into two categories: the major, or greater disbelief, which takes one out of Islaam, and the minor, or lesser disbelief, which does not take one out of Islaam.

3. Major, or greater, disbelief, is of five categories:

   - *Kufr of denial and falsehood-* and this is the person who denies something from that which Allaah revealed to His Final Prophet and Messenger, may Allaah's praise and salutations be upon him, or the one who invents a lie against Allaah.
   - *Kufr of rejection and pride, along with affirmation of the truth-* This is that which Fir'awn and Iblees fell into, as well as many amongst the People of the Book. They know the truth of Allaah's Lordship, yet they reject the message out of their own arrogance. And the People of the Book rejected the Prophet, may Allaah's peace and salutations be upon him, even though they knew that he was indeed the prophet which had been prophesied in their books.
   - *Kufr of doubt and uncertainty-* and this is two fold. It encompasses the one who doubts that the Day of Judgment will ever come, or that it is so far away as to not be important. It also includes those who believe that they will enter into *Jennah* due solely to their own deeds- rather, it is Allaah's mercy alone that will gain them entrance to *Jennah* in the end- his ultimate end is known only to Allaah, Glorified and Exalted is He.
   - *Kufr of abandonment-* This is abandoning anything from that which the Messenger of Allaah, may Allaah's praise and salutations be upon him brought from the Lord of the Worlds. Again, for this to be major *shirk*, it must include *istihlaal al-qalbiyyah*, in which one abandons that which is obligatory with his heart, in his belief.
   - *Kufr of hypocrisy-* This is entering into Islaam, and performing acts of worship, for a reason other than sincere devotion and belief in Allaah.

4. The minor, or lesser, *kufr*, does not take one outside of the religion of Islaam. So while it is lesser in degree than the major *kufr*, we must still guard ourselves against it as wrongdoing often leads to wrongdoing, and so also can something which starts out as minor, become major.

5. Minor *kufr* is disbelief in the beneficence of Allaah, and His blessings. We must constantly remind ourselves of the blessings of Allaah upon us, and that no good can come to us, unless it be by Allaah's will. We must foster gratitude within ourselves, in times of ease as well as hardship, so that we stay far away from this minor *kufr*- which could lead to major *kufr* by causing us to either doubt Allaah Himself in times of hardship, or to become arrogant and give credit to other than Allaah in times of ease.

6. Sheikh Saalih ibn Fauzaan ibn 'Abdullaah al-Fauzaan, may Allaah preserve him, says, concerning the difference between the two categories of *kufr*:

    - The major *kufr*, or disbelief, causes one to leave the religion, and righteous works to be lost, while the minor *kufr* does not cause one to leave the religion, or the works to be lost; however it decreases their worth according to the extent of the disbelief, and it exposes the one who falls into it to the promised punishment.
    - The major *kufr* causes the one who falls into it to enter into the Hellfire forever. As for the minor *kufr*, if the one who performs it enters into the Hellfire, he will not be in it forever. And Allaah may pardon the one who performs it, so that He will not enter him into the Hellfire at all
    - The blood and wealth of the one who falls into major disbelief is permitted, while the minor *kufr* does not cause it to be permissible.
    - The major *kufr* makes absolute enmity obligatory between the one who falls into it and the Believers, so that it is not permissible for the Believers to love him, or support him even if he is from the closest family. As for the minor disbelief, then it does not make forbidden support in all cases. Rather, the one who falls into it may be loved and supported for that which is with him of faith, and is hated and made an enemy for that which is with him of disobedience

Lesson 18

1. *An-nifaaq*, or hypocrisy is to manifest Islaam and the good outwardly, but to harbor inside disbelief and evil. It is called that because one enters into the religion from one door, and exits from it by another door.

2. Hypocrisy existed at the time of the Prophet, may Allaah's praise and salutations be upon him, and it exists today- and the scholars have said that it is to a worse degree today because at the time of the Prophet, may Allaah's praise and salutations be upon him, the hypocrites hid their *nifaaq*, while today they people can manifest it outwardly.

3. The two categories of hypocrisy are hypocrisy of belief, and hypocrisy of action. As for the first, then it is the major hypocrisy which takes one out of Islaam. As for the second, it does not immediately take one outside of Islaam; rather it is to manifest any of the characteristics of the hypocrite mentioned in the two hadeeth.

4. The ones who fall into hypocrisy of belief, then they will be in the lowest depths of the Hellfire, as Allaah has informed us in His Noble Book.

5. The six categories of hypocrisy of belief are:

   - Denial of the Messenger, may Allaah's praise and good mention be upon him
   - Denial of some of what the Messenger, may Allaah's praise and good mention be upon him, came with
   - Hatred of the Messenger, may Allaah's praise and good mention be upon him
   - Hatred of some of what the Messenger, may Allaah's praise and good mention be upon him, came with
   - Happiness with a lowering of the religion of the Messenger, may Allaah's praise and good mention be upon him
   - Dislike with the victory of the religion of the Messenger, may Allaah's praise and good mention be upon him

These are the categories of the hypocrisy of belief. They take place in the heart, and, as the nature of hypocrisy is deceit, are not clearly evident from what a person manifests on the outside. We must guard ourselves from these beliefs, through increasing in asking forgiveness of Allaah, and supplicating to Him, and gaining knowledge of Allaah, our religion, and the Messenger of Allaah, may Allaah's praise and salutations be upon him.

Lesson 19

1. Concerning hypocrisy of action, then the characteristics of a hypocrite are five:

    - Whenever he is entrusted, he betrays the trust (proves dishonest and untrustworthy- if you leave something with him, he will not return it)
    - Whenever he speaks, he tells a lie
    - Whenever he promises, he breaks his promise
    - Whenever he quarrels, he behaves in a very imprudent (excessive), evil and insulting manner
    - Whenever he makes a covenant, he proves treacherous

2. So the hypocrisy of action is to perform any of these acts from the acts of the hypocrites, while retaining faith and belief in one's heart. It is to be feared, as the Messenger of Allaah, may Allaah's praise and salutations be upon him, warned in an authentic hadeeth that whoever combines (the four characteristics mentioned in that hadeeth) is a *pure hypocrite*!! So we should be careful not to make any of these actions a habit, or it may grow and become something that makes us a hypocrite in truth.

3. Sheikh Fauzaan listed the differences between major hypocrisy, which is hypocrisy of belief, and minor hypocrisy, which is hypocrisy of action:

    - Major hypocrisy causes one to leave the religion, while minor hypocrisy does not.
    - In major hypocrisy, there is a difference between that which is concealed and that which is made public, in belief. In minor hypocrisy, the difference between the inner and outer is a matter of actions, only, without belief.
    - Major hypocrisy cannot come from a believer, but minor hypocrisy can come from a believer.
    - A person who falls into major hypocrisy does not usually repent, and if he does repent, scholars differ in regards to the acceptance of his repentance with a judge. This differs from the minor hypocrisy- as the one who falls into it, and repents to Allaah, then Allaah will accept his repentance. (Translator's note: In other words, the public repentance of the one who commits major hypocrisy, may not be accepted by a judge. As for his private repentance between himself and Allaah, then that matter lies between himself and Allaah.)

4. Concerning this hypocrisy of action, Sheikh al-Islaam ibn Taymiyyah, may Allaah have mercy upon him, said, "*Often a believer manifests a branch from the branches of hypocrisy, then Allaah forgives him this. And some of that which indicates hypocrisy may reach his heart, and Allaah protects him from it. The believer may be subjected to the whispers of ash-Shaytaan, and the whispers of disbelief, by which his heart becomes straitened. As one of the Companions said, "Oh Messenger of Allaah, one of us may find in his self that which it would be more beloved to him to fall from the sky to the earth than to speak them." He, may Allaah's praise and salutations be upon him, said, {That is the pure eemaan (faith)}* (Related in Imam Ahmad's Musnad and Saheeh Muslim) *And in another version, when to speak of these things becomes intense, say, {All praise is due to Allaah, who reduced the plot of ash-Shaytaan to mere whispering.} Meaning, these whisperings occur, along with intense hatred (of them), and repulsing them from the heart- this is an expression of pure eemaan.*"

5. Concerning hypocrisy of belief, Sheikh al-Islaam Ibn Taymiyyah said, "*Scholars differ as to the acceptance of their public repentance, as it cannot be verified, even if they were to always manifest Islaam outwardly.*"

6. There are many well known narrations from the Companions and the Pious Predecessors, which show how much they feared any type of hypocrisy for themselves- if these noble people feared it, then how much more must we fear it for ourselves, and guard ourselves against it??

Lesson 20

1. The first thing that Allaah made obligatory upon the sons of Aadam was the disbelief in *at-taaghoot* and belief in Allaah.

2. The religious meaning of *at-taaghoot* is anything which is worshipped along with or instead of Allaah, the Most High. And Ibn Qayyim, may Allaah have mercy upon him, says that *at-taaghoot* is *"…anything, regarding which the servant exceeds the due limits, whether it is someone worshipped, obeyed, or followed."* And Sheikh 'Utheimeen and others say that the righteous one who is worshipped after his death, and he had not called the people to this- then he is not *at-taaghoot*. Some of the scholars, however, say that in this case it still falls under the general definition of *at-taaghoot* as being that which is worshipped other than Allaah. And Allaah knows best.

3. The heads of *at-taaghoot* listed in *al-Waajibaat* are:

    - ash-Shaytaan, the one who calls to worship of other than Allaah
    - The unjust judge who alters the rulings of Allaah- and this is the one who says that what he rules or judges by is better than that which Allaah has legislated.
    - The one who judges by other than that which Allaah has revealed- and this is the one who does not believe that it is better than Allaah's legislation, yet he judges by it for another reason, such as bribery or personal advancement.
    - The one who professes to have knowledge of the unseen other than Allaah
    - The one who is worshipped other than Allaah, and he is pleased with that worship- and this is whether or not he himself has called the people to this worship.

4. For a person's faith to be complete, he must affirm every aspect of worship, all of them, to Allaah alone, conversely, he must negate every category of worship to other than Allaah, the Most High. He must believe in Allaah AND reject and turn away from any of *at-taaghoot*. And this is *"…the most trustworthy handhold that will never break…"*

Conclusion

Alhamdulillah, these chapters have been meant as an introductory foundation of the correct Islamic *'aqeedah*. And again, along with the knowledge comes the action upon that knowledge, and teaching and guiding others to that knowledge. By following the guidelines put forth in *"al-Waajibaat"*, one has a strong foundation on which to base his or her understanding of the religion, and his or her actions upon that understanding, insh'Allaah. It is merely a key to understanding the guidance which has been revealed to us, in the Book of Allaah, and in the Sunnah of the Messenger of Allaah, may Allaah's praise and salutations be upon him, with the understanding of the Pious Predecessors. May Allaah purify our intentions, and make all that we do solely seeking His Face. May He accept the good deeds that are done solely for Him alone. May Allaah guide us all further along the path to beneficial knowledge, that knowledge that benefits us in this life, and in the Hereafter.

All praise is due to Allaah alone, who has made possible this endeavor, and through Whom all good deeds are performed.

AL-WAAJIBAAT- FINAL EXAM

This is a closed-book exam. You cannot use your notes or the book to answer the questions. Please write neatly and answer each question as completely as you are able. Use as many sheets of notebook paper needed to answer the questions fully and legibly. Write your name and number each answer clearly. you are encouraged to write the Arabic for terms used throughout the course whenever you are able!

Definitions: Be sure to give their religious meaning. If you know their meaning in the language, then write it also, for extra points:

al-'aqeedah:

at-tawheed:

ash-shahadah:

ash-shirk:

al-kufr:

al-walaa:

al-baraa:

al-'ibaadah:

al-ikhlaas:

ad-daleel:

ash-shari'ah:

at-taaghoot:

Short Answer:

1. Why is it important to study *al-'aqeedah*? What is the Islamic ruling on studying it?

2. What are the sources from which we can learn the correct Islamic *'aqeedah*?

3. What did the prophets, may Allaah's praise and good mention be upon them all, call to? Why is it important that we understand this?

4. Why is it vital that we learn about the life of the Prophet, may Allaah's praise and good mention be upon him, his Companions, and those who followed them in righteousness?

5. Who wrote *"al-Waajibaat"*? Briefly tell me something about his life and his call.

6. All actions must fall into one of five categories. List them, define them, and give me an example of each.

7. Who is your Lord?

8. Who is your prophet?

9. What is your religion?

10. Why is it obligatory that we know and understand these three things?

11. What two conditions must be fulfilled for an action to count as a righteous or accepted action?

12. What are the three categories of *at-tawheed*? Briefly explain each one.

13. List the conditions of *ash-shahadah*. List their opposites. For EXTRA CREDIT give me at least one proof for each.

14. List those things listed in the text which nullify one's Islaam. For EXTRA CREDIT give me at least one proof for each.

15. Explain how Islaam is a matter which encompasses the heart, tongue, and limbs.

16. List five ways in which we must refrain from supporting or showing love to the disbelievers.

17. What conditions must be met before the scholars may declare someone a disbeliever?

18. List the four categories of major *shirk*.

19. List the five categories of major *disbelief*.

20. What is minor disbelief?

21. What is the major difference between these major and minor categories?

22. List the six categories of major hypocrisy.

23. In general, how does *ahl-as-Sunnah wa ahl-al-Jama'ah* understand Allaah's names and attributes?

Multiple Choice

1. Which of the following is not one of the conditions that must be met for an action to be in conformance of the *Shari'ah?*
   A. The action must be done for the correct reason
   B. The action must be done at the correct time, in the correct place
   C. The person must state out loud his intention to perform that action
   D. The action must be done in the correct form or manner

2. What is the difference between a prophet and a messenger, according to Sheikh al-Islaam ibn Taymiyyah?
   A. The messenger receives revelation, but the prophet does not
   B. They both receive revelation, but the prophet does not call to that which has been revealed
   C. The prophet receives revelation, but the messenger does not
   D. They both receive revelation. However, a prophet calls to the *Shari'ah* of a previous messenger, while the messenger calls to a new *Shari'ah*

3. Which of the following is NOT a legislated way to protect oneself from the harm of magic?
   A. Wearing an amulet with a piece of paper with a verse of Qur'aan in it
   B. Trusting in Allaah, the Most High to protect you from the magic
   C. Reading legislated verses of Qur'aan over the one inflicted with magic
   D. Attaching one's heart to Allaah through reading His Book, and increasing in supplication

4. Which of the following acts does NOT fall under minor *shirk?*
   A. Swearing by other than Allaah with the tongue, but not believing it in one's heart
   B. Having love for someone that equals the love one has for Allaah
   C. Saying, "If Allaah and so and so wills it."
   D. *ar-riyaa*

5. What is the first thing that Allaah made obligatory upon the Tribe of Aadam?
   A. Prayer
   B. Righteous actions
   C. Worshipping Allaah
   D. Disbelief in *at-taaghoot* and belief in Allaah

6. Which of the following is not one of the heads of *at-taaghoot?*
   A. The one who is worshipped other than Allaah, and he is pleased with that
   B. The one who alters the rulings of Allaah, the Most High
   C. The one who makes that which is forbidden, permissible in his actions, not in his heart
   D. The one who professes to have knowledge of the unseen other than Allaah

7. Which one of the following is NOT one of the actions of the hypocrite mentioned by the Prophet?
   A. When he is not in public, he commits sins
   B. When he speaks, he lies
   C. When you entrust him with something, he betrays the trust
   D. When he quarrels, he behaves in an evil manner

8. Which of the following is NOT from those things which stand between the one who commits an act of disbelief and disbelief itself?
   A. Ignorance
   B. Forgetting
   C. Planning on repenting afterwards
   D. Incorrect understanding

9. What is the general ruling on commanding the good and forbidding the evil?
   A. It is obligatory upon every Muslim to command the good and forbid the evil
   B. It is obligatory upon a Muslim to command the good and forbid the evil if he is able to, and there is no one else fulfilling this obligation
   C. It is a recommended action
   D. It is neither rewarded, nor punished

10. The type of knowledge that is referred to in the conditions of *ash-shahadah* is:
    A. That which one believes to be true, and the finds evidences in the Book and the Sunnah to support it
    B. That which benefits us solely in worldly matters, such as engineering and medicine
    C. Knowledge of Allaah, His Prophet, and the religion of Islaam, with the proofs from the Book and the Sunnah
    D. That which comes solely from one's intellect and observation

Life Application Questions

1. It is obligatory upon the Muslim to have love and support for the believers and hatred and enmity and disassociation for the disbelievers. Give an example of how can you put this into action in your own life?

2. What is the most important thing for the Muslims to understand and then begin to implement in their lives? Why?

3. In our study, we sometimes encounter instances when the scholars often divide things into different categories, such as major and minor disbelief. Why do they do this?

4. You are now responsible for the knowledge gained in this course. List three things that you, personally, feel are the most important things that have learned, and which you wish to implement in your life, NOW?

5. What place should Islaam take in your life? How can you strive to make this a reality for YOU.

Additional Book Notes

Additional Book Notes

LESSON / QUIZ /EXAM ANSWER KEY

Key Terms in Lesson 1

Define these terms:

'aqeedah: the system of beliefs by which we run our lives

al-eemaan: faith

at-tawheed: oneness of Allaah, worshipping Allaah alone

waajib: obligatory

mustahab: recommended

mubah: neutral

makrooh: disliked

haraam: forbidden

Lesson 1 Questions

Level 1: [required]

1. What is *'aqeedah*?

Aqeedah is the system of beliefs which should guide the life of every Muslim and Muslimah.

2. What is the ruling on learning correct *'aqeedah*?

It is waajib.

3. Where was Sheikh Muhammad ibn 'Abdul Wahaab born?

In 'Uyaynah , Saudi Arabia.

4. What did he call to?

He called to *at-tawheed*, or the worship of Allaah alone without any partners. He took a firm stance against innovation and changes in the religion and gained many followers and students.

5. List the five categories that all actions fall into, and briefly describe them.

Waajib, obligatory: A Muslim will be punished by Allaah if he does not carry these acts out and rewarded if he does.

Mustahab, recommended: These acts are pleasing to Allaah and the doer will be rewarded by Allaah if he carries them out, but not punished if he does not.

Mubah, neutral: The doer will not be punished or rewarded for doing them.

Makrooh, disliked: These actions do not please Allaah, but there is no specific punishment stated for them.

Haraam, forbidden: If one does them, he may be punished by Allaah, and if he leaves them he will be rewarded.

Level 2: [supplementary]

1. How does *'aqeedah* help a Muslim in everyday life?

(The answer should contain some of the benefits mentioned in the lesson)

2. Why is a sound *'aqeedah* so important?

Because it is the foundation on which our actions and our life proceeds. If the aqeedah is correct, then the actions and one's course in life will also be correct, inshAllaah.

3. Why was it clearly a blessing from Allaah that Sheikh Muhammad ibn 'Abdul Wahaab was so successful in his call?

(The answer should include how the Sheikh revived the message of *tawheed* to the Hijaaz even though its people were steeped in the practice of idolatry, and that this is not something he could have done without the aid of Allaah)

4. Give an example of each type of the five categories of actions

Obligatory: praying the five prayers a day

Recommended: praying the late night *witr* prayer

Neutral: cooking rice or pasta

Disliked: wearing only one shoe

Forbidden: making supplication for your needs to other than Allaah or drinking alcohol

5. Briefly explain the sources for learning the correct *'aqeedah*, and the importance of taking them as our guides.

The correct aqeedah is found in the Qur'aan and the Sunnah, based upon the understanding of the Pious Predecessors from the first three generations of Muslims. In order to follow the truth , one must look to these sources or he will be misguided to some degree and in some matters.

Key Terms in Lesson 2

Define these terms:

basmalah: the Arabic statement Bismillaah ir Rahman ir Raheem
(In the name of Allaah the Most Gracious, the Most Merciful.)

usool: Principles

du'a: supplication

Lesson 2 Questions:

Level 1: [required]

1. What is the ruling on beginning a book with the *Basmalah*?

The scholars has stated that it is *mustahab* (recommended), as it was the practice of the Messenger of Allaah, may Allaah's praise and salutations be upon him, to do so when writing letters, and also the Qur'aan begins with the *basmalah*.

2. What are the three principles stated in the text that it is obligatory on every male and female Muslim to understand?

That he know his Lord

That he know his religion

That he know his Prophet Muhammad, may Allaah's praise and salutations be upon him.

He must know all of this, with their basic evidences.

3. Where do these three principles come from?

Their foundation is the hadeeth of Al-Baraa' ibn Aazib

4. What is the stance of *ahl-as-Sunnah wa ahl-al-Jama'ah* in regards to the names and attributes of Allaah?

In summary, they affirm everything that Allaah and his Messenger affirmed, without interpretation, distortion, negation, without adding or taking away, without asking how.

5. What are the benefits of learning and understanding the names and attributes of Allaah?

A. Knowledge of the names and attributes of Allaah is the way to knowledge of Allaah.

B. Purification and correction of the soul through the worship of the One , the Unique Lord.

C. Knowledge of His names and attributes is from the most excellent knowledge.

D. Knowledge of the names and attributes of Allaah is the root of all knowledge

E. A way to increase in ones faith

F. The tremendous reward for whoever memorizes and comprehends the names of Allaah

G. The exaltation and glorification of Allaah and supplication to him using His affirmed names and attributes.

Level 2: [supplementary]

1. Why does the Sheikh specify both male and female Muslims?

Because the knowledge referred to is obligatory on both males and females, and both are responsible for this in front of Allaah- it is not like those matters such as the various rulings concerning menses or other matters, which are specific to the female worshipers of Allaah.

2. What are some of the ways that we can know about our Lord?

We can know about Allaah through His Book, the Qur'aan, through His Prophet, and from His various signs in that which He has created.

3. What are some of the deviations and innovations concerning the beliefs in Allaah's names and attributes?

(Answer should include some of the misguided beliefs of the sects specifically mentioned in the lesson)

4. List five names of Allaah in Arabic and English. You may want to use your translation of the Qur'aan for this. Memorize these names and understand their meanings so that you can use them in your *du'a*.

Ar-Rahmaan, Ar-Raheem, Al-Khaaliq, Al-Majeed, Ar-Ra'uf, As-Samee' as well as other affirmed authentic names.

5. Is it permissible to ask about the "how" of Allaah's attributes? Why or why not? How do we understand His names and attributes?

It is not permissible to ask "how" about Allaah's attributes. No one knows this , as it is one of the matters of the unseen. We must understand His names and attributes as understood by the Pious Predecessors did without interpretation, changing , negation, adding or taking away, only affirming of them that which Allaah and His Messenger have affirmed of them.

Key Terms in Lesson 3

Define these terms:

al-inqiyaad: compliance

at-taa'a: obedience

ash-shirk   associating others in worship with Allaah

al-baraa':   disassociation

Lesson 3 Questions

Level 1: [required]

1. What is the religious definition of *al-Islaam*?

To submit to Allaah alone with *at-tawheed*- joining none along with Him in worship, and complying with Him with obedience, and being free from associating others with Allaah and those who do so.

2. What are the two conditions put forth by the scholars for an act to be considered a righteous action?

A. Purity of intention

B. Conformance with the guidance of the Qur'an and Sunnah

3. How did ibn Qayyim, may Allaah have mercy upon him, define *al-Islaam*?

As belief in the oneness of Allaah and worshipping Him alone, without associating any partners with Him, and belief in His Messenger, and following that which he came with.

4. Why is Ibraaheem a good example for us concerning *al-baraa'* from *ash-shirk* and its people?

Because he separated himself from his people, even his father, when his people refused to worship Allaah without associating partners to him, even though they were from his loved ones.

5. What is a main difference between a believer and a disbeliever?

It is that the believer pronounces the shahadatain with truthfulness and sincerity and its other conditions, and makes that a reality in his life, while the disbeliever does not.

Level 2: [supplementary]

1. Why is the one who submits totally to Allaah alone considered one of the *ghuraba* (the strangers)?

One who submits to Allaah in all things is a stranger, because the normal thing is for people to be misguided and following nothing but their whims and desires.

2. Why did Ibn Mas'ood chastise the ones who were making *dhikr* in the *masjid* collectively with the stones?

Because they were doing an act of worship, in a manner that was not done by the Messenger, rather, it was being done an innovated way not known by the Prophet, may Allaah's praise and salutations be upon him nor known by his Companions, may Allaah be pleased with them all, despite the fact that many of those who learned directly from the Prophet were living from whom they could learn the religion without such changes and innovations.

3. A man wants to please Allaah so he decides to *wear hijaab*. Will his act be accepted? Why or why not?

This action will never please Allaah, for it is not one of the acts that Allaah desired and has legislated for men to wear hijaab. This contradicts the second condition for acts to be accepted,(Conformance with the guidance of the Quran and Sunnah)

4. A woman wants to please Allaah so she swears that she will live a life of austerity. She wears old clothes and eats only old rice and regularly prays an extra prayer *after 'Asr*. She does not consult her husband about this. Will her action be accepted? Why or why not?

No, because she is committing mistakes in her practice. It is not from the Sunnah to regularly pray an extra prayer after 'Asr, or to eat only old food and wear only old clothes with holes. Also, she is doing all of this without consulting her husband, and perhaps he will be unhappy with this or she will fall short in giving him his rights which are obligatory upon her.

5. Explain how *al-Islaam* is a matter of the heart, the tongue, and the limbs.

The heart by belief, the tongue by giving utterance to the shahadatain, and the limbs by complying with Allaah's commands and leaving off that which He has forbidden.

Key Terms in Lesson 4

Define these terms:

dhariyah: descendants

shar'iah: legislation

Lesson 4 Questions:

Level 1: [required]

1. What are the five matters that Sheik Utheimeen mentions that make up knowledge of the Prophet?

A. His lineage

B. The place he was born, the place he migrated to, and the age he attained

C. Knowledge of his life as a prophet

D. Through what did he become a prophet and a messenger

E. What the message he was sent with and why was he sent

2. What is the Prophet's, may Allaah's praise and salutations be upon him, name and his lineage?

Muhammad Ibn 'Abdullah Ibn Abdul-Muttalib Ibn Haashim, from the tribe of the Quraish, from the Arabs

3. Where was he born? What age was he when prophethood came to him? When he died?

He was born in Makkah, he was forty years old when prophethood came to him, and he died when he was sixty three years old.

4. What Message was he, may Allaah's praise and salutations be upon him, sent with?

He was sent with the call to *at-tawheed*, meaning the worship of Allaah alone, doing that which He commands and shunning that which He forbids, and warning against as-*shirk*.

5. What is the difference between a prophet and a messenger?

One of the strongest explanations of the difference is that a messenger is sent with a new Shar'iah, while a prophet is sent to spread the Shar'iah of the prophet before him.

Level 2: [supplementary]

1. How did revelation of the Qur'aan descend upon the Prophet, may Allaah's praise and salutations be upon him, the first time?

(The answer should include the details of the affirmed story mentioned, that was related on 'Aishah.)

2. How did Khadijah react to this? How is she a good example for all of us? If there is anything else that you know authentically related about her, share this, and tell me how it shows her as a good example.

(The answers will vary, but should include how she helped and reassured him calmly and that this showed support and patience, which all of us must attempt to attain.)

3. What are some of the benefits of knowing our Prophet, may Allaah's praise and salutations be upon him?

(Various answers are possible including)
To follow his good example, to increase our love for him, to increase our understanding of our religion, etc.

4. List five of the characteristics of the Prophet.

(Answers will vary but could include :)
He was truthful, handsome, well-mannered, kind, gentle, and generous.

5. How can we implement some of these characteristics and make them a part of our character?

By striving our utmost to emulate these characteristics , and remembering that these were the characteristics of the most perfect of human beings , whom we must strive to be like.

Key Terms in Lesson 5

Define these terms:

asl-	origin, basis
qaa'idah-	principle, rule
at-tahreed-	inciting , urging, motivating
al-mawaalah-	support, adherence
tark-	forsake, leave
al-in'thaar-	warning
at-taghleedh-	strength
al-mu'aadah-	enmity, hostility
'ibaadah-	simply put, worship- all that Allaah is pleased with, done for the His pleasure

Lesson 5 Questions:

Level 1: [required]

1. What are these two matters stated in the text referring to?

To the commanding of the good and the forbidding of the evil- here, specifically related to spreading *at-tawheed* and warning against *ash-shirk*

2. What is the meaning of *al-amr bi al-ma'roof wa an-nahi 'an al-munkar?*

Commanding the good and forbidding the evil

3. What is its general ruling, according to Ibn Taymiyyaah?

It is obligatory on every Muslim. However, if there are enough people doing so, then it becomes a community obligation rather than an individual one. Also, there are conditions that must be met, such as the good outweighing the harm and that the one has the ability to do so.

4. Who was Ibn Qayyim al-Jawziyyah's most well known teacher?

Sheikh Al-Islaam Ibn Taymiyyah

5. List the two conditions mentioned by Ibn Taymiyyah for commanding the good and forbidding the evil?

A. Capability of doing so
B. Security of the person who is doing so

Level 2: [supplementary]

1. Is a person who leaves off performing the obligatory acts of Islaam a disbeliever? Why or why not?

If he does not say the shahadatain, and he does not pray, and leaves off worship entirely, including the worship of the heart, then he is a disbeliever. But if he says the shahadatain, and he prays, and does the worship of the heart then he is a Muslim.

2. What characteristics did Sheikh al-Islaam Ibn Taymiyyah put forth for the one who commands the good and forbids the evil? Why do you think these are important?

(Answers will vary but must include the three conditions mentioned in the lesson, gentleness, tolerance, and patience. These are important because without them one will not be successful in bringing a wrongdoing person to the right way. The Prophet exhibited all these characteristics in his call to Islaam, as did his companions and the pious predecessors, whose examples we must follow.)

3. Briefly explain the weighing of potential harm against potential good.

(Answers will vary , but should include the explanations by Ibn Taymiyyah and Ibn Qayyim that are in the lesson)

4. Give an example of when one SHOULD command the good and forbid the evil.

Answers will vary, but for example one hears a sister talking badly about someone else, and she wishes to remind her that this is not permissible, and she has the ability to do so and she is not in any danger if she does so, then it is necessary for her to command the good and forbid the evil.

5. Give an example of when one SHOULD NOT command the good and forbid the evil.

Answers will vary, but for example one sees a man on the street drinking alcohol, so she decides to go and try to stop him. This will obviously result in more harm than good, and she will probably get hurt, while bringing about no benefit.

QUIZ NUMBER ONE (KEY)

This is a closed-book quiz. You cannot use your notes or the book to answer the questions. Please write neatly and answer each question as completely as you are able. Use as many sheets of notebook paper needed to answer the questions fully and legibly. Write your name and the quiz number, number each answer clearly.

1. Define these terms:

al-'aqeedah:	beliefs- the system of belief by which we live our lives
basmalah:	Bismillaah ir Rahmaan ir Raheem (In the name of Allaah, the Most Gracious Most Merciful)
at-tawheed:	worshipping Allaah alone, oneness of Allaah
al-istislaam:	submission
al-inqiyaad:	compliance, yielding
ash-shirk:	associating others in worship with Allaah
al-walaa:	support, have allegiance to
al-baraa:	dissassociation
asl:	principle, root
amr:	matter, command, order
qaa'idah:	fundamental, rule, principle
al-'ibaadah:	simply put, worship- all that Allaah is pleased with, done for the His pleasure

Questions:

1. Why is it important to study *al-'aqeedah*? What is the Islamic ruling on studying it?

It is important to study *al-aqeedah* because this is what we must build our lives on it. If we do not have the correct *aqeedah* then we cannot be successful. It is *waajib* to study *aqeedah*.

2. Write a short paragraph about the life of Sheikh Muhammad ibn 'Abdul Wahaab, *rahimahu Allaah*.

Answers will vary, but should include mention of his place of birth, his message, how he brought the people to the truth, etc.

3. What two conditions must be met for an act to count as a righteous action?

A. Purity of intention
B. Following the Qur'aan and the Sunnah

4. Give an example of someone trying to do a good deed, but whose action will not be accepted. Explain why her action will not be accepted. (Hint: Remember the six points needed for an act to conform to the *shari'iah*)

Answers will vary, but should be based upon the six points mentioned by Sheikh 'Utheimeen, may Allaah have mercy upon him

5. Explain how we can practice *al-walaa* and *al-baraa* in our everyday lives.

We can practice it by always supporting and helping the Muslims, while separating ourselves from the disbelievers. We should, for example, choose to buy from a store owned by a Muslim rather than one owned by a disbeliever.

6. Explain how faith is an action of the heart, the tongue, and the limbs.

The heart by belief, the tongue by giving utterance to the *shahadatain*, and the limbs by complying to Allaah's commands.

7. What is the ruling of beginning a book with the *basmalah*? What two examples are being followed by doing so?

It is *mustahab*, and in doing this we are following the example of the Qur'aan, as it is started with Basmalah, and the Sunnah, as our Prophet used to begin his letters with Basmalah as well.

8. List the five categories of actions, beginning with *waajib*, and list one thing that falls under each ruling.

(Examples will vary)

Obligatory: praying the five prayers a day.

Recommended: praying the late night *witr* prayer

Neutral: cooking rice or pasta

Disliked: spitting over the right shoulder

Forbidden: making supplication for your needs to other than Allaah or drinking alcohol

9. What three fundamentals must each Muslim know and understand? Where does the Sheikh, *rahimahu Allaah*, find this list of three?

A. His lord

B. His religion

C. His prophet Muhammad

This list of three is found in the Hadeeth of Al-Baraa' Ibn 'Aazib

10. What are some of the benefits of knowing the names and attributes of Allaah?

A. Knowledge of the names and attributes of Allaah is the way to knowledge of Allaah.

B. Purification and correction of the souls through the worship of the one , the unique.

C. Knowledge of His names and attributes is the most excellent knowledge.

D. Knowledge of the names and attributes of Allaah is the root of all knowledge

E. Increase of faith

F. The greatness of the reward for whoever memorizes and comprehends the names of Allaah

G. Exaltation and glorification of Allaah and supplication of him using his names and attributes.

11. Briefly explain the belief of *Ahl-as-Sunnah wa al-Jama'ah* in regards to Allaah's names and attributes.

We believe in them without interpretation, changing , negation, adding or taking away, only affirming of them what Allaah and His Messenger have affirmed of them, without asking how.

12. Tell me about our Prophet, may Allaah's praise and salutations be upon him, and try to mention all of the five things that Sheikh 'Utheimeen mentions are included in knowledge of the Prophet.

Answers will vary in content but should include the things mentioned by Sheikh 'Utheimeen. It should include all of the basic information presented in the lesson, in abbreviated form

13. What are the two conditions for commanding the good and forbidding the evil?

The conditions are:

Capability of doing so

Security of the one doing so

14. Give an example wherein one should command the good and forbid the evil, and how she should do it. Then give an example of a time when one should remain silent.

One should command the good and forbid the evil, if one sees his brother toss the Mushaf on the floor. He should explain to him with love, patience, and kindness why it is not permissible to do so.

One should remain silent, if one sees someone smoking, and this person is known for violence and the like, so he would likely harm anyone who tried to stop him or advise him.

Key Terms in Lesson 6

Define these terms:

ash-shahadah: It refers to these words, *Ash'hadu an la ilaaha ila Allaah wa ash-hadu anna Muhammadan 'abdahu wa rasulahu*

al-jamhoor: the majority of the scholars

al-yaqeen: certainty

al-ikhlaas: sincerity and purity of intention

Lesson 6 Questions:

Level 1: [required]

1. What is the meaning of *ash-shahadah*?

There is no god worthy of worship except Allaah, and Muhammad is his servant and messenger

2. Why is it incorrect to translate it as "There is no god but Allaah"?

Because there are gods worshipped other than Allaah, even though they are not worthy of it. As well, grammatically this is not correct.

3. Who wrote "*Fath al-Majeed*"? What is it an explanation of?

Shaykh 'Abdur-Rahmaan ibn Hasn is the author. It is an explanation of "*Kitaab At-Tawheed*".

4. What are the meanings of *al-'ilm* mentioned, and which is correct? 1.

A. It is that which Allaah says and his Messenger said, on the understanding of the Pious Predecessors.

B. It to know Allaah with the evidences and to know His Messenger with the evidences and to know the religion of Islaam with the evidences.

C. It is to know Allaah and his prophet and the religion of Allaah with the evidences.

And all of them are correct, as they all have the same meaning.

5. Discuss the meaning of *shart / sharoot*. Give an example other than the one I have given.

It means condition, and *sharoot* is the plural. Religiously it means that which if it is not present, the act is not valid, and it's presence does not make the act obligatory. (Examples will vary, but may be *wudhoo* for *salaat*, or something similar)

1. Why is it important to know the *sharoot* of an action before doing it?

Because without fulfilling the *sharoot* the act will not be correct and accepted.

2. Is it enough that a person says *ash-shahadah*? Why or why not?

No, they must fulfill the *sharoot* and also act upon their utterance.

3. What is meant by the Prophet's, may Allaah's praise and salutations be upon him, saying, *"The one who testifies…"*?

It means the one who states it, understanding its meaning, and acting upon its requirements, both hidden and apparent.

4. Why does the Sheikh mention the opposite of many of the conditions?

Because it is easier to understand something through its opposite.

5. A young man prays to Allaah because his father tells him to. He has no knowledge of Allaah, he just thinks it is a good thing to pray. He makes sure his friends see him. Based upon what was presented, do you think his prayer will be accepted? (and only Allaah knows if it will, in truth, be accepted)

No, because he is now fulfilling the conditions of *ash-shahadah*. He is not praying to Allaah alone, or seeking His pleasure, and he does not have knowledge of Allaah..

Key Terms in Lesson 7

Define these terms:

as-sidq:	truthfulness, sincerity, honesty
al-kadhab:	lying, falsehood, deceitfulness
an-nifaaq:	hypocrisy
al-muhabbah:	love, attachment, inclination
as-suroor:	contentment, joy delight
al-inqiyaad:	compliance, submission
al-qabool:	acceptance, assent
ar-rad:	rejection, refusal
al-adilah:	plural of daleel: proofs, evidences
at-taaghoot:	The religious meaning of at-taaghoot is anything which is worshipped along with or instead of Allaah, the Most High. And Ibn Qayyim, may Allaah have mercy upon him, says that at-taaghoot is "…anything, regarding which the servant exceeds the due limits, whether it is someone worshipped, obeyed, or followed."

Lesson 7 Questions:

Level 1: [required]

1. How does truthfulness negate hypocrisy?

Because if one is truthful and sincere, then they cannot have hypocrisy, which is the opposite, at the same time.

2. How does love for Allaah help us to worship Him better?

If we love Him we will strive to earn His pleasure, and will appreciate all that He does for us.

3. *al-inqiyaad* was mentioned in a previous lesson. What are the two conditions we mentioned before for an action to be accepted?

A. Purity of intention

B. That it is done according to the Qur'aan and Sunnah

4. What condition do some of the scholars add to the ones that Sheikh Muhammad ibn 'Abdul Wahhab listed in *"al-Waajibaat"*? What is its proof?

Disbelief in *at-taaghoot* and its proof is in Surat Al-Baqarah ayat 256

Level 2: [supplementary]

1. How is truthfulness the opposite of hypocrisy?

Because truthfulness cancels out hypocrisy

2. Why is contentment with that which Allaah has commanded and decreed for us such a blessing?

Because if we are content then that is the highest degree of happiness that we can attain

3. How do the Muslims who adhere to the sunnah differ with those who are upon a way of innovation, in how they deal with evidence?

The Muslims look at the evidence and derive the rulings from all of the applicable evidence, whereas the people of innovation bring rulings and then search for evidence to support it.

4. Give an example of someone rejecting something from the Qur'aan and Sunnah.

(Examples will vary, but should be similar to the examples in the lesson)

For example some people reject the *hijaab* as old-fashioned and incorrect, while this is clearly brought in the Qur'aan and Sunnah.

Key Terms in Lesson 8

Define these terms:

al-ikhlaas: sincerity, purity of intention
al-yaqeen: certainty- knowledge without doubt or uncertainty
al-jahl: ignorance

Lesson 8 Questions:

Level 1: [required]

1. *What sort of knowledge is being referred to in the first condition?*

    That which will increase us in obedience to Allaah and His Messenger, the true authentic knowledge

    2. *What are some of the fruits of al-yaqeen?*

    If one has certainty in the meaning of the *shahadah*, then he will proceed to follow the commands of Allaah with sincerity. If one believes in the *shahadah* with *al-yaqee*n, he will enter paradise

    3. *What is the meaning of al-ikhlaas?*

    It means that all acts of worship are done for Allaah alone, without directing any of them to anything else

    4. *What do you call a person who claims to be Muslim, but is not truthful in this statement?*

    A hypocrite, as his inward state does not reflect his outward claim.

Level 2: [supplementary]

    1. *How were the people at the time of the Prophet, may Allaah's praise and good mention be upon him, ignorant?*

    They did not understand the proper meaning of god, or one that is worshipped.

    2. *Why will a person who has doubts in his heart concerning the shahadah not be successful?*

    If one does not have certainty in the meaning of the *shahadah* then it will not be accepted from him.

    3. *How is following the Sunnah a matter of al-ikhlaas?*

    By limiting ourselves to the Sunnah and leaving innovation and differing. Sincerity should bring with it the desire to do all that one can to please one's Lord, and this includes following His Messenger.

4. After marrying a Muslim man, a woman takes her *shahadah*. She does it because she thinks it would be best for their children to be raised in one faith, and she thinks that there is a lot of good to be found in Islaam in a general sense. She does not know much about the belief system, but she knows there is no drinking or adultery, so that is good. Do you think her *shahadah* be correct? Why or why not? (and only Allaah knows if it would, indeed, be correct)

Her *shahadah* will not be accepted unless she truly believes in it and acts upon it and fulfills its conditions.

Key Terms in Lesson 9

Define these terms:

al-inqiyaad: compliance, submission
al-qabool: acceptance, verification

Lesson 9 Questions:

Level 1: [required]

1. What is the love that is spoken of in this condition? What does it include?

It is loving Allaah, loving His Messenger, and loving all that which has been made obligatory. It also includes love of his supporters and those who are obedient to him.

2. What is the proof that following the Prophet, may Allaah's praise and salutations be upon him, is part of this love?

It is the saying of the Most High: ﴿ *Say (O Muhammad to mankind) " If you (really) love Allaah then follow me. Allaah will love you and forgive your sins. And Allaah is Oft-forgiving, Most Merciful.*﴾ (Surat aal-Imraan, Ayat 31)

3. Explain the difference between *al-inqiyaad* and *al-qabool?*

Inqiyaad is following with actions, while *al-qabool* is demonstrating the truth of the meaning of that through ones speech and the belief of the heart.

Level 2: [supplementary]

1. How do we show love for Allaah by following His Messenger, may Allaah's praise and salutations be upon him?

(Answers will vary but should include the information found in the lesson under the proofs of love) Allaah has commanded us to follow His Messenger, may Allaah's praise and salutations be upon him, and so by following him in all aspects of what he taught we are obeying our Lord, and showing our love for Allaah and His messenger.

2. Give an example of *al-inqiyaad*. Give an example of *al-qabool*.

(Examples will vary) For example:

> *Inqiyaad*: Performing Salaat because you know that Allaah ordered us to.
>
> *Qabool*: accepting the fact that Allaah is the only one worthy of worship and that Muhammad is His Messenger

3. Explain how pride and envy leads to disbelief. Give examples of this.

Pride and envy lead to disbelief because a person may be too proud to admit that this religion is the truth, or too proud to acknowledge that there is only worthy of submission and worship. also he may be envious that he was not guided to the truth first, so he denies that it is the truth, etc. The examples that are correct will vary. So, for example, when Musailamah, who falsely claimed to be a prophet appeared, some of his people followed him even thought they believed that he was a liar, because they were too proud to admit that the man from their people was in the wrong while Prophet Muhammad was in the right. Therefore their pride lead them to disbelief.

4. How can someone who verbally states *ash-shahadah* still be a disbeliever? Who has the right to make the statement that one has disbelieved?

If he does not comply with all that it signifies and requires inwardly and outwardly, and associates others with Allaah, then he is a liar in his spoken *shahadah*, and it will not benefit him. It is only for the people of knowledge to make this statement of disbelief, based upon the evidences presented to them.

<h1 style="text-align:center">Key Terms in Lesson 10</h1>

Define these terms:

naaqid/nawaaqid:	departing or deviating from the legislation to other than it. It is that which nullifies or cancels something else
waseetah/ wasaa'it:	intercession, intermediation
hadee:	guidance
al-bughd:	to hate, to detest

<h1 style="text-align:center">Lesson 10 Questions:</h1>

Level 1: [required]

1. Does all *shirk* take us outside of Islaam? Explain your answer.

Only the greater *shirk* takes one out of Islaam, while the lesser *shirk* does not. However, the lesser *shirk* is a significant sin may lead to the greater, so we must be on guard and seek refuge in Allaah against falling into either of them.

2. List four of the punishments for *ash-shirk* mentioned in the *ayat*.

A. He is forbidden from Paradise

B. The Fire will be his abode

C. There will be no helpers for him

D. He will be from the *dhaalimoon*, the people of injustice.

3. Explain the two types of *al-waseetah* discussed in the lesson.

A. legislated *waseetah*, which is the *waseetah* of the prophets, scholars, and pious people because they carry knowledge to us.

B. Forbidden *waseetah* that involves some aspect of associating others with Allaah, and this is making someone an intermediary between you and your Lord.

4. What is the proof from the Qur'aan that the disbelievers will not be successful in the Hereafter?

It is in the saying of the Most High ◈ ***Verily whoever sets up partners (in worship) with Allaah...*** ◈ to the end of the Ayat, (Surat al-Maaidah, Ayat 72)

5. Give two of your own examples of following guidance other than the guidance of Muhammad, may Allaah's praise and salutations be upon him.

(Examples will vary) For example, believing that democracy is a better form of government than that which is provided in the *Shari'ah*, or the laws of the disbelievers are more just and suitable than those of the *Shari'ah*. Another example would be intentionally not wearing hijaab or abandoning the growing the beard because one considers them old fashioned, misguided, or not socially acceptable to the disbelievers.

6. What are the two types of hatred? Which one nullifies one's Islaam?

A. Natural hatred and dislike

B. Intellectual dislike of what has been legislated for us by Allaah and His Messenger

The second one is the one which can nullify your Islaam.

Level 2: [supplementary]

1. Why do we need to be aware of those things which nullify one's Islaam?

In order that we can stay away from them, and be aware of them so that we do not fall into them. Also, we must warn others away from them when possible, and guard our families from them.

2. Allaah states that He will forgive any sin other than *ash-shirk*. Does that mean that if one commits any *shirk*, and repents from that, that he will not be forgiven? Why or why not?

If one commits *shirk* and repents sincerely in his lifetime, then Allaah will accept his repentance. The Ayat quoted in the question is referring to one who dies upon *ash-shirk*, without repenting before his death.

3. Give an example of *ash-shirk* in speech, and one in action, and one in intention.

(Examples will vary) In speech, saying "If Allaah and His Messenger will it to be", in action by prostrating oneself to an idol, in intention by praying with the intention of showing off to people.

4. How is the *waseetah* that includes associating other with Allaah, likening the Creator to the created?

It means that we do not understand that Allaah listens to all supplications and answers them directly, unlike a king, for example, whom you cannot reach except through many intermediaries. Allaah does not need these intermediaries, for He is above that and is not like the creation.

5. Explain how committing *shirk* is having the bad suspicion of Allaah? And having *tawakkul* is having the good suspicion of Allaah?

If we commit *shirk* this means that we do not believe that Allaah is able to fulfill our needs, and that He has some deficiency requiring that we turn towards another or an intermediary, which is having the bad suspicion of Allaah. And if we have *ikhlaas*, this means that we are placing our trust in Allaah and trusting that He, in His knowledge and wisdom, will always guide us to that which is best for us, which is having the good suspicion of Allaah.

6. As long as we act upon Allaah's legislation, we are successful. Is this true? Why or why not?

No, because we must also believe in its truth, and stay away from those things which nullify ones Islaam. That being said, we should act upon all that we learn to truly be part of Islaam, and pray that our intentions remain correct and our hearts content with that action.

Key Terms in Lesson 11

Define these terms:

al-istihzaa': distaining, mocking, ridiculing

as-sihr: the use of spells, charms and tying knots, in order to influence the body and heart, and it causes illness, ineffectiveness, and differences between husband and wife.

al-mudhaahirah: to help and protect

Lesson 11 Questions:

Level 1: [required]

1. List the two categories of *al-istihzaa'*, and give an example of each.
A. explicit (*sareeh*), for example ridiculing the *hijaab* that Muslim women wear.
B. not explicit (*ghairu sareeh*) for example throwing the *mushaf* to the side or sitting on it.

2. Is *sihr*, or magic, real, or is it an illusion? Explain your answer with proofs.
There is magic that is a reality, which is mentioned in the Qur'aan: ❨ ***And from the evil of those who practice witchcraft when they blow in the knots.*** ❩ And there is magic which is an illusion, which is mentioned in Surat Taa Haa: ❨ ***(Moosa said) ' Nay, throw you (first)! Then behold! Their ropes and their sticks, by their magic, appeared to him as though they moved fast.*** ❩

3. What are the two ways that magic enters into associating others with Allaah?
A. That which makes use of the shayaateen and attachment to them and coming near to them, so that they will carry out his desires and perform that which he cannot do without them.
B. That which contains claiming the knowledge of the unseen, and claiming partnership with Allaah in that, which is disbelief.

4. What are two proofs from the Qur'aan that we must show enmity to the disbelievers?
❨ ***O you who believe! Take not the Jews and the Christians as auliyaa' (friends, protectors, helpers), they are but auliyaa' of each other. And if any amongst you takes them as auliyaa', then surely, he is one of them. Verily, Allaah guides not those people who are the polytheists and wrong doers and unjust.*** ❩ and Surat al-Mumtahanah, Ayat 4.
❨ ***Indeed there has been an excellent example for you in Ibraaheem and those with him, when they said to their people: "Verily, we are free from you and whatever you worship besides Allaah, we have rejected you, and there has appeared between us and you, hostility and hatred for ever until you believe in Allaah Alone," – except the saying of Ibraaheem to his father: "Verily, I will ask forgiveness (from Allaah) for you, but I have no power to do anything for you before Allaah." "Our Lord! In You (Alone) we put our trust, and to You (Alone) we turn in repentance, and to You (Alone) is (our) final Return.*** ❩

5. Is it permissible to send our mothers a card on Mother's Day to show her how much we love her? Explain.

The scholars have said that it is not permissible, because this is not from the ways of showing ones loved to your mother which is found in the Qur'aan or the Sunnah, but it is only imitation and following in the footsteps of the disbelievers. Rather we should show our mothers special love and respect all the time, not just one day of the year.

Level 2: [supplementary]

1. A brother jokingly says that he must have really tough knees from prostrating all day. He says this, not meaning to show disdain for the prayer. Is this *istihzaa'*? Why or why not?

Yes this is definitely *istihzaa'*, even if it is not his intention, because it is not permissible to joke about our religion at all. Our religion is a serious significant matter which should not be joked about, as is shown in the example which occurred during the battle of Tabook this involving the Prophet himself and his and Allaah's rejection of the peoples claim that they were "only joking".

2. Give two examples of *as-sihr*.

(Examples will vary).

A. A man who has two wives, and one becomes very jealous, so she goes to a magician and asks for help. Then the next day the man suddenly conceives an intense dislike for the other wife. This is a frequently heard of occurrence.

B. A magician ties knots in some of a cut pieces of a woman's hair and blows on it, and then the woman grows very ill for no apparent reason.

3. How can we protect ourselves from magic? Should we be afraid of it?

We can protect ourselves from magic by using the legislated supplications, making dhikr, and attaching our heart to Allaah. We should not fear it, because Allaah holds the Shaytaan by his forelock, and he can do nothing except by the will of Allaah.

4. How should we act towards the disbelievers who do not harm us or stop us from worship?

We should treat them with kindness, but we must remember that they are committing the gravest of sins, and limit our love for them accordingly.

5. Choose five of the ways in which one falls into showing support for the disbelievers, and give an example for each of them. (Answers will vary)

A. Resembling them in their clothes and speech and other than that. For example, wearing

jeans which is hallmark of the disbelievers, and previously unknown in Muslim culture.

B. To name our children with their names. For example to name your son Alex or your daughter Mary, rather than the Muslim names of Muhammad or 'Asma.

C. Participating with them in their holidays and helping them to prepare for them. For example, sending your nephew presents for Christmas or candy on Easter.

D. Travelling to their lands as tourists, or for one's own pleasure, such as traveling from the

Muslims lands to Hawaii for vacation. Using their calendar instead of the Muslim calendar, For example, saying that the month is January, when you could use the Muslim month instead.

Key Terms in Lesson 12

Define these terms:

al-i'raad: abandonment by one's hearing and one's heart- one does not necessarily verify the Messenger's truthfulness, nor say that he was a liar, nor does he have to support him or attack him, and he does not pursue or endeavor to perform that which he came with at all.

al-istihlaal :   considering in ones heart that something which is forbidden by the Qur'aan or Sunnah is actually permissible, which is disbelief. Secondly, committing the forbidden act even if one does not say it is actually permissible, which is a sin.

Lesson 12 Questions:

Level 1: [required]

1. What are the proofs that the legislation of Muhammad is the final legislation?

From the Sunnah, the hadeeth narrated by Nawas in which the Prophet, may Allaah's praise and salutations be upon him states that at the end of time 'Eesaa, *aleihi salaam*, will descend and judge by the *Shari'ah* of Muhammad, may Allaah's praise and good mention be upon him. And from the Qur'aan, **"This day I have completed your religion for you, and perfected My blessings upon you, and am pleased with Islaam as your religion."** (Surat al-Maa'idah, Ayat 3)

2. What was al-Khidr?

He was a prophet, according to the most correct opinion.

3. List and explain the two types of *al-i'raad.*

A. That which is major disbelief (which Ibn Qayyim mentioned in his definition)

B. That which is not disbelief (this is when one commits a prohibited act, but not with saying that the act which is prohibited is permissible (without making *al-istihlaal al-qalbiyyah*)

4. What conditions must be fulfilled before a person can be considered a disbeliever?

A. That it is established in the texts (the Qur'aan and the Sunnah) that this act is disbelief

B. The proofs of the person's disbelief must be used in the correct manner and context

C. That the barriers which stood between him and the ruling of disbelief must be removed.

1. How do some of the Sufees use the story of Moosaa and al-Khidr to justify some of them leaving the Islamic legislation? Is this correct? Explain.

They use it to prove that some people do not have to follow the legislation because Al-Khidr did not follow the legislation of Moosa. This is incorrect because Muhammad, may Allaah's praise and salutations be upon him, is the Final Messenger was sent to all mankind, and the *Shari'ah* he was sent with abrogated all previous revealed *shari'ahs*, and applies to everyone up until the Day of Judgment.

2. Why must all of mankind, the *jinn* and the men, adhere to the legislation that the Messenger of Allaah, may Allaah's praise and salutations be upon him, came with?

Because this is the final and complete legislation, which Allaah sent to all mankind.

3. List and explain the two types of *al-istihlaal*. Give an example of each.

A. *Qalbiyyan*, or with the heart, such as believing that it is permissible to eat pork despite the fact that the Qur'an explicitly forbids it. This is disbelief.

B. *Fi'liyyan*, or through the actions, such as eating pork, even if one does not believe that it is permissible.

4. What are those things which prevent a person who has committed an act of disbelief, from falling into disbelief.

1. Being forced
2. Incorrect understanding
3. Ignorance
4. Mistake
5. Forgetting

5. We see that a person among us commits at least one of these things which nullify Islaam. We don't think that she is being forced or is ignorant…do we say that she is a disbeliever and separate from her? What would you do if this was one of your friends?

The answer could include:

First we must consider whether advising her would bring more harm than good or if it would benefit her. If you decide that you should advise her than do so with knowledge, using love, gentleness and tolerance. If you do not have enough knowledge to advise her yourself then direct her to someone who is more knowledgeable than you, or you could give her a book on the subject.If she still persists after she knows the truth then you cannot call her a disbeliever, because you do not have sufficient knowledge to do so. This case should be referred to the knowledgeable scholars

However, you may decide not sit with her and socialize with her, because of what you have seen in her in compliance with the necessity to stay away from harmful companionship.

QUIZ NUMBER TWO (KEY)

This is a closed-book quiz. You cannot use your notes or the book to answer the questions. Please write neatly and answer each question as completely as you are able. Use as many sheets of notebook paper needed to answer the questions fully and legibly. Write your name and the quiz number, number each answer clearly.

1. Define these terms:

shart / sharoot:	condition/conditions
shahadah:	It refers to these words, *Ash'hadu an la ilaaha ila Allaah wa ash-hadu anna Muhammadan 'abdahu wa rasulahu* which means, I bear witness that there is no god worthy of worship except Allaah, and I bear witness that Muhammad is his servant and messenger.
at-taaghoot:	Anything that is worshipped other than Allaah
al-'ilm:	knowledge
al-yaqeen:	certainty
al-Ikhlaas:	sincerity, purity of intention
as-sidq:	truthfulness
al-muhabbah:	love
al-inqiyaad:	compliance
al-qabool:	acceptance
ad-daleel/al-adilah:	proof/proofs
naaqid/nawaaqid:	those things which nullify
waseetah/wasaa'it:	intermediaries
hadee:	guidance
hukm:	ruling
al-istihzaa':	ridiculing
al-i'raad	abandonment, turning away

1. List the conditions of *ash-shahadah* and their opposites (in Arabic or English).

A. Knowledge/ignorance

B. Certainty/doubt and uncertainty

C. Sincerity/*shirk*

D. Truthfulness/insincerity

E. Love and contentment/ hate and discontentment

F. Compliance/resistance

G. Acceptance/rejection

2. Which condition or conditions of *ash-shahadah* negate hypocrisy?

Truthfulness and sincerity

3. How can love of Allaah bring about contentment in our hearts?

Answer should include:

> If we love Allaah than we will be content to follow his commands and will accept whatever befalls us because we know that Allaah knows best what is beneficial for us. This will lead to happiness and contentment which is the true achievement.

4. What is the eighth condition, as mentioned by Ibn Qayyim?

Disbelief in *at-taaghoot*

5. How do *Ahl-as-Sunnah wa al-Jama'ah* understand and use the evidences? How does this differ from the people of innovations and desires?

They first look to the evidences and then bring the ruling according to what they see in the evidences. This is contrary to the practice of people of innovations and desires in that these people first decide what they think the ruling should be and then search for and find evidences to support it.

6. What sort of knowledge is intended in the first condition? What is its opposite?

What is meant here by *al-ilm*, is that which increases us in obedience to Allaah and His Messenger, may Allaah's praise and salutations be upon him, as well as that which increases us in fear and reverence for Allaah, the Most High. And it is the true, authentic, knowledge, with the meaning and significance of the *shahadatan* and that which both of them make obligatory from action. And the opposite of *al-ilm*, is *al-jahl*, or ignorance.

7. Explain how certainty leads to worshipping Allaah with our tongues and limbs.

If we have certainty in the meaning of the *shahadah* then our limbs and tongues will then definitely proceed in worshipping him and glorifying him.

8. Explain the saying of Dhu Noon al-Misree, when he was asked about when one loves Allaah: "If what He hates is more bitter to you than *as-sabr*."

As-sabr is a very bitter type of plant which is hateful to the taste, so if we hate that which Allaah hates even more than this, then we truly love Allaah and wish to please him and stay away from that which he dislikes. The first thing one does upon tasting something bitter is to spit it out and try to remove any taste of it from his mouth- so we should do with the things which do not please Allaah.

9. What are the two categories of *ash-shirk*? Give an example of each. Which is the one mentioned here?

A. *shirk akbar*, or greater *shirk*

B. *shirk asghar*, or lesser *shirk*

The one that is mentioned in the *nawaaqid* is the greater *shirk*.

10. What are the two types of *al-waseetah*? How could this be considered *ash-shirk*?

A. legislated *waseetah*

B. forbideen *waseetah* that involves associating others with Allaah

This is considered *shirk* because it is making someone an intermediary between you and Allaah, because you do not think that Allaah will answer you without an intermediary. This is likening Allaah to his creation, which is forbidden.

11. How do we implement this *ayat* of Allaah in our lives: ﴾ *You will not find any people who believe in Allaah and the Last Day, making friendship with those who oppose Allaah and His Messenger , even though they were their fathers or their sons or their brothers or their kindred.* ﴿ –(Surat al-Mujaadilah, From Ayat 22)

By distancing oneself from the disbelievers in every way indicated by Islaam and not supporting them even if they are our relatives. We also commit ourselves to its opposite, supporting the Muslims and helping them.

12. What is the problem with accepting that which has been proven scientifically over something which comes in the Qur'aan and the Sunnah?

Because this is accepting something other than the guidance of Allaah and His Messenger over their guidance and what has been revealed, as is mentioned in the *nawaaqid* of Islaam. This means that we believe that these scientists know more than our Lord, who created everything and is the All-Knowing, Exalted is He above what they claim.

13. How can natural hatred lead to that hatred which may nullify one's Islaam?

Because we continue to hate something from the religion without attempting to change our hate to love, and this leads to hating the fact that Allaah legislated this, which can nullify ones Islaam.

14. Explain how *al-istihzaa* can be intended, or not intended. Is there a difference in their rulings?

Some people might willfully ridicule Islaam, intending to belittle it, while others do not intend this but are just playing around. In general their ruling does not differ.

15. What is *as-sihr*? Is it real, or illusion? How can we protect or cure ourselves from it?

There is both real magic and magic that is an illusion. We can protect ourselves with the legislated supplications and making *dhikr* often.

16. List five of the ways that Sheikh Fauzaan mentioned as being examples of supporting the disbelievers.

(Answers will vary)

A. Resembling them in their clothing and manners of speech and other than that.

B. To name our children with their names.

C. Participating with them in their holidays and helping them to prepare for them

D. Travelling to their lands as tourists, or for one's own pleasure

E. Using their calendar instead of the Muslim calendar,

17. How do some of the Sufees use the story of al-Khidr to allow them to leave off practicing that which was legislated by Allaah and His Messenger? Why is this incorrect?

Some of them say that certain privileged or elite people do not have to practice any of the legislated guidelines, commandments or prohibitions, because Al-Khidr did not follow the legislation of Moosaa. This is incorrect because Muhammad was sent to all mankind, not a specific people or class of people, and everybody must follow his legislation.

18. What is the difference between abandoning an act, and it is a sin, and abandoning an act and it is disbelief?

If you abandon the act while believing that it is obligatory, then you are committing a sin, but if you leave the act while believing that it is not legislated then it could take you out of Islaam.

19. What are the three conditions that the scholars use when determining if one of these *nawaaqid* of Islaam has, in reality, nullified someone's Islaam?

A. That the proofs that this act is disbelief are found in the Qur'aan and Sunnah

B. That these proofs are used in the correct manner

C. That the barriers which are between him and the ruling of disbelief have been removed.

Lesson 13 Questions:

Level 1: [required]

1. Why is Islaam known by *at-tawheed?*

The religion of Islaam is designated by *at-tawheed*, because it is first and foremost based upon the fact that Allaah is One, matchless in His dominion and His actions, with no partners ascribed to Him. He is Unique in His nature and His attributes, and none is equal to Him. He is alone in His status as God, and the worship of Him, and nothing is equal to Him.

2. What are the three mentioned categories of *at-tawheed?* Write their names, English meanings, and give a brief description of each.

A. *Tawheed ar-rububiyyah, tawheed* in the Lordship of Allaah, This is accepting that Allaah is the Lord of everything, and its Master, and the One who created it, and the one who provides for it that which it needs, and the One who gives life and causes death, the One who allows any harm, and Who brings any benefit, the Sole Possessor of the ability to answer the supplications of the one in need.

B. *Tawheed al-uloohiyyah*, which is *tawheed* in worship. This is built upon sincerity and purity in worshipping Allaah, the Most High, alone. This includes love, fear, hope, reliance, desire, reverence, supplication to Allaah alone; and purity in that all acts of worship.

C. *Tawheed al-asmaa was-sifaat* which is *tawheed* in Allaah's being, names and attributes. This is to affirm whatever names or attributes Allaah affirmed for Himself in His Book, or in the Sunnah of His Messenger, may Allaah's praise and salutations be upon him, in a manner which befits Him, without changing or distorting their wording or their meaning, without denial of them, without putting forth how they are, and without declaring them to be like the attributes of creation."

3. Why were the disbelievers not successful, even though they affirmed *tawheed ar-ruboobiyyah?*

Because they did not affirm the other types of *tawheed*, and one by itself without the others is not sufficient. The Quraish at the time of the Prophet, may Allaah's praise and salutations be upon him, affirmed *tawheed ar-ruboobiyyah*, and they were not successful until they embraced Islaam and affirmed the other two aspects of *at-tawheed*.

4. How is it that *tawheed al-uloohiyyah* differentiates between the People of Paradise and the People of Hellfire?

Because those who affirm and act upon *tawheed al-uloohiyyah* will be successful and enter paradise, while those who did not will be from the unhappy inhabitants of the hellfire.

5. How do we understand Allaah's names and attributes?

We affirm whatever names or attributes Allaah affirmed for Himself in His Book, or in the Sunnah of His Messenger, may Allaah's praise and salutations be upon him, in a manner which befits Him, without changing or distorting their wording or their meaning, without denial of them, without putting forth how they are, and without declaring them to be like the attributes of creation.

Level 2: [supplementary]

1. Ibn Taymiyyah and Ibn Qayyim divided *at-tawheed* into two categories. What are they? Where do the three categories of *at-tawheed* mentioned here fit into them?

They are *tawheed al-ma'rifa wa al-ithbaat* (comprehending and affirming), and this is *tawheed ar-ruboobiyyah* and *tawheed al-asmaa wa as-sifaat*, and secondly *tawheed at-talib wa al-qasd*, (seeking and intention) which is *tawheed al-uloohiyyah wa al-'ibaadah*

2. How do we make *at-tawheed* a reality with our hearts, tongues and limbs?

Tawheed occurs within the heart, which is the knowledge, and the tongue, which is the speech, and the action, which is compliance with the commands and the leaving off of forbidden things.

3. The scholars have said that people commit *ash-shirk* through ignorance or through arrogance. Explain this as best as you are able, and give an example of each.

Because either they are ignorant of the truth, such as many of the idolators were, or they are too arrogant to accept it, like Fir'awn was too ignorant to accept the truth from Moosaa.

4. *Tawheed al-uloohiyyah* was mentioned as the meaning of *la ilaaha ila Allaah*. Explain this.

Tawheed al-uloohiyyah is the meaning of *la ilaaha ila Allaah*, because this category of *Tawheed* is affirming that no one has the right to be worshipped other than Allaah, and leaving off all worship of other than Him.

5. Is it sufficient for one to have any one of the categories of *at-tawheed* without the others? Why or why not?

No, it is not sufficient, one must have all the categories to be a believer, as is shown by the fact that the Arabs affirmed *tawheed ar-ruboobiyyah* while denying the others, and this did not enter them into Islaam.

Lesson 14 Questions:

Level 1: [required]

1. What is the definition of *ash-shirk?*

It is to divert something from the categories of worship to other then Allaah, such as supplication, sacrifice, swearing, and asking for help from other than Allaah in that which nothing has any power over except for Allaah.

2. What are the three categories listed here? Is this the only way one can classify *ash-shirk?*

Greater, lesser, and hidden *shirk*. These are not the only way to classify as-*shirk*, as some scholars mention less and some scholars mention more.

3. What is the punishment of one who commits major *shirk*, and dies upon it?

He will be thrown into the Hellfire and be denied the forgiveness of Allaah and all of his good deeds will be of no use to him.

4. What are the two classes of supplication? Give an example of each.

A. Supplication of worship (*du'a al-'ibaadah*), such as making dhikr

B. Supplication concerning a matter, question, or problem (*du'a al-masa'lah*), such as asking Allaah for forgiveness

5. When is it permissible to disobey our husbands, parents, or those with power over us? Why?

It is permissible to disobey them when they order us to do something which is contrary to the commands of Allaah, because we cannot obey anyone in the disobedience of Allaah.

Level 2: [supplementary]

1. The Quraish loved Allaah, and called upon him. Why were the ones who did not embrace Islaam, not successful?

Because in addition to this, they also associated others in worship with Him.

2. Which type of major *shirk* is an example of hypocrisy in belief? Why?

Shirk of intention desire and purpose. This is an example of hypocrisy because the one who commits this *shirk* is really worshipping Allaah for a worldly purpose, while outwardly it seems as if he is worshipping for the sake of Allaah.

3. Explain the *shirk* of intention. Give an example of it other than mine.

Shirk of intention is when one worships Allaah outwards but only for worldly reasons, like someone who pretends to be a Muslim so that he can receive charity from the Muslims, etc.

4. How did the Jews and Christians take their rabbis and monks as lords other than Allaah?

They obeyed them in what they wrong stated what Allaah's commands and religion.

5. How could love for a person turn into the love that leads to *ash-shirk*?

If one loves a person more or as much as one loves Allaah than this would enter into *shirk*. He may obey him in those things which are not established in the Qur'aan and Sunnah because of this love, and may begin to act as though the person is like a god, and can do those things which only Allaah can do.

Key Terms in Lesson 15

Define these terms:

al-khafee: hidden

al-jalee: apparent, visible

ar-riyaa: to perform an act for the notice and admiration of the people.

Lesson 15 Questions:

Level 1: [required]

1. List three examples of minor *shirk.*

Answers will vary

A. Saying "By the Ka'bah" without believing that it deserves to be worshipped along with Allaah.

B. Saying "If Allaah and my parents will, such and such" without believing that their power is like that of Allaah.

C. Giving charity whenever anyone you know is around so that they will be impressed with your generosity.

2. When is swearing by other than Allaah minor *shirk*? When does it become major *shirk*?

If one does not believe that the thing which he swore by deserves to worshipped along with Allaah, but it just an empty statement from his tongue then this is minor *shirk*. However if he believes that this thing should be worshipped along with Allaah or the like then he has fallen into major *shirk*.

3. How can *ar-riyaa* lead to major *shirk*?

If one does not try to cure himself from *ar-riyaa*, then this will decrease his faith, until perhaps he will fall into doing all of the action for the sake of something other than Allaah.

4. What is the punishment of one who commits minor *shirk* and does not repent from it? How does this differ from the punishment for major *shirk*?

The punishment for minor *shirk* is that which Allaah has decreed of punishment for it, such as punishment in Hellfire- he will not be in the fire forever, due to it, if he enters it. As the individual who commits this he is like all those who commit major sins. Whereas this differs from major *shirk*, for the one who does not repent before his death, the reality is that he leaves the religion of Islaam, and will be punished in the Hellfire forever.

Level 2: [supplementary]

1. Give me two examples of *ar-riyaa* other than that which I have given you.

Answers will differ

A. A woman who fasts every Monday and Thursday whenever she has guests in order to impress them.

B. A man who gives away a lot of food and clothes to poor people so that the people will say that he is pious.

2. Is hidden *shirk* from the major or minor *shirk*? Explain, and give examples.

It could be from either major or minor. An example of the hidden major *shirk*, would be the belief that there are gods other than Allaah. An example of hidden minor *shirk*, is *ar-riyaa*.

3. What is the state of one who begins an act solely for Allaah's sake, but somewhere in the act he falls into *ar-riyaa*? What affect can this have upon his faith?

The value of the deed diminishes, resulting in a weakening of his faith in proportion to the amount of *ar-riyaa* that remained in his heart. Still, the deed remains for Allaah, but whatever portion of it he mixed up and was confused about is *ar-riyaa*.

4. What are some ways to guard ourselves against *ar-riyaa*?

We must strive to purify our intention in all that we do. We have to be diligent in steering any change in intention back to Allaah alone. The Companions used to hide their good deeds as they hid their bad deeds, in order to avoid falling into *ar-riyaa*. Also, avoid talking too much, as this can lead to bragging or saying things to get the praise of the people.

5. Why is it important to be aware of the categories of *ash-shirk* and their rulings?

So that we can stay away from them and be aware of their categories and rulings, and we can teach others about them and warn them away from them.

Key Terms in Lesson 16

Define these terms:

al-kufr: disbelief

What it means in the language:

> enveloping or concealing

What the religious meaning is:

> It is the absence of faith in Allaah, and His Messenger, whether or not this is with denial, or not with denial. Rather, it is merely doubt and uncertainty or abandonment of faith, or envy, or pride, or following some of the desires that repel the following of the Messenger.

al-ibaa: rejection

al-kibr: pride

Lesson 16 Questions:

Level 1: [required]

1. What conditions cause *al-kufr* which take one out of Islaam?
A. That it is established in the texts (the Qur'aan and the Sunnah) that this act is disbelief
B. The proofs of the person's disbelief must be used in the correct manner and context
C. That those barriers which stood between him and the ruling of disbelief must be removed.

2. What is the most unjust act a person can commit?
Creating a lie against Allaah, because this misguides himself and others.

3. Who are two examples of disbelief out of arrogance that we know of from the Qur'aan? Explain
A. Iblees, when he disbelieved and refused to follow the command of Allaah because of his pride.
B. Fir'awn, when he refused to believe in Moosaa because he was too proud and conceited.

4. What is the stance of *ahl-as-Sunnah wa ahl-al-Jamaáh* in regards to entrance to Paradise?
We believe and testify that no one is entitled to Paradise, even if he has performed good deeds and his worship was the most sincere, or his obedience was the purest obedience, and his way was a pleasing to Allaah, unless Allaah favors him, thus granting it to him, through His Blessings and Graciousness. Since the good deeds which the person performed were not made easy for him, except by the facilitation of Allaah.

Level 2: [supplementary]

1. Give two examples other than those stated of someone inventing a lie against Allaah.

Answers will vary

A. Someone claiming that he knows the unseen, when only Allaah knows the unseen.

B. The Christians who hold such beliefs as that Allaah grew tired or that He forgot such and such a matter.

2. How can an increase in wealth or knowledge, lead to disbelief? How can we protect against this?

Because it may lead us to pride and can make us forget that Allaah gave us everything we have, so we disbelieve in Him. We can protect ourselves by humbling ourselves to Allaah and remembering that He gave us everything we have, even our own bodies.

3. Knowing that we will only gain Paradise through the mercy of Allaah, do we still have to do good deeds? Explain.

Yes, we must strive to gain the pleasure of Allaah and know that we will be rewarded for them. If we stop performing good deeds, then we have fallen into a trap of the Shaytaan, and will be responsible for this.

4. How do we fight against the possibility of falling into the disbelief of doubt?

We must strive to have certainty in our hearts about Allaah, and His religion, including the rewards and the punishments, and the Divine Decree, among other things through studying with reliable scholars and students of knowledge. We must increase in remembrance of Allaah, and asking His forgiveness, and making *du'a* that our knowledge increase, along with our acting upon it, so that our scales will be heavy on the Day of Judgment, and that we increase in certainty in Allaah's Mercy and Justice, so that we can be of the people of Paradise, if Allaah so wills.

Key Terms in Lesson 17

Define these terms:

al-i'raad :   abandonment, rejection

an-nifaaq: hypocrisy

ash-shukr: thankfulness

Lesson 17 Questions:

Level 1: [required]

1. Explain the *kufr* of abandonment, in the context of *istihlaal al-qalbiyyah,* and *istihlaal al-fi'liyyah.*

For abandonment fall into this category, one must make the *istihlaal al-qalbiyyah*, in which one abandons that which is obligatory with his heart, in his belief. This is in opposition to the one who does *istihlaal al-fi'liyyah*, in which he abandons acting upon that thing, but does not in his heart believe that the thing is not obligatory.

2. What is the effect of hypocrisy on the heart?

It seals their hearts from Allaah's light and guidance.

3. Whom is the *ayat* of Surat an-Nahl referring to? What blessings did they deny?

This example refers to the people of Makkah, which had been secure, peaceful and stable but they denied the blessings of Allaah towards them, the greatest of which was Muhammad, may Allaah's praise and salutations be upon him, being sent to them.

4. List and explain the differences between the major and minor disbelief.

1. The major *kufr*, or disbelief, causes one to leave the religion, and all righteous works to be lost in the next life, while the minor *kufr* does itself not cause one to leave the religion, nor ones works to be lost in the next life; however it decreases their worth according to the extent of the disbelief, and it exposes the one who falls into it to the promised punishment.

2. The major *kufr* causes the one who falls into it to enter into the Hellfire forever. As for the minor *kufr*, if the one who performs it enters into the Hellfire, he will not be in it forever. And Allaah may pardon or expiate the sin of the one who performs it, so that He will not enter him into the Hellfire at all.

3. The blood and wealth of the one who falls into major disbelief is permitted when fighting under the legitimate Muslim ruler, while the minor *kufr* does not cause it to be permissible.

4. The major *kufr* makes absolute enmity obligatory between the one who falls into it and the Believers, so that it is not permissible for the Believers to love him, or support him even if he is from the closest family. As for the minor disbelief, then it does not make forbidden support in all cases. Rather, the one who falls into it may be loved and supported for that which he possesses of faith, and is hated and made an enemy for that which is with him of disobedience.

Level 2: [supplementary]

1. Give an example of *kufr* of abandonment.

(Answers will vary) For example, someone decides that it is not necessary for him to pray, so he stops praying. He has committed *kufr* of abandonment.

2. How is hypocrisy an action of the heart? What two other actions of the heart negate it? Explain

Hypocrisy is an action of the heart because it is not believing in ones heart, despite your outward appearance. One acts upon that which he does not actually believe inside. Sincerity and truthfulness negate it. If one has these two within his heart, there is no place for their opposite, which is hypocrisy. One cannot be truthful and sincere, and also be a liar and insincere, which is the state of the hypocrites.

3. Give your own example of disbelief in the blessings of Allaah in times of hardship and ease.

(Examples will vary) For example, someone plants a garden and it grows and provides them with food for years and years. However, instead of thanking Allaah for that, he thinks he has done it from himself. Then when the garden ceases to produce, he says "Allaah has never blessed me in anything!" May Allaah protect us from that.

4. Is it okay for us to fall into minor disbelief since it won't take us out of Islaam? Explain.

NO! It is one of the worst of sins against Allaah that we should stay very far away from, as it can lead to that which is worse- wrongdoing often leads to more wrongdoing, and we should strive to stay away from anything that will displease Allaah.

Key Terms in Lesson 18

Define these terms:

an-nifaaq:

Linguistically: it is derived from the hole of *al-yarbu'*, (a rodent like burrowing animal) from which he leaves his burrow. As if he is being chased from one, he flees to the other, and exits from it. And it is said, it is a tunnel, and it is a tunnel which he hides in.

The religious meaning: to manifest Islaam and the good outwardly, but to harbor inside disbelief and evil.

Lesson 18 Questions:

Level 1: [required]

1. What are the proofs that hypocrisy is more evil than disbelief?

The verse of the Qur'aan, ❅ *Verily the hypocrites are in the lowest level of the fire (ad-dirk al-asfal min an-naar)* ❅-(Surat an-Nisaa, Ayat 145)

2. What is meant by Allaah's stating that the hypocrites are in the lowest level of the fire?

That they will have the most severe of punishments in Hellfire.

3. What are two proofs that we must follow the Messenger of Allaah?

Two proofs of this from the Qur'aan are, ❅ *And whatsoever the Messenger (Muhammad) gives you, take it; and whatsoever he forbids you, abstain (from it).* ❅-(Surat al-Hashr, From Ayat 7) And He, Glorified and Exalted is He, statement, ❅ *Say (O Muhammad to mankind): "If you (really) love Allaah, then follow me (i.e. accept Islaam, follow the Qur'aan and the Sunnah)* ❅ (Surat al-'Imraan, from Ayat 31)

4. Give an example of being happy over the lowering or decline of the religion, other than what I gave.

(Answers will vary) For example, being happy when one sees Muslim men wearing the clothing of the disbelievers, or is happy with the situation of injustice which is happening in Palestine, where the Jews are oppressing the Muslims.

5. Give an example of resenting the victory of Islaam, other than what was mentioned.

(Answers will vary)

For example, upset when the *Shari'ah* is properly implemented in a country, thinking that the women who obey the commandments of the Qur'aan are oppressed and the punishments of the *Shari'ah* too harsh. Or being pleased with the private schools in a Muslim country teaching a curriculum designed by the disbelievers in order to educate the children upon their way of life.

Level 2: [supplementary]

1. There were no hypocrites in al-Madinah. Is this statement true? Explain your answer.

No, it is not. There were many hypocrites in Al-Madinah, who were known to the Prophet and to some of his companions.

2. Why would anyone become a hypocrite?

Sometimes because Islaam is strong, and they cannot resist it openly- so they publicly enter into it for the purpose of plotting against it and its people in private. And because they live with the Muslims, they want to ensure the safety of their blood and their wealth.

3. Was Muhammad the only prophet who was denied? Give another example of this.

(Examples will vary) No, many of the prophets were denied for example Lut was denied by his people so they were destroyed.

4. Is a person clearly a hypocrite if he acts upon that which he dislikes about the religion? Explain

No, he is not, because he is acting on that which he dislikes so it is not clear that he is a hypocrite. He should act upon the commands of Allaah, and pray for love of these acts to fill his heart, and contentment with that which is decreed for him.

5. What are some ways to guard ourselves against hypocrisy of belief?

By increasing in asking forgiveness of Allaah, and supplicating to Him, and gaining knowledge of Allaah, our religion, and the Messenger of Allaah, may Allaah's praise and salutations be upon him.

Lesson 19 Questions:

Level 1: [required]

1. What are the signs of the hypocrite, as mentioned in the two hadeeth?

Whenever he is entrusted, he betrays (proves dishonest and untrustworthy)

Whenever he speaks, he tells a lie

Whenever he makes a covenant, he proves treacherous

Whenever he quarrels, he behaves in a very imprudent (excessive), evil and insulting manner

Whenever he promises, he always breaks it (his promise)

2. How do we understand this, as explained by the scholars?

That these are all characteristics of the hypocrite, and the one who possesses one of them or some of them is resembling the hypocrites in these characteristics, and behaving as they behave to some degree.

3. In what way do hypocrites resemble the Jews?

In that they have the knowledge, but do not act upon it in reality.

4. Why does Sheikh al-Islaam ibn Taymiyyah say that the public repentance of a hypocrite may not be accepted, according to some of the scholars?

Because it cannot be verified, even if they were to always manifest Islaam outwardly.

5. What are the differences between the hypocrisy of belief and the hypocrisy of action? Why must we guard against them both?

Hypocrisy of belief is major hypocrisy while hypocrisy of action is minor, and their differences are: Major hypocrisy causes one to leave the religion, while minor hypocrisy does not. In major hypocrisy, there is a difference between that which is concealed and that which is made public, in belief. In minor hypocrisy, the difference between the inner and outer is a matter of actions, only, without belief.

Major hypocrisy cannot come from a believer, but minor hypocrisy can come from a believer.

A person who falls into major hypocrisy does not usually repent, and if he does repent, scholars differ in regards to the acceptance of his repentance with a judge. This differs from the minor hypocrisy- as the one who falls into it, and repents to Allaah, then Allaah will accept his repentance

Level 2: [supplementary]

1. If a person performs some of the actions of a hypocrite, is he a hypocrite?

No, but he has one of the traits of a hypocrite which may lead him further into hypocrisy.

2. How can these characteristics lead to hypocrisy of belief, which takes one out of Islaam?

Because wrongdoing will often lead to more wrong doing, so these characteristics can lead on into what is worse than it.

3. You lend some money to Brother So and So. He is supposed to return it on Friday, but he does not. Should you immediately believe that he has one of these signs of hypocrisy? Explain.

No. He may have some excuse, maybe he forgot, and you must have the good suspicion of your brother. It is importance to distinguish between an isolated occurrence of something and when something is a consistent trait of characteristic.

4. Explain that which Sheikh Fauzaan said, "*Major hypocrisy cannot come from a believer, but minor hypocrisy can come from a believer.*"

Even when one commits hypocrisy of action one still has belief in his heart, but with the Major hypocrisy the belief is not present within one's heart.

5. Explain the statement of the Prophet, may Allaah's praise and salutations be upon him, "*That is the pure eemaan (faith)*"

Meaning, these whisperings occur, along with intense hatred (of them), and repulsing them from the heart- this is an expression of pure *eemaan*, because the believer hated these whisperings and repulsed them. Indeed, the believer is not the one who is complacent in his faith but he is the one who fears for himself.

Lesson 20 Questions:

Level 1: [required]

1. What is the linguistic meaning of *at-taaghoot*?

It is derived from *tughyaan*, which means to exceed the boundaries

2. How does Ibn Qayyim define *at-taaghoot*?

At-taaghoot is anything, regarding which the servant exceeds the due limits, whether it is someone worshipped, obeyed, or followed.'

3. Who is the head of the *shayateen*? What is his goal in life?

Iblees, and his goal in life is to lead mankind astray from the right path.

4. What is another category of *at-taaghoot*, as stated in *"Usool ath-Thalaathah"*?

Whoever calls the people to worship of himself.

5. What is *al-ghaib*? Who has knowledge of it besides Allaah?

It is the unseen, and no one has knowledge of it except Allaah, and if He chooses to reveal some of it to one of His chosen Messengers He does so.

Level 2: [supplementary]

1. What does staying away from *at-taaghoot* encompass?

It encompasses believing that worship of anything other than Allaah is false, and to leave it, to dislike it, and to know that the ones who engage in it are disbelievers, and are enemies of the truth.

2. What does belief in Allaah encompass?

It encompasses believing that Allaah is the only god worthy of worship, without anything other than Him being worthy of worship, and to make all acts of worship intended solely for Allaah alone, and to deny all that is worshipped other than Him, and to love the people of faith and devotion (*al-ikhlaas*) and to have hatred for the people who associate others with Allaah and make them enemies.

3. How is an evil scholar a *taaghoot*? What is the role of the righteous scholar?

Because he calls the people to following a legislation and rulings other than the actual legislation of Allaah and His Messenger, and in this he has exceeded his limits. The role of the righteous scholar is that of the inheritor of the Messengers guiding to that which they brought directly and indirectly.

4. What is the difference between the second and third categories of *at-taaghoot*?

The difference is that in the second category the person does not believe or say that that which he is judging by is better than Allaah's legislation.

5. What is *al-'urwat al-wuthqa:* (the trustworthy handhold that will never break)? What does it entail?

It is to testify that there is none worthy of worship other than Allaah. This entails negation of all worship of other than Allaah and affirmation of all aspects of worship to Allaah.

AL-WAAJIBAAT- FINAL EXAM (KEY)

This is a closed-book exam. You cannot use your notes or the book to answer the questions. Please write neatly and answer each question as completely as you are able. Use as many sheets of notebook paper needed to answer the questions fully and legibly. Write your name and number each answer clearly. you are encouraged to write the Arabic for terms used throughout the course whenever you are able!

Definitions: Be sure to give their religious meaning. If you know their meaning in the language, then write it also, for extra points:

al-'aqeedah: creed, or belief system

at-tawheed: oneness ; worshipping Allaah alone, with no partners

ash-shahadah: it refers to these words, *Ash'hadu an la ilaaha ila Allaah wa ash-hadu anna Muhammadan 'abdahu wa rasulahu*

ash-shirk: associating others in worship with Allaah

al-kufr: disbelief

al-walaa: supporting

al-baraa: disassociation

al-'ibaadah: worship; doing those things that Allaah loves and He is pleased with, in order to please Him

al-ikhlaas: sincerity

ad-daleel: proof

ash-shari'ah: legislation

at-taaghoot: The religious meaning of *at-taaghoot* is anything which is worshipped along with or instead of Allaah, the Most High. And Ibn Qayyim, may Allaah have mercy upon him, says that *at-taaghoot* is "…anything, regarding which the servant exceeds the due limits, whether it is someone worshipped, obeyed, or followed."

Short Answer:

1. Why is it important to study *al-'aqeedah*? What is the Islamic ruling on studying it?

It is important to study Aqeedah because it is the basis of our religion. In order for our actions to be correct, we must have correct understanding of the true 'aqeedah. It is obligatory to study aqeedah.

2. What are the sources from which we can learn the correct Islamic *'aqeedah*?

From the Qur'aan, the Sunnah with the understanding and the examples of the pious predecessors.

3. What did the prophets, may Allaah's praise and good mention be upon them all, call to? Why is it important that we understand this?

They called to *tawheed* in all of its divisions, and this is the essential matter which distinguishes between the believers and the disbelievers.

49. Why is it vital that we learn about the life of the Prophet, may Allaah's praise and good mention be upon him, his Companions, and those who followed them in righteousness?

We have commanded to obey and follow the Messenger this requires knowing about his life and deeds. The Messenger, may Allaah's praise and salutations, be upon him, commanded us to follow the way of his rightly guided successor, so we must also know about their lives and deeds. Additionally, knowing about his life, and that of his Companions, will increase our love of them, insh'Allaah, and assist us in doing righteous deeds. By knowing about them, we can also follow their examples, and they were the best of people.

5. Who wrote *'al-Waajibaat'*? Briefly tell me something about his life and his call.

It was compiled from the works of Sheikh Muhammad Ibn Abdul-Wahhaab, may Allaah have mercy upon him. Answers after this will vary, they should include where he was born, and a bit about his life and his call. Basically, he was born in 'Uyaynah and lived his life calling to *tawheed*. Allaah blessed his efforts and the whole of Najd was brought to the truth through him.

6. All actions must fall into one of five categories. List them, define them, and give me an example of each.

(Examples will vary)
Obligatory: praying the five prayers a day.
Recommended: praying the late night *witr* prayer
Neutral: cooking rice or pasta
Disliked: wearing one shoe

Forbidden: making supplication for your needs to other than Allaah or drinking alcohol

7. Who is your Lord?

Allaah is our lord, and He alone we worship.

8. Who is your prophet?

Muhammad Ibn 'Abdullah, and he is the last of the prophets, may Allaah's praise and salutations, be upon him.

9. What is your religion?

Our religion is Islaam.

10. Why is it obligatory that we know and understand these three things?

Because they are the basis for our religion. Also, we will be asked about them in the grave, as is stated in the authentic hadeeth of al-Baraa ibn Aazib.

11. What two conditions must be fulfilled for an action to count as a righteous or accepted action?

Purity of Intention and following the Qur'aan and Sunnah.

12. What are the three categories of *at-tawheed*? Briefly explain each one.

Tawheed ar-rububiyyah, tawheed in the Lordship of Allaah, This is accepting that Allaah is the Lord of everything, and its Master, and the One who created it, etc.

Tawheed al-uloohiyyah, which is *tawheed* in worship. This is built upon sincerity and purity in worshipping Allaah, the Most High, alone.

Tawheed al-asmaa was-sifaat which is *tawheed* in Allaah's being, names and attributes.

13. List the conditions of *ash-shahadah*. List their opposites. For EXTRA CREDIT give me at least one proof for each.

Knowledge/ignorance
Certainty/doubt and uncertainty
Sincerity/*shirk*
Truthfulness/insincerity
Love and contentment/ hate and discontentment
Compliance/resistance
Acceptance/rejection

14. List those things listed in the text which nullify one's Islaam. For EXTRA CREDIT give
me at least one proof for each.

The proofs are in the text:

   A. *Shirk*

   B. Placing intermediaries between oneself and Allaah

   C. Not believing that those people who commit *shirk* have disbelieved

   D. Believing that a guidance other than the guidance of Muhammad is better than his guidance or that the ruling of other than him is better than his.

   E. Whoever hates some thing from what the Messenger of Allaah brought

   F. Whoever ridicules anything of the religion

   G. Magic

   H. Helping the Disbelievers against the Muslims

   I. Whoever believes that some people can leave the *Shari'ah* of Muhammad like Khidr did not follow the *sharee'ah* of Moosaa

   J. Abandoning the religion of Allaah, Not learning it or acting upon it.

15. Explain how Islaam is a matter which encompasses the heart, tongue, and limbs.

The tongue through saying the shahadatain, the heart through belief and the other actions of the heart and the limbs by following Allaah's legislation.

16. List five ways in which we must refrain from supporting or showing love to the disbelievers.

(Answers will vary)

A. Resembling them in their clothes and speech and other than that.

B. To name our children with their names.

C. Participating with them in their holidays and helping them to prepare for them.

D. Travelling to their lands as tourists, or for one's own pleasure

E. Using their calendar instead of the Muslim calendar,

17. What conditions must be met before the scholars may declare someone a disbeliever?

A. That the proof that this action is disbelief is found in the Qur'aan and Sunnah

B. That the proofs are used in the correct context

C. That The barriers which were between him And the ruling of disbelief have been removed

18. List the four categories of major *shirk*.

A. *Shirk* of supplication

B. *Shirk* of intention, desire and purpose

C. *Shirk* of obedience

D. *Shirk* of love

19. List the five categories of major *disbelief.*

A. Kufr of falsehood
B. Kufr of denial and pride
C. Kufr of doubt
D. Kufr of abandonment
E. Kufr of hypocrisy

20. What is minor disbelief?

Not giving thanks for the blessings Allaah has given you, as well as other actions affirmed in
the Book and the authentic sunnah.

21. What is the major difference between these major and minor categories?

That the major one takes one out of Islaam while the minor one does not. Both must be
avoided, as even if the minor one does not take you directly out of Islaam, it is still a great
sin, and can lead to that which DOES take one out or Islaam.

22. List the six categories of major hypocrisy.

A. Denial of the Messenger, may Allaah's praise and salutations be upon him
B. Denial of some of what the Messenger, may Allaah's praise and salutations be upon him,
came with
C. Hatred of the Messenger, may Allaah's praise and salutations be upon him
D. Hatred of some of what the Messenger, may Allaah's praise and salutations be upon him,
came with
E. Happiness with a lowering of Islaam
F. Hating the victory of Islaam

23. In general, how does *ahl-as-Sunnah wa ahl-al-Jama'ah* understand Allaah's names and
attributes?

They affirm whatever names or attributes Allaah affirmed for Himself in His Book, or in the
Sunnah of His Messenger, may Allaah's praise and salutations be upon him, in a manner
which befits Him, without changing or distorting their wording or their meaning,
without denial of them, without putting forth how they are, and without declaring them
to be like the attributes of creation."

Multiple Choice

1. Which of the following is not one of the conditions that must be met for an action to be
in conformance of the *Shari'ah?*
   A. The action must be done for the correct reason
   B. The action must be done at the correct time, in the correct place
   C. The person must state out loud his intention to perform that action
   D. The action must be done in the correct form or manner

2. What is the difference between a prophet and a messenger?

   A. The messenger receives revelation, but the prophet does not

   B. They both receive revelation, but the prophet does not call to that which has been revealed

   C. The prophet receives revelation, but the messenger does not

   D. They both receive revelation. However, a prophet calls to the *Shari'ah* of a previous messenger, while the messenger calls to a new *Shari'ah*

3. Which of the following is NOT a legislated way to protect oneself from the harm of magic?

   A. Wearing an amulet with a piece of paper with a verse of Qur'aan in it

   B. Trusting in Allaah, the Most High to protect you from the magic

   C. Reading legislated verses of Qur'aan over the one inflicted with magic

   D. Attaching one's heart to Allaah through reading His Book, and increasing in supplication

4. Which of the following acts does NOT fall under minor *shirk*?

   A. Swearing by other than Allaah with the tongue, but not believing it in one's heart

   B. Having love for someone that equals the love one has for Allaah

   C. Saying, "If Allaah and so and so wills it."

   D. ar-riyaa

5. What is the first thing that Allaah made obligatory upon the Tribe of Aadam?

   A. Prayer

   B. Righteous actions

   C. Worshipping Allaah

   D. Disbelief in *at-taaghoot* and belief in Allaah

6. Which of the following is not one of the heads of *at-taaghoot?*

    A. The one who is worshipped other than Allaah, and he is pleased with that

    B. The one who alters the rulings of Allaah, the Most High

    C. The one who makes that which is forbidden, permissible in his actions, not in his heart

    D. The one who professes to have knowledge of the unseen other than Allaah

7. Which one of the following is NOT one of the actions of the hypocrite mentioned by the Prophet?

    A. When he is not in public, he commits sins

    B. When he speaks, he lies

    C. When you entrust him with something, he betrays the trust

    D. When he quarrels, he behaves in an evil manner

8. Which of the following is NOT from those things which stand between the one who commits an act of disbelief and disbelief itself?

    A. Ignorance

    B. Forgetting

    C. Planning on repenting afterwards

    D. Incorrect understanding

9. What is the general ruling on commanding the good and forbidding the evil?

    A. It is obligatory upon every Muslim to command the good and forbid the evil

    B. It is obligatory upon a Muslim to command the good and forbid the evil if he is able to, and there is no one else fulfilling this obligation

    C. It is a recommended action

    D. It is neither rewarded, nor punished

10. The type of knowledge that is referred to in the conditions of *ash-shahadah* is:

    A. That which one believes to be true, and the finds evidences in the Book and the Sunnah to support it

    B. That which benefits us solely in worldly matters, such as engineering and medicine

    C. Knowledge of Allaah, His Prophet, and the religion of Islaam, with the proofs from the Book and the Sunnah

    D. That which comes solely from one's intellect and observation

1. It is obligatory upon the Muslim to have love and support for the believers and hatred and enmity and disassociation for the disbelievers. Give an example of how can you put this into action in your own life?

The answer should include some examples of how you think you can start putting this principle into action in your life.

2. What is the most important thing for the Muslims to understand and then begin to implement in their lives? Why?

The correct aqeedah is the most Important thing because It is your whole belief system. If your aqeedah is wrong than your beliefs are wrong, and you cannot understand your religion. It is the proper foundation for all of the other beliefs and practices of Islaam.

3. In our study, we sometimes encounter instances when the scholars often divide things into different categories, such as major and minor disbelief. Why do they do this?

They do it to make things easier for us to understand, to facilitate our comprehension of what is already found within the guidance of Islaam not to bring something new.

4. You are now responsible for the knowledge gained in this course. List three things that you, personally, feel are the most important things that have learned, and which you wish to implement in your life. NOW?

This is a personal question, so answers will vary

5. What place should Islaam take in your life? How can you strive to make this a reality for YOU

Answers will vary, but should include that Islaam should take the foremost place in your life, etc.

END OF COMPILATION

متن الواجبات المتحتمات المعرفة
على كل مسلم ومسلمة

للإمام محمد بن عبد الوهاب

الأصول الثلاثة التي يجب على كل مسلم ومسلمة تعلمها ...

وهي : معرفة العبد ربه ودينه ونبيه محمداً صلى الله عليه وسلم :

فإن قيل لك : من ربك ؟ فقل : ربي الله الذي رباني وربى جميع العالمين بنعمته ، وهو معبودي ،

ليس لي معبود سواه .

وإذا قيل لك : ما دينك ؟ فقل : ديني الإسلام ، وهو الاستسلام لله بالتوحيد والانقياد وبالطاعة

والبراء من الشرك وأهله .

وإذا قيل لك : من نبيك ؟ فقل : محمد بن عبد الله بن عبد المطلب بن هاشم ، وهاشم من قريش

، وقريش من العرب ، والعرب من ذرية إسماعيل بن إبراهيم عليهما وعلى نبينا أفضل الصلاة

والتسليم.

أصل الدين وقاعدته أمران...

الأول : الأمر بعبادة الله وحده لا شريك له ، والتحريض على ذلك ، والموالاة فيه ، وتكفير من

تركه .

الثاني : الإنذار عن الشرك في عبادة الله ، والتغليظ في ذلك ، والمعاداة فيه ، وتكفير من فعله .

شروط لا إله إلا الله ...

الأول : العلم بمعناها نفياً وإثباتاً.

الثاني : اليقين ، وهو : كمال العلم بها ، المنافي للشك والريب .

الثالث : الإخلاص المنافي للشرك .

الرابع : الصدق المنافي للكذب .

الخامس : المحبة لهذه الكلمة ، ولما دلت عليه ، والسرور بذلك .

السادس : الانقياد لحقوقها ، وهي : الأعمال الواجبة ، إخلاصاً لله ، وطلباً لمرضاته .

السابع : القبول المنافي للرد .

أدلة هذه الشروط من كتاب الله تعالى ومن سنة رسول الله صلى الله عليه وسلم :

دليل العلم : قوله تعالى : { فاعلم أنه لا إله إلا الله } وقوله : { إلا من شهد بالحق وهم يعلمون

} أي بـ « لا إله إلا الله » { وهم يعلمون } بقلوبهم ما نطقوا به بألسنتهم .

ومن السنة : الحديث الثابت في الصحيح عن عثمان رضي الله عنه قال : (قال رسول الله صلى الله عليه وسلم : من مات وهو يعلم أنه لا إله إلا الله دخل الجنة) .

ودليل اليقين : قوله تعالى : { إنما المؤمنون الذين ءامنوا بالله ورسوله ثم لم يرتابوا وجاهدوا بأموالهم وأنفسهم في سبيل الله أولئك هم الصادقون } فاشترط في صدق إيمانهم بالله ورسوله كوهم لم يرتابوا –أي لم يشكوا – فأما المرتاب فهو من المنافقين .

ومن السنة : الحديث الثابت في الصحيح عن أبي هريرة رضي الله عنه ، قال : (قال رسول الله صلى الله عليه وسلم : أشهد أن لا إله إلا الله وأني رسول الله ، لا يلقى الله بهما عبد غير شاك فيهما إلا دخل الجنة) وفي رواية : (لا يلقى الله بهما عبد غير شاك فيهما فيحجب عن الجنة) . وعن أبي هريرة أيضاً من حديث طويل : (من لقيت من وراء هذا الحائط يشهد أن لا إله إلا الله مستيقناً بها من قلبه فبشره بالجنة) .

ودليل الإخلاص : قوله تعالى : { ألا لله الدين الخالص } وقوله سبحانه : { وما أمروا إلا ليعبدوا الله مخلصين له الدين حنفاء } .

ومن السنة : الحديث الثابت في الصحيح عن أبي هريرة رضي الله عنه عن النبي صلى الله عليه وسلم : (أسعد الناس بشفاعتي من قال لاإله إلا الله خالصاً من قلبه –أو من نفسه –) وفي الصحيح عن عتبان بن مالك رضي الله عنه عن النبي صلى الله عليه وسلم : (إن الله حرم على النار من قال لا إله إلا الله يبتغي بذلك وجه الله عز وجل) وللنسائي في '' اليوم والليلة '' من حديث رجلين من الصحابة عن النبي صلى الله عليه وسلم : (من قال لا إله إلا الله وحده لا شريك له ، له الملك ، وله الحمد ، وهو على كل شيء قدير ، مخلصاً بها من قلبه ، يصدق بها لسانه . . . إلا فتق الله السماء فتقاً ، حتى ينظر إلى قائلها من أهل الأرض ، وحق لعبد نظر إليه الله أن يعطيه سؤله) .

ودليل الصدق : قوله تعالى : { الم * أحسب الناس أن يتركوا أن يقولوا ءامنا وهم لا يفتنون * ولقد فتنا الذين من قبلهم فليعلمن الله الذين صدقوا وليعلمن الكاذبين } وقوله تعالى : { ومن الناس من يقول ءامنا بالله واليوم الآخر وما هم بمؤمنين * يخادعون الله والذين ءامنوا وما يخدعون إلا أنفسهم وما يشعرون * في قلوبهم مرض فزادهم الله مرضاً ولهم عذاب أليم بما كانوا يكذبون } .

ومن السنة : ما ثبت في الصحيحين عن معاذ بن جبل رضي الله عنه عن النبي صلى الله عليه وسلم : (ما من أحد يشهد أن لا إله إلا الله وأن محمداً رسول الله ، صادقاً من قلبه ، إلا حرمه الله على النار) .

ودليل المحبة : قوله تعالى : { ومن الناس من يتخذ من دون الله أنداداً يحبونهم كحب الله والذين آمنوا أشد حباً لله } وقوله : { يأيها الذين آمنوا من يرتد منكم عن دينه فسوف يأتي الله بقوم يحبهم ويحبونه أذلة على المؤمنين أعزة على الكافرين يجاهدون في سبيل الله ولا يخافون لومة لائم } .

ومن السنة : ما ثبت في الصحيح عن أنس رضي الله عنه ، قال : (قال رسول الله صلى الله عليه وسلم : ثلاث من كن فيه وجد حلاوة الإيمان : أن يكون الله ورسوله أحب إليه مما سواهما ، وأن يحب المرء لا يحبه إلا لله ، وأن يكره أن يعود في الكفر بعد إذ أنقذه الله منه كما يكره أن يقذف في النار) .

ودليل الانقياد : ما دل عليه قوله تعالى : { وأنيبوا إلى ربكم وأسلموا من قبل أن يأتيكم العذاب ثم لا تنصرون } وقوله : { ومن أحسن ديناً ممن أسلم وجهه لله وهو محسن } وقوله : { ومن يسلم وجهه لله وهو محسن فقد استمسك بالعروة الوثقى } أي بـ « لا إله إلا الله » ، وقوله تعالى : { فلا وربك لا يؤمنون حتى يحكموك فيما شجر بينهم ثم لا يجدوا في أنفسهم حرجاً مما قضيت ويسلموا تسليماً } .

ومن السنة : قوله صلى الله عليه وسلم : (لا يؤمن أحدكم حتى يكون هواه تبعاً لما جئت به) وهذا هو تمام الانقياد وغايته .

ودليل القبول : قوله تعالى : { وكذلك ما أرسلنا من قبلك في قرية من نذير إلا قال مترفوها إنا وجدنا آباءنا على أمة وإنا على آثارهم مقتدون * قال أولو جئتكم بأهدى مما وجدتم عليه آباءكم قالوا إنا بما أرسلتم به كافرون * فانتقمنا منهم فانظر كيف كان عاقبة المكذبين } وقوله تعالى : { إنهم كانوا إذا قيل لهم لا إله إلا الله يستكبرون * ويقولون أإنا لتاركوا آلهتنا لشاعر مجنون } .

ومن السنة : ما ثبت في الصحيح عن أبي موسى رضي الله عنه عن النبي صلى الله عليه وسلم : (مثل ما بعثني الله به من الهدى والعلم كمثل الغيث الكثير أصاب أرضاً ، فكان منها نقية قبلت الماء فأنبتت الكلأ والعشب الكثير ، وكانت منها أجادب أمسكت الماء فنفع الله به الناس فشربوا وسقوا وزرعوا ، أصاب منها طائفة أخرى إنما هي قيعان لا تمسك الماء ولا تنبت كلأ ، فذلك مثل من فقه في دين الله ونفعه ما بعثني الله به فعلم وعلّم ، ومثل من لم يرفع بذلك رأساً ولم يقبل هدى الله الذي أرسلت به).

نواقض الإسلام ...

اعلم أن نواقض الإسلام عشرة :

الأول : الشرك في عبادة الله تعالى ، قال الله تعالى : { إن الله لا يغفر أن يشرك به ويغفر ما دون ذلك لمن يشاء } وقال : { إنه من يشرك بالله فقد حرم الله عليه الجنة ومأواه النار وما للظالمين من أنصار } ومنه الذبح لغير الله ، كمن يذبح للجن أو للقبر .

الثاني : من جعل بينه وبين الله وسائط يدعوهم ويسألهم الشفاعة ويتوكل عليهم ، كفر إجماعاً .

الثالث : من لم يكفر المشركين أو شك في كفرهم أو صحح مذهبهم .

الرابع : من اعتقد أن غير هدي النبي صلى الله عليه وسلم أكمل من هديه ، أو أن حكم غيره أحسن من حكمه – كالذي يفضل حكم الطواغيت على حكمه – فهو كافر .

الخامس : من أبغض شيئاً مما جاء به الرسول صلى الله عليه وسلم ولو عمل به ، كفر .

السادس : من استهزأ بشيء من دين الرسول صلى الله عليه وسلم أو ثوابه أو عقابه ، والدليل قوله تعالى : { ولئن سألتهم ليقولن إنما كنا نخوض ونلعب قل أبالله وآياته ورسوله كنتم تستهزءون * لا تعتذروا قد كفرتم بعد إيمانكم } .

السابع : السحر ، ومنه الصرف والعطف ، فمن فعله أو رضي به كفر ، والدليل قوله تعالى : { وما هم بضارين به من أحد إلا بأذن الله ويتعلمون ما يضرهم ولا ينفعهم } .

الثامن : مظاهرة المشركين ومعاونتهم على المسلمين ، والدليل قوله تعالى : { ومن يتولهم منكم فإنه منهم إن الله لا يهدي القوم الظالمين } .

التاسع : من اعتقد أن بعض الناس يسعه الخروج عن شريعة محمد صلى الله عليه وسلم ، كما وسع الخضر الخروج عن شريعة موسى عليه السلام ، فهو كافر .

العاشر : الإعراض عن دين الله تعالى ، لا يتعلمه ولا يعمل به ، والدليل قوله تعالى : { ومن أظلم ممن ذكر بآيت ربه ثم أعرض عنها إنا من المجرمين منتقمون } .

ولا فرق في جميع هذه بين الهازل والجاد والخائف إلا المكره ، وكلها من أعظم ما يكون خطراً وأكثر ما يكون وقوعاً ، فينبغي للمسلم أن يحذرها ويخاف منها على نفسه ، نعوذ بالله من موجبات غضبه وأليم عقابه.

التوحيد ثلاثة أنواع...

الأول : توحيد الربوبية : وهو الذي اقر به الكفار على زمن رسول الله صلى الله عليه وسلم ، وقاتلهم رسول الله صلى الله عليه وسلم ، و لم يدخلهم في الإسلام ، واستحل دماءهم وأموالهم ، وهو توحيد الله بفعله تعالى ، والدليل قوله تعالى : { قل من يرزقكم من السماء والأرض أمن يملك السمع والأبصار ومن يخرج الحي من الميت ويخرج الميت من الحي ومن يدبر الأمر فسيقولون الله فقل أفلا تتقون } والآيات على هذا كثيرة جداً .

الثاني : توحيد الألوهية : وهو الذي وقع فيه النزاع من قديم الدهر وحديثه ، وهو توحيد الله بأفعال العباد ، كالدعاء والنذر والنحر والرجاء والخوف والتوكل والرغبة والرهبة والإنابة ، وكل نوع من هذه الأنواع عليه دليل من القرآن .

الثالث : توحيد الذات والأسماء والصفات : قال الله تعالى : { قل هو الله أحد * الله الصمد * لم يلد و لم يولد * و لم يكن له كفواً أحد } وقوله تعالى : { ولله الأسماء الحسنى فادعوه بها وذروا الذين يلحدون في أسمائه سيجزون ما كانوا يعملون } وقوله تعالى : { ليس كمثله شيء وهو السميع البصير } .

ضد التوحيد الشرك...

وهو ثلاثة انواع : شرك اكبر ، وشرك اصغر ، وشرك خفي .

النوع الأول من انواع الشرك : الشرك الأكبر ، لا يغفره الله ولا يقبل معه عملاً صالحاً ، قال الله عز وجل : { إن الله لا يغفر أن يشرك به ويغفر ما دون ذلك لمن يشاء ومن يشرك بالله فقد ضل ضلالاً بعيداً } وقال سبحانه : { لقد كفر الذين قالوا إن الله هو المسيح ابن مريم وقال المسيح يابني إسرائيل اعبدوا الله ربي وربكم إنه من يشرك بالله فقد حرم الله عليه الجنة ومأواه النار وما للظالمين من أنصار } وقال تعالى : { وقدمنا على ما عملوا من عمل فجعلناه هباءً منثوراً } وقال سبحانه : { لئن أشركت ليحبطن عملك ولتكونن من الخاسرين } وقال سبحانه : { ولو اشركوا لحبط عنهم ما كانوا يعملون } .

والشرك الأكبر أربعة أنواع :

الأول : شرك الدعوة : والدليل قوله تعالى : { فإذا ركبوا في الفلك دعوا الله مخلصين له الدين فلما نجاهم الله إلى البر إذا هم يشركون } .

الثاني : شرك النية والإرادة والقصد : والدليل قوله تعالى : { من كان يريد الحياة الدنيا وزينتها نوف إليهم اعمالهم فيها وهم لا يبخسون * أولئك الذين ليس لهم في الآخرة إلا النار وحبط ما صنعوا وباطل ما كانوا يعملون } .

الثالث : شرك الطاعة : والدليل قوله تعالى : { اتخذوا أحبارهم ورهبانهم أرباباً من دون الله والمسيح ابن مريم وما أمروا إلا ليعبدوا إلهاً واحداً لا إله إلا هو سبحانه عما يشركون } وتفسيرها الذي لا إشكال فيه : طاعة العلماء والعباد في المعصية ، لا دعاؤهم إياهم ، كما فسرها النبي صلى الله عليه وسلم لعدي بن حاتم لما سأله ، فقال : (لسنا نعبدهم !) فذكر له أن عبادتهم طاعتهم في المعصية .

الرابع : شرك المحبة : والدليل قوله تعالى : { ومن الناس من يتخذ من دون الله أنداداً يحبوهم كحب الله } .

النوع الثاني من أنواع الشرك : شرك اصغر : وهو الرياء ، والدليل قوله تعالى : { فمن كان يرجو لقاء ربه فليعمل عملاً صالحا ولا يشرك بربه أحداً } .

النوع الثالث من أنواع الشرك : شرك خفي : والدليل قوله صلى الله عليه وسلم : (الشرك في هذه الأمة أخفى من دبيب النملة السوداء على صفاة سوداء في ظلمة الليل) ، وكفارته قوله صلى الله عليه وسلم : (اللهم إني أعوذ بك أن أشرك بك شيئاً وأنا أعلم ، وأستغفرك من الذنب الذي لا أعلم).

296

الكفر كفران...

النوع الأول : كفر يخرج من الملة : وهو خمسة أنواع :

النوع الأول : كفر التكذيب : والدليل قوله تعالى : { ومن اظلم ممن افترى على الله كذباً أو كذب بالحق لما جاءه أليس في جهنم مثوى للكافرين } .

النوع الثاني : كفر الإباء والاستكبار مع التصديق : والدليل قوله تعالى : { وإذ قلنا للملائكة اسجدوا لادم فسجدوا إلا إبليس أبى واستكبر وكان من الكافرين } .

النوع الثالث : كفر الشك : وهو كفر الظن ، والدليل قوله تعالى : { ودخل جنته وهو ظالم لنفسه قال ما أظن ان تبيد هذه أبداً * وما أظن الساعة قائمة ولئن رددت إلى ربي لأجدن خيراً منها منقلباً * قال له صاحبه وهو يحاوره أكفرت بالذي خلقك من تراب ثم من نطفة ثم سواك رجلاً * لكنا هو الله ربي ولا أشرك بربي أحداً } .

النوع الرابع : كفر الإعراض : والدليل قوله تعالى : { والذين كفروا عما أنذروا معرضون } .

النوع الخامس : كفر النفاق : والدليل قوله تعالى : { ذلك بإنهم ءامنوا ثم كفروا فطبع على قلوبهم فهم لا يفقهون } .

النوع الثاني من نوعي الكفر : وهو كفر اصغر لا يخرج من الملة ، وهو كفر النعمة : والدليل قوله تعالى : { وضرب مثلاً قرية كانت ءامنة مطمئنة يأتيها رزقها رغداً من كل مكان فكفرت بأنعم الله فأذاقها الله لباس الجوع والخوف بما كانوا يصنعون } .

أنواع النفاق...

النفاق نوعان : اعتقادي وعملي :

النفاق الاعتقادي : ستة أنواع ، صاحبها من أهل الدرك الأسفل من النار :

الأول : تكذيب الرسول صلى الله عليه وسلم .

الثاني : تكذيب بعض ما جاء به الرسول صلى الله عليه وسلم .

الثالث : بغض الرسول صلى الله عليه وسلم .

الرابع : بغض بعض ما جاء به الرسول صلى الله عليه وسلم .

الخامس : المسرة بانخفاض دين الرسول صلى الله عليه وسلم .

السادس : الكراهية بانتصار دين الرسول صلى الله عليه وسلم .

النفاق العملي : خمسة أنواع : والدليل قوله صلى الله عليه وسلم : (آية المنافق ثلاث : إذا حدث كذب ، وإذا وعد أخلف ، وإذا ائتمن خان) وفي رواية : (إذا خاصم فجر ، وإذا عاهد غدر) .

معنى الطاغوت ورؤوس أنواعه...

اعلم رحمك الله تعالى أنَّ أول ما فرض الله على ابن آدم الكِفر بالطاغوت والإيمان بالله ، والدليل قوله تعالى : { ولقد بعثنا في كل أمة رسولاً أنِ اعبدوا الله واجتنبوا الطاغوت } .

فأمّا صفة الكفر بالطاغوت أن تعتقد بطلان عبادة غير الله وتتركها وتبغضها وتكفِّر أهلها وتعاديهم .

وأمّا معنى الإيمان بالله أن تعتقد أنَّ الله هو الإله المعبود وحده دون سواه. وتخلص جميع أنواع العبادة كلها لله. وتنفيها عن كل .... سواه ،وتحب أهل الإخلاص وتواليهم. وتبغض أهل الشرك وتعاديهم. وهذه ملّة إبراهيم التي سفه نفسه مَن رغب عنها. وهذه هي الأسوة التي أخبر الله بها في قوله تعالى : { قد كانت لكم أسوة حسنة في إبراهيم والذين معه إذ قالوا لقومهم إنّا بُرَآءُ منكم وممّا تعبدون من دون الله كفرنا بكم وبدا بيننا وبينكم العداوة والبغضاء أبداً حتى تؤمنوا بالله وحده } .

والطاغوت عام في كل ما عُبد من دون الله ورضي بالعبادة من معبود أو متبوع أو مطاع في غير طاعة الله ورسوله فهو طاغوت.

والطواغيت كثيرة ورؤوسهم خمسة :

الأول : الشيطان الداعي إلى عبادة غير الله ، والدليل قوله تعالى : { ألم أعهد إليكم يا بني ءادم أن لا تعبدوا الشيطان إنه لكم عدو مبين} .

الثاني : الحاكم الجائر المغير لأحكام الله ، والدليل قوله تعالى : { ألم تر إلى الذين يزعمون أنهم ءامنوا بما أنزل إليك وما أنزل من قبلك يريدون أن يتحاكموا إلى الطاغوت وقد أمروا أن يكفروا به ويريد الشيطان أن يضلهم ضلالاً بعيداً} .

الثالث : الذي يحكم بغير ما أنزل الله ، والدليل قوله تعالى : { ومن لم يحكم بما أنزل الله فأولئك هم الكافرون } .

الرابع : الذي يدّعي علم الغيب من دون الله ، والدليل قوله تعالى : { عالم الغيب فلا يظهر على غيبه أحداً إلا من ارتضى من رسول فإنه يسلُك من بين يديه ومن خلفه رصداً } ، وقال تعالى : { وعنده مفاتح الغيب لا يعلمها إلا هو ويعلم ما في البر والبحر وماتسقط من ورقة إلا يعلمها ولا حبة في ظلمات الأرض ولا رطب ولا يابس إلا في كتاب مبين } .

الخامس : الذي يعبد من دون الله وهو راض بالعبادة ، والدليل قوله تعالى : { ومن يقل منهم إني إله من دونه فذلك نجزيه جهنم كذلك نجزي الظالمين } .

واعلم أن الإنسان ما يصير مؤمنا بالله إلا بالكفر بالطاغوت ، والدليل قوله تعالى : { فمن يكفر بالطاغوت ويؤمن بالله فقد استمسك بالعروة الوثقى لا انفصام لها والله سميع عليم } ، الرشد : دين محمد صلى الله عليه وآله وسلم ، والغي : دين أبي جهل ، والعروة الوثقى : شهادة أن لا إله إلا الله ، وهي متضمنة للنفي والإثبات ، تنفي جميع أنواع العبادة عن غير الله ، وتثبت جميع أنواع العبادة كلها لله وحده لا شريك له .

والحمد لله الذي بنعمته تتم الصالحات.

THE NAKHLAH
EDUCATIONAL SERIES:

MISSION

The Purpose of the 'Nakhlah Educational Series' is to contribute to the present knowledge based efforts which enable Muslim individuals, families, and communities to understand and learn Islaam and then to develop withi,n and truly live, Islaam. Our commitment and goal is to contribute beneficial publications and works that:

Firstly, reflect the priority, message and methodology of all the prophets and messengers sent to humanity, meaning that single revealed message which embodies the very purpose of life, and of human creation. As Allaah the Most High has said,

❝ *We sent a Messenger to every nation ordering them that they should worship Allaah alone, obey Him and make their worship purely for Him, and that they should avoid everything worshipped besides Allaah. So from them there were those whom Allaah guided to His religion, and there were those who were unbelievers for whom misguidance was ordained. So travel through the land and see the destruction that befell those who denied the Messengers and disbelieved.*❞ —(Surah an-Nahl: 36)

Sheikh Rabee'a ibn Haadee al-Madkhalee in his work entitled, '*The Methodology of the Prophets in Calling to Allaah, That is the Way of Wisdom and Intelligence.*' explains the essential, enduring message of all the prophets:

"*So what was the message which these noble, chosen men, may Allaah's praises and salutations of peace be upon them all brought to their people? Indeed their mission encompassed every matter of good and distanced and restrained every matter of evil. They brought forth to mankind everything needed for their well-being and happiness in this world and the Hereafter. There is nothing good except that they guided the people towards it, and nothing evil except that they warned the people against it. ...*

This was the message found with all of the Messengers; that they should guide to every good and warn against every evil. However where did they start, what did they begin with, and what did they concentrate upon? There are a number of essentials, basic principles, and fundamentals which all their calls were founded upon, and which were the starting point for calling the people to Allaah. These fundamental points and principles are: 1. The worship of Allaah alone without any associates 2. The sending of prophets to guide creation 3. The belief in the resurrection and the life of the Hereafter

These three principles are the area of commonality and unity within their calls, and stand as the fundamental principles which they were established upon. These principles are given the greatest importance in the Qur'aan and are fully explained in it. They are also its most important purpose upon which it centers and which it continually mentions. It further quotes intellectual and observable

OUR MISSION & METHODOLOGY

proofs for them in all its chapters as well as within most of its accounts of previous nations and given examples.

This is known to those who have full understanding, and are able to consider carefully and comprehend well. All the Books revealed by Allaah have given great importance to these points and all of the various revealed laws of guidance are agreed upon them. And the most important and sublime of these three principles, and the most fundamental of them all, is directing one's worship only towards Allaah alone, the Blessed and the Most High."

Today one finds that there are indeed many paths, groups, and organizations apparently presenting themselves as representing Islaam, which struggle to put forth an outwardly pleasing appearance to the general Muslims; but when their methods are placed upon the precise scale of conforming to priorities and methodology of the message of the prophets sent by Allaah, they can only be recognized as deficient paths- not simply in practice but in principle- leading not to success, but rather only to inevitable failure.

As Sheikh Saaleh al-Fauzaan, may Allaah preserve him, states in his introduction to the same above-mentioned work on the methodology of all the prophets,

"So whichever call is not built upon these foundations, and whatever methodology is not from the methodology of the Messengers - then it will be frustrated and fail, and it will be effort and toil without any benefit. The clearest proofs of this are those present-day groups and organizations which set out a methodology and program for themselves and their efforts of calling the people to Islaam which is different from the methodology of the Messengers. These groups have neglected the importance of the people having the correct belief and creed - except for a very few of them - and instead call for the correction of side-issues."

There can be no true success in any form for us as individuals, families, or larger communities without making the encompassing worship of Allaah alone, with no partners or associates, the very and only foundation of our lives. It is necessary that each individual knowingly choose to base his life upon that same foundation taught by all the prophets and messengers sent by the Lord of all the worlds, rather than simply delving into the assorted secondary concerns and issues invited to by the various numerous parties, innovated movements, and groups. Indeed Sheikh al-Albaanee, may Allaah have mercy upon him, stated:[1]

"...We unreservedly combat against this way of having various different parties and groups. As this false way- of group or organizational allegiances - conforms to the statement of Allaah the Most High, ﴿ **But they have broken their religion among them into sects, each group rejoicing in what is with it as its beliefs. And every party is pleased with whatever they stand with.**﴾ –(Surah al-Mu'minoon: 53) And in truth they are no separate groups and parties in Islaam itself. There is only one true party, as is stated in a verse in the Qur'an, ﴿ **Verily, it is the party of Allaah that will be the successful.** ﴾–(Surah al-Mujadilaah: 58). The party of Allaah are those people who stand with the Messenger of Allaah, may Allaah's praise and salutations be upon him, meaning that an individual proceeds upon the methodology of the Companions of the Messenger. Due to this we call for having sound knowledge of the Book and the Sunnah."

---

[1]   Knowledge Based Issues & Sharee'ah Rulings: The Rulings of The Guiding Scholar Sheikh Muhammad Naasiruddeen al-Albaanee Made in the City of Medina & In the Emirates – [Emiratee Fatwa no 114. P.30]

TWO ESSENTIAL FOUNDATIONS

Secondly, building upon the above foundation, our commitment is to contributing publications and works which reflect the inherited message and methodology of the acknowledged scholars of the many various branches of Sharee'ah knowledge, who stood upon the straight path of preserved guidance in every century and time since the time of our Messenger, may Allaah's praise and salutations be upon him. These people of knowledge, who are the inheritors of the Final Messenger, have always adhered closely to the two revealed sources of guidance: the Book of Allaah and the Sunnah of the Messenger of Allaah- may Allaah's praise and salutations be upon him, upon the united consensus, standing with the body of guided Muslims in every century - preserving and transmitting the true religion generation after generation. Indeed the Messenger of Allaah, may Allaah's praise and salutations be upon him, informed us that, *{ A group of people amongst my Ummah will remain obedient to Allaah's orders. They will not be harmed by those who leave them nor by those who oppose them, until Allaah's command for the Last Day comes upon them while they remain on the right path. }*[2]

We live in an age in which the question frequently asked is, "*How do we make Islaam a reality?*" and perhaps the related and more fundamental question is, "*What is Islaam?*", such that innumerable different voices quickly stand to offer countless different conflicting answers through books, lectures, and every available form of modern media. Yet the only true course of properly understanding this question and its answer- for ourselves and our families -is to return to the criterion given to us by our beloved Messenger, may Allaah's praise and salutations be upon him. Indeed the Messenger of Allaah, may Allaah's praise and salutations be upon him, indicated in an authentic narration, clarifying the matter beyond doubt, that the only "Islaam" which enables one to be truly successful and saved in this world and the next is as he said, *{... that which I am upon and my Companions are upon today.}*[3] referring to that Islaam which stands upon unchanging revealed knowledge. While every other changed and altered form of Islaam, whether through some form of extremism or negligence, or through the addition or removal of something, regardless of whether that came from a good intention or an evil one- is not the religion that Allaah informed us about when He revealed, *◊ This day, those who disbelieved have given up all hope of your religion; so fear them not, but fear Me. This day, I have perfected your religion for you, completed My Favor upon you, and have chosen for you Islaam as your religion.◊*–(Surah al-Maa'idah: 3)

[2]   Authentically narrated in Saheeh al-Bukhaaree
[3]   Authentically narrated in Jaam'ea at-Tirmidhee

The guiding scholar Sheikh al-Albaanee, may have mercy upon him, said,

"...And specifically mentioning those among the callers who have taken upon themselves the guiding of the young Muslim generation upon Islaam, working to educate them with its education, and to socialize them with its culture. Yet they themselves have generally not attempted to unify their understanding of those matters about Islaam regarding which the people of Islaam today differ about so severely.

And the situation is certainly not as is falsely supposed by some individuals from among them who are heedless or negligent - that the differences that exist among them are only in secondary matters without entering into or affecting the fundamental issues or principles of the religion; and the examples to prove that this is not true are numerous and recognized by those who have studied the books of the many differing groups and sects, or by the one who has knowledge of the various differing concepts and beliefs held by the Muslims today." [4]

Similarly he, may Allaah have mercy upon him, explained:[5]

"Indeed, Islaam is the only solution, and this statement is something which the various different Islamic groups, organizations, and movements could never disagree about. And this is something which is from the blessings of Allaah upon the Muslims. However there are significant differences between the different Islamic groups, organizations, and movements that are present today regarding that domain which working within will bring about our rectification. What is that area of work to endeavor within, striving to restore a way of life truly reflecting Islaam, renewing that system of living which comes from Islaam, and in order to establish the Islamic government? The groups and movements significantly differ upon this issue or point. Yet we hold that it is required to begin with the matters of tasfeeyah –clarification, and tarbeeyah -education and cultivation, with both of them being undertaken together.

As if we were to start with the issue of governing and politics, then it has been seen that those who occupy themselves with this focus firstly possess beliefs which are clearly corrupted and ruined, and secondly that their personal behavior, from the aspect of conforming to Islaam, is very far from conforming to the actual guidance of the Sharee'ah. While those who first concern themselves with working just to unite the people and gather the masses together under a broad banner of the general term "Islaam," then it is seen that within the minds of those speakers who raise such calls -in reality there is in fact no actual clear understanding of what Islaam is. Moreover, the understanding they have of Islaam has no significant impact in starting to change and reform their own lives. Due to this reason, you find that many such individuals from here and there, who hold this perspective, are unable to truly realize or reflect Islaam, even in areas of their own personal lives in matters which it is in fact easily possible for them to implement. Such an individual holds that no one - regardless of whether it is because of his arrogance or pridefulness - can enter into directing him in an area of his personal life!

---

[4]   Mukhtasir al-'Uloo Lil'Alee al-Ghafaar, page 55

[5]   Quoted from the work, 'The Life of Sheikh al-Albaanee, His Influence in Present Day Fields of Sharee'ah Knowledge, & the Praise of the Scholars for Him.' volume 1 page 380-385

Yet at the same time these same individuals are raising their voices saying, "Judgment is only for Allaah!" and "It is required that judgment of affairs be according to what Allaah revealed." And this is indeed a true statement, but the one who does not possess something certainly cannot give or offer it to others. The majority of Muslims today have not established the judgment of Allaah fully upon themselves, yet they still seek from others to establish the judgment of Allaah within their governments...

...And I understand that this issue or subject is not immune from there being those who oppose our methodology of tasfeeyah and tarbeeyah. As there is the one who would say, "But establishing this tasfeeyah and tarbeeyah is a matter which requires many long years!" So, I respond by saying, this is not an important consideration in this matter, what is important is that we carry out what we have been commanded to do within our religion and by our Mighty Lord. What is important is that we begin by properly understanding our religion first and foremost. After this is accomplished then it will not be important whether the road itself is long or short.

And indeed, I direct this statement of mine towards those men who are callers to the religion among the Muslims, and towards the scholars and those who direct our affairs. I call for them to stand upon complete knowledge of true Islaam, and to fight against every form of negligence and heedlessness regarding the religion, and against differing and disputes, as Allaah has said, ❧...and do not dispute with one another for fear that you lose courage and your strength departs ❧—(Surah al-Anfaal: 46).

The guiding scholar Sheikh Zayd al-Madkhalee, may Allaah protect him, stated in his writing, 'The Well Established Principles of the Way of the First Generations of Muslims: It's Enduring & Excellent Distinct Characteristics' that,

"From among these principles and characteristics is that the methodology of tasfeeyah -or clarification, and tarbeeyah -or education and cultivation- is clearly affirmed and established as a true way coming from the first three generations of Islaam, and is something well known to the people of true merit from among them, as is concluded by considering all the related evidence. What is intended by tasfeeyah, when referring to it generally, is clarifying that which is the truth from that which is falsehood, what is goodness from that which is harmful and corrupt, and when referring to its specific meanings, it is distinguishing the noble Sunnah of the Prophet and the people of the Sunnah from those innovated matters brought into the religion and the people who are supporters of such innovations.

As for what is intended by tarbeeyah, it is calling all of the creation to take on the manners and embrace the excellent character invited to by that guidance revealed to them by their Lord through His worshiper and Messenger Muhammad, may Allaah's praise and salutations be upon him; so that they might have good character, manners, and behavior. As without this they cannot have a good life, nor can they put right their present condition or their final destination. And we seek refuge in Allaah from the evil of not being able to achieve that rectification."

Thus the methodology of the people of standing upon the Prophet's Sunnah, and proceeding upon the 'way of the believers' in every century is reflected in a focus and concern with these two essential matters: tasfeeyah- or clarification of what is original, revealed message

from the Lord of all the worlds, and tarbeeyah- or education and raising of ourselves, our families, and our communities, and our lands upon what has been distinguished to be that true message and path.

METHODOLOGY:

The Roles of the Scholars & General Muslims In Raising the New Generation

The priority and focus of the 'Nakhlah Educational Series' is reflected within in the following statements of Sheikh al-Albaanee, may Allaah have mercy upon him:

"As for the other obligation, then I intend by this the education of the young generation upon Islaam purified from all of those impurities we have mentioned, giving them a correct Islamic education from their very earliest years, without any influence of a foreign, disbelieving education."[6]

"...And since the Messenger of Allaah, may Allaah's praise and salutations be upon him, has indicated that the only cure to remove this state of humiliation that we find ourselves entrenched within, is truly returning back to the religion, then it is clearly obligatory upon us - through the people of knowledge- to correctly and properly understand the religion in a way that conforms to the sources of the Book of Allaah and the Sunnah, and that we educate and raise a new virtuous, righteous generation upon this."[7]

It is essential, in discussing our perspective upon this obligation of raising the new generation of Muslims, that we highlight and bring attention to a required pillar of these efforts as indicated by Sheikh al-Albaanee, may Allaah have mercy upon him, and others- in the golden words, *"through the people of knowledge."* Something we commonly experience today is that many people have various incorrect understandings of the role that the scholars should have in the life of a Muslim, failing to understand the way in which they fulfill their position as the inheritors of the Messenger of Allaah, may Allaah's praise and salutations be upon him, and stand as those who preserve and enable us to practice the guidance of Islaam. Indeed, the noble Imaam Sheikh as-Sa'dee, may Allaah have mercy upon him, in his work, *"A Definitive and Clear Explanation of the Work 'A Triumph for the Saved Sect'"* [8], has explained this crucial issue with an extraordinary explanation full of remarkable benefits:

---

[6]   Silsilaat al-Hadeeth ad-Da'eefah, Introduction pg. 2
[7]   Clarification and Cultivation and the Need of the Muslims for Them
[8]   A Definitive and Clear Explanation of the Work 'A Triumph for the Saved Sect'" pages 237-240

"Section: Explaining the Conditions for These Two Source Texts to Suffice You -or the Finding of Sufficiency in these Two Sources of Revelation.

Overall the conditions needed to achieve this and bring it about return to two matters:

Firstly, the presence of the requirements necessary for achieving this; meaning a complete devotion to the Book and the Sunnah, and the putting forth of efforts both in seeking to understand their intended meanings, as well as in striving to be guided by them. What is required secondly is the pushing away of everything which prevents achieving this finding of sufficiency in them.

This is through having a firm determination to distance yourself from everything which contradicts these two source texts in what comes from the historical schools of jurisprudence, assorted various statements, differing principles and their resulting conclusions which the majority of people proceed upon. These matters which contradict the two sources of revelation include many affairs which, when the worshiper of Allaah repels them from himself and stands against them, the realm of his knowledge, understanding, and deeds then expands greatly. Through a devotion to them and a complete dedication towards these two sources of revelation, proceeding upon every path which assists one's understanding them, and receiving enlightenment from the light of the scholars and being guided by the guidance that they possess- you will achieve that complete sufficiency in them. And surely, in the positions they take towards the leading people of knowledge and the scholars, the people are three types of individuals:

The first of them is the one who goes to extremes in his attachment to the scholars. He makes their statements something which are infallible as if their words held the same position as those of the statements of the Messenger of Allaah, may Allaah's praise and salutations be upon him, as well as giving those scholars' statements precedence and predominance over the Book of Allaah and the Sunnah. This is despite the fact that every leading scholar who has been accepted by this Ummah was one who promoted and encouraged the following of the Book and the Sunnah, commanding the people not to follow their own statements nor their school of thought in anything which stood in opposition to the Book of Allaah and the Sunnah.

The second type is the one who generally rejects and invalidates the statements of the scholars and forbids the referring to the statements of the leading scholars of guidance and those people of knowledge who stand as brilliant lamps in the darkness. This type of person neither relies upon the light of discernment with the scholars, nor utilizes their stores of knowledge. Or even if perhaps they do so, they do not direct thanks towards them for this. And this manner and way prohibits them from tremendous good. Furthermore, that which motivates such individuals to proceed in this way is their falsely supposing that the obligation to follow the Messenger of Allaah, may Allaah's praise and salutations be upon him, and the giving of precedence to his statements over the statements of anyone else, requires that they do so without any reliance upon the statements of the Companions, or those who followed them in goodness, or those leading scholars of guidance within the Ummah. This is a glaring and extraordinary mistake.

Indeed the Companions and the people of knowledge are the means and the agency between the Messenger of Allaah, may Allaah's praise and salutations be upon him, and his Ummah- in the transmission and spreading his Sunnah in regard to both its wording and texts, as well as its

meanings and understanding. Therefore the one who follows them in what they convey in this is guided through their understandings, receives knowledge from the light they possess, benefits from the conclusions they have derived from these sources -of beneficial meanings and explanations, as well as in relation to subtle

matters which scarcely occur to the minds of some of the other people of knowledge, or barely comes to be discerned by their minds. Consequently, from the blessing of Allaah upon this Ummah is that He has given them these guiding scholars who cultivate and educate them upon two clear types of excellent cultivation.

The first category is education from the direction of one's knowledge and understanding. They educate the Ummah upon the more essential and fundamental matters before the more complex affairs. They convey the meanings of the Book and the Sunnah to the minds and intellects of the people through efforts of teaching which rectifies, and through composing various beneficial books of knowledge which a worshiper doesn't even have the ability to adequately describe what is encompassed within them of aspects of knowledge and benefits. These works reflect the presence of a clear white hand in deriving guidance from the Book of Allaah and the Sunnah, and through the arrangement, detailed clarification, division and explanation, through the gathering together of explanations, comparisons, conditions, pillars, and explanations about that which prevents the fulfillment of matters, as well as distinguishing between differing meanings and categorizing various knowledge based benefits.

The second category is education from the direction of one's conduct and actions. They cultivate the peoples characters encouraging them towards every praiseworthy aspect of good character, through explaining its ruling and high status, and what benefits comes to be realized from it, clarifying the reasons and paths which enable one to attain it, as well as those affairs which prevent, delay, or hinder someone becoming one distinguished and characterized by it. Because they, in reality, are those who bring nourishment to the hearts and the souls; they are the doctors who treat the diseases of the heart and its defects. As such, they educate the people through their statements, and actions, as well as their general guided way. Therefore the scholars have a tremendous right over this Ummah. A portion of love and esteem, respect and honor, and thanks, are due to them because their merits and their various good efforts stand above every other right after establishing the right of Allaah, and the right of His Messenger, may Allaah's praise and salutations be upon him.

Because of this, the third group of individuals in respect to the scholars are those who have been guided to understand their true role and position, and establish their rights, thanking them for their virtues and merits, benefiting by taking from the knowledge they have, while acknowledging their rank and status. They understand that the scholars are not infallible and that their statements must stand in conformance to the statements of the Messenger of Allaah, may Allaah's praise and salutations be upon him, and that each one from among them has that which is from guidance, knowledge, and correctness in his statements taken and benefited from, while turning away from whatever in mistaken within it.

Yet such a scholar is not to be belittled for his mistake, as he stands as one who strove to reach the truth; therefore his mistake will be forgiven, and he should be thanked for his efforts. One clarifies what was stated by of any one of these leaders from among men, when it is recognized that

it has some weakness or conflict to an evidence of the Sharee'ah, by explaining its weakness and the level of that weakness, without speaking evilly of the intention of those people of knowledge and religion, nor defaming them due to that error. Rather we say, as it is obligatory to say, "And those who came after them say: ﴾

Our Lord! forgive us and our brethren who have preceded us in faith, and put not in our hearts any hatred against those who have believed. Our Lord! You are indeed full of kindness, Most Merciful. ﴿ *-(Surah al-Hashr: 10).*

Accordingly, individuals of this third type are those who fulfill two different matters. They join together on one hand between giving precedence to the Book and the Sunnah over everything else, and, on the other hand, between comprehending the level and position of the scholars and the leading people of knowledge and guidance, and establishing this even if it is only done in regard to some of their rights upon us. So we ask Allaah to bless us to be from this type, and to make us from among the people of this third type, and to make us from those who love Him and love those who love Him, and those who love every action which brings us closer to everything He loves."

Upon this clarity regarding the proper understanding of our balanced position towards our guided Muslim scholars, consider the following words about the realm of work of the general people of faith, which explains our area of efforts and struggle as Muslim parents, found in the following statement by Sheikh Saaleh Fauzaan al-Fauzaan, may Allaah preserve him.

"Question: Some people mistakenly believe that calling to Allaah is a matter not to be undertaken by anyone else other than the scholars without exception, and that it is not something required for other than the scholars, according to that which they have knowledge of, to undertake any efforts of calling the people to Allaah. So what is your esteemed guidance regarding this?"

The Sheikh responded by saying:[9]

"This is not a misconception, but is in fact a reality. The call to Allaah cannot be established except through those who are scholars, and I state this. Yet, certainly there are clear issues which every person understands. As such, every individual should enjoin the good and forbid wrongdoing according to the level of his understanding, such that he instructs and orders the members of his household to perform the ritual daily prayers and other matters that are clear and well known.

Undertaking this is something mandatory and required even upon the common people, such that they must command their children to perform their prayers in the masjid. The Messenger of Allaah, may Allaah praise and salutations be upon him, said, { **Command you children to pray at seven, and beat them due to its negligence at ten.**} *(Authentic narration found in Sunan Abu Dawood). And the Messenger of Allaah, may Allaah praise and salutations be upon him, said, {* **Each one of you is a guardian or a shepherd, and each of you is responsible for those under his guardianship....**} *(Authentic narration found in Saheeh al-Bukhaaree). So this is called guardianship, and this is also called enjoining the good and forbidding wrongdoing. The Messenger of Allaah, may Allaah praise and salutations be upon him, said, {* **The one from among you who sees a wrong should change it with his hand, and if he is unable to do so, then with his tongue, and**

---

[9]   Beneficial Responses to Questions About Modern Methodologies, Question 15, page 22

if he is not able to do this, then with his heart. } (Authentic narration found in Saheeh Muslim).

So in relation to the common person, that which it is required from him to endeavor upon is that he commands the members of his household-as well as others -with the proper performance of the ritual prayers, the obligatory charity, with generally striving to obey Allaah, to stay away from sins and transgressions, that he purify and cleanse his home from disobedience, and that he educate and cultivate his children upon the obedience of Allaah's commands. This is what is required from him, even if he is a general person, as these types of matters are from that which is understood by every single person. This is something which is clear and apparent.

But as for the matters of putting forth rulings and judgments regarding matters in the religion, or entering into clarifying issues of what is permissible and what is forbidden, or explaining what is considered associating others in the worship due to Allaah and what is properly worshiping Him alone without any partner- then indeed these are matters which cannot be established except by the scholars"

Similarly the guiding scholar Sheikh 'Abdul-'Azeez Ibn Baaz, may Allaah have mercy upon him, also emphasized this same overall responsibility:

"...It is also upon a Muslim that he struggles diligently in that which will place his worldly affairs in a good state, just as he must also strive in the correcting of his religious affairs and the affairs of his own family. The people of his household have a significant right over him that he strive diligently in rectifying their affair and guiding them towards goodness, due to the statement of Allaah, the Most Exalted, **Oh you who believe! Save yourselves and your families Hellfire whose fuel is men and stones** -(Surah at-Tahreem: 6)

So it is upon you to strive to correct the affairs of the members of your family. This includes your wife, your children- both male and female- and such as your own brothers. This concerns all of the people in your family, meaning you should strive to teach them the religion, guiding and directing them, and warning them from those matters Allaah has prohibited for us. Because you are the one who is responsible for them as shown in the statement of the Prophet, may Allaah's praise and salutations be upon him, **{ Every one of you is a guardian, and responsible for what is in his custody. The ruler is a guardian of his subjects and responsible for them; a husband is a guardian of his family and is responsible for it; a lady is a guardian of her husband's house and is responsible for it, and a servant is a guardian of his master's property and is responsible for it....}** Then the Messenger of Allaah, may Allaah's praise and salutations be upon him, continued to say, **{...so all of you are guardians and are responsible for those under your authority.}** (Authentically narrated in Saheeh al-Bukhaaree & Muslim)

It is upon us to strive diligently in correcting the affairs of the members of our families, from the aspect of purifying their sincerity of intention for Allaah's sake alone in all of their deeds, and ensuring that they truthfully believe in and follow the Messenger of Allaah, may Allaah's praise and salutations be upon him, their fulfilling the prayer and the other obligations which Allaah the Most Exalted has commanded for us, as well as from the direction of distancing them from everything which Allaah has prohibited.

It is upon every single man and woman to give advice to their families about the fulfillment of what is obligatory upon them. Certainly, it is upon the woman as well as upon the man to perform this. In this way our homes become corrected and rectified in regard to the most important and essential matters. Allaah said to His Prophet, may Allaah's praise and salutations be upon him, ❧ **And enjoin the ritual prayers on your family...** ❧ *(Surah Taha: 132) Similarly, Allaah the Most Exalted said to His prophet Ismaa'aeel,* ❧ **And mention in the Book, Ismaa'aeel. Verily, he was true to what he promised, and he was a Messenger, and a Prophet. And he used to enjoin on his family and his people the ritual prayers and the obligatory charity, and his Lord was pleased with him.** ❧ *-(Surah Maryam: 54-55)*

As such, it is only proper that we model ourselves after the prophets and the best of people, and be concerned with the state of the members of our households. Do not be neglectful of them, oh worshipper of Allaah! Regardless of whether it is concerning your wife, your mother, father, grandfather, grandmother, your brothers, or your children; it is upon you to strive diligently in correcting their state and condition..." [10]

---

[10] Collection of Various Rulings and Statements- Sheikh 'Abdul-'Azeez Ibn 'Abdullah Ibn Baaz, Vol. 6, page 47

CONTENT & STRUCTURE:

We hope to contribute works which enable every striving Muslim who

acknowledges the proper position of the scholars, to fulfill the recognized duty and obligation which lays upon each one of us to bring the light of Islaam into our own lives as individuals, as well as into our homes and among our families. Towards this goal we are committed to developing educational publications and comprehensive educational curricula -through cooperation with and based upon the works of the scholars of Islaam and the students of knowledge. Works which, with the assistance of Allaah, the Most High, we can utilize to educate and instruct ourselves, our families and our communities upon Islaam in both principle and practice. The publications and works of the Nakhlah Educational Series are divided into the following categories:

Basic / Elementary: Ages 4-11   *Secondary: Ages 11-14*

High School: Ages 14- Young Adult   *General: Young Adult –Adult*

Supplementary: All Ages

Publications and works within these stated levels will, with the permission of Allaah, encompass different beneficial areas and subjects, and will be offered in every permissible form of media and medium. Certainly, the guiding scholar Sheikh Saaleh ibn Fauzaan al-Fauzaan, may Allaah preserve him, has stated,

"Beneficial knowledge is itself divided into two categories. Firstly is that knowledge which is tremendous in its benefit, as it benefits in this world and continues to benefit in the Hereafter. This is religious Sharee'ah knowledge. And second, that which is limited and restricted to matters related to the life of this world, such as learning the processes of manufacturing various goods. This is a category of knowledge related specifically to worldly affairs.

…As for the learning of worldly knowledge, such as knowledge of manufacturing, then it is legislated upon us collectively to learn whatever the Muslims have a need for. Yet, if they do not have a need for this knowledge, then learning it is a neutral matter upon the condition that it does not compete with or displace any areas of Sharee'ah knowledge…"

("Explanations of the Mistakes of Some Writers", Pages 10-12)

So we strive always to remind ourselves and our brothers of this crucial point also indicated by Sheikh Sadeeq Ibn Hasan al-Qanoojee, may Allaah have mercy upon him, in: '*Abjad al-'Uloom*',[11]

"…What is intended by knowledge in the mentioned hadeeth is knowledge of the religion and the distinctive Sharee'ah, knowledge of the Noble Book and the pure Sunnah, of which there is no third along with them. But what is not meant in this narration are those invented areas of knowledge, whether they emerged in previous ages or today's world, which the people in these present

---

[11] 'Abjad al-'Uloom', pg. 89

times have devoted themselves to. They have specifically dedicated themselves to them in a manner which prevents them from looking towards those areas of knowledge related to faith, and in a way which has preoccupied them from occupying themselves from what is actually wanted or desired by Allaah, the

Most High, and His Messenger, who is the leader of men and Jinn. Due to this, the knowledge in the Qur'aan has become something abandoned and the sciences of hadeeth have become obscure, while these new areas of knowledge related to manufacturing and production continually emerge from the nations of disbelief and apostasy, and they are called, "sciences", "arts", and "ideal development". This sad state increases every day, indeed from Allaah we came and to Him shall we return....

...Additionally, although the various areas of beneficial knowledge all share some level of value, they all have differing importance and ranks. Among them is that which is to be considered according to its subject, such as medicine, and its subject is the human body. Or such as the sciences of 'tafseer' and its subject is the explanation of the words of Allaah, the Most Exalted and Most High, and the value of these two areas is not in any way unrecognized.

And from among the various areas, there are those areas which are considered according to their objective, such as knowledge of upright character, and its goal is understanding the beneficial merits that an individual can come to possess. And from among them there are those areas which are considered according to the people's need for them, such as 'fiqh' which the need for it is urgent and essential. And from among them there are those areas which are considered according to their apparent strength, such as knowledge of physical sports and exercise, as it is something openly demonstrated.

And from the areas of knowledge are those areas which rise in their position of importance through their combining all these different matters within them, or the majority of them, such as revealed religious knowledge, as its subject is indeed esteemed, its objective one of true merit, and its need is undeniably felt. Likewise one area of knowledge may be considered of superior rank than another in consideration of the results that it brings forth, or the strength of its outward manifestation, or due to the essentialness of its objective. Similarly, the result that an area produces is certainly of higher estimation and significance in appraisal than the outward or apparent significance of some other areas of knowledge.

For that reason, the highest ranking and most valuable area of knowledge is that of knowledge of Allaah the Most Perfect and the Most High, of His angels, and messengers, and all the particulars of these beliefs, as its result is that of eternal and continuing happiness."

We ask Allaah, the most High to bless us with success in contributing to the many efforts of our Muslim brothers and sisters committed to raising themselves as individuals, and the next generation of our children, upon that Islaam which Allaah has perfected and chosen for us, and which He has enabled the guided Muslims to proceed upon in each and every century. We ask him to forgive us, and forgive the Muslim men and the Muslim women, and to guide all the believers to everything He loves and is pleased with. The success is from Allaah, the Most High the Most Exalted, alone and all praise is due to Him.

Abu Sukhailah Khalil Ibn-Abelahyi
Taalib al-Ilm Educational Resources

Publication Translators:

We are presently looking for competent translators in several languages to help translate publications from the English language.

Spanish, French, German, Portuguese, Russian, Turkish, Indonesian, Urdu, Bengali, Russian, & other languages

---

For further information, please visit our affiliate web page here:

http://taalib.com/translate

http://taalib.com/translate

Online Sales Affiliates:

We now have an affiliate program that enables Muslim around the world to earn affiliate income of any sales they refer to us through the system. With simple sign up, you can download a banner or images and earn permissible income through any sales that coms from your social media account, website. or direct promotional efforts.

25% referred fee for any product order directly referred by you to our sites

+ additional 5% retail amount for any order from individual referred by you who also joins the affiliate program

---

For further information, please visit our affiliate web page here:

http://taalib.com/earn

http://taalib.com/earn

BELIEFS & WORSHIP

30 Days of Guidance [Book 1]: Learning Fundamental Principles of Islaam

A Short Journey Within the Work Al-Ibaanah al-Sughrah With Sheikh 'Abdul-'Azeez Ibn 'Abdullah ar-Raajhee

AUTHOR - COMPILER - TRANSLATOR

Abu Sukhailah Khalil Ibn-Abelahyi

BOOK OVERVIEW

- Interactive course book
- Focused upon both beliefs & principles
- 1st book in 30 Day Series

AVAILABLE LANGUAGES

English

WHO IS THIS BOOK FOR

All age levels

For every Muslim who wishes to live their life in a way pleasing to Allaah it is essential that they ensure that their beliefs and practices actually have evidence and support from within the sources of Islaam. This work approaches this challenge in a way that allows an individual to proceed through discussions related to this a day at a time over thirty days, based upon explanations from one of today's noble scholars.

"...Allaah, the Most Glorified and the Most Exalted, according to a wisdom that is with Him, places those who would oppose the truth in order that the truth be known, and in order that it become something which manifests as something clear and dominant over falsehood."
Sheikh al-'Utheimeen. - Open Door Gatherings 3/66.

WHAT YOU WILL LEARN IN THIS BOOK

Related to essential basic principles of guidance

The role of Islaam in today's world is something which is indisputable and often contested. There are many different understandings of Islaam which range from dangerous extremism, all the way to vulnerable laxity. Yet our well-known scholars continue to work diligently in openly examining and clarifying the false ideas and practices that are attributed to Islaam.

VERSIONS - PRICING

- *Self-Study Edition (hardcover)*   USD $42.50
- *Self-Study Edition (soft cover)*   USD $27.50
- *Directed Study Edition*   USD $25.00
- *Workbook*   USD $12.50
- *Kindle edition*   USD $09.99

PDF PREVIEW	PURCHASE BOOK

https://ilm4.us/30daybook1   http://taalib.com/4134

30 Days of Guidance [Book 2]: Cultivating The Character & Behavior of Islaam

A Short Journey Within The Work Al-Adab Al-Mufrad
With Sheikh Zayd Ibn Muhammad Ibn Haadee al-Madkhalee

> "It is predominant over the other religions and ways of life, as it enjoins the best of deeds, as well as the most excellent aspects of good character, and enjoins the overall well-being of those who worship Allaah."
>
> *Imaam Sa'dee. - "A Summarized Jewel..."*

WHAT YOU WILL LEARN IN THIS BOOK

Related to the subject of perfecting ones character
Some of the questions that this course book helps us answer are: Are you prepared for your reckoning? Are you always working for good while you can? Do you remember the benefit in your difficulties? Is your life balanced as was the lives of the Companions? How do you deal with your own faults and those of others? Do you know what things bring you closer to Jannah?....and more

VERSIONS - PRICING

- *Self-Study Edition (hardcover)*   USD $42.50
- *Self-Study Edition (soft cover)*   USD $27.50
- *Directed Study Edition*   USD $25.00
- *Workbook*   USD $12.50
- *Kindle edition*   USD $09.99

AUTHOR - COMPILER - TRANSLATOR

Abu Sukhailah Khalil Ibn-Abelahyi

BOOK OVERVIEW

- Interactive course book
- Focused upon both character & behavior
- 2nd book in 30 Day Series

AVAILABLE LANGUAGES

English

WHO IS THIS BOOK FOR

All age levels
This course book is intended for the Muslim individual for self-study, as well as for us as Muslim parents in our essential efforts to educate our children within Islaam and our ongoing endeavor of cultivating them upon the extraordinary character and behavior of our beloved Prophet. It is also intended to be an easy to use classroom resource for our Muslim teachers in the every growing numbers of Islamic centers, masjids, and Islamic weekend and full-time schools.

PDF PREVIEW

https://ilm4.us/30daybook2

PURCHASE BOOK

http://taalib.com/4137

30 Days of Guidance [Book 3]: Signposts Towards Rectification & Repentance

A Short Journey through Selected Questions & Answers with Sheikh Muhammad Ibn Saaleh al-'Utheimeen

AUTHOR - COMPILER - TRANSLATOR

Abu Sukhailah Khalil Ibn-Abelahyi

BOOK OVERVIEW

- Interactive course book
- Focused upon both change & growth in Islaam
- 3rd book in 30 Day Series

AVAILABLE LANGUAGES

English

WHO IS THIS BOOK FOR

All age levels

This course book is intended for any Muslim who wishes to improve his life and rectify his heart. Yet this self rectification or purification of the soul must be done in the correct way and upon the correct foundation of knowledge from the Sunnah, if it is to lead to true success in both this life and the next.

Ibn al-Qayyim, may Allaah have mercy upon him, also stated, '*The true purification of the soul and the self is directly connected to those messengers sent to humanity...*'

'The purification of the self or soul and its becoming rectified is dependent upon it being called to account and assessed. There is no purification or rectification nor any possibility of it being brought to a state of well-being except through calling oneself to account.'

Ibn al-Qayyim - Madaarij as-Saalikeen

WHAT YOU WILL LEARN IN THIS BOOK

Related to the Subject of perfecting ones character

This course discusses in detail the inward and outward changes and steps we must take as striving Muslims to improve and bring our lives into a better state after mistakes, sins, slips, and negligence. Discussing real life problems and issues faced by Muslim of all ages and situations -the Sheikh advises and indicates the road to reform, repentance, and true rectification.

VERSIONS - PRICING

- *Self-Study Edition (hardcover)*   USD $42.50
- *Self-Study Edition (soft cover)*   USD $27.50
- *Directed Study Edition*   USD $25.00
- *Workbook*   USD $12.50
- *Kindle edition*   USD $09.99

PDF PREVIEW   PURCHASE BOOK

https://ilm4.us/30daybook3   http://taalib.com/4150

Foundations For The New Muslim & Newly Striving Muslim

A Short Journey through Selected Questions & Answers with Sheikh 'Abdul-'Azeez Ibn 'Abdullah Ibn Baaz

"Proceed upon the straight path, even if with limited good deeds. As proceeding along with the obedient worshippers doing limited deeds, is better that to proceeding upon any of the various paths or ways which have deviated away from the way of truth...."
Sheikh Ibn Baaz - "Comments Upon the Book..."

WHAT YOU WILL LEARN IN THIS BOOK

Related to building a firm foundation for our Islaam
This course book discusses What are the conditions of correct Islaam? Is faith only what is in our hearts? When is it necessary for me to ask a scholar? What is the guidance of Islaam about our health? What should I do after falling into sin again and again? Do I have to make up for my previous negligence? How should I interact with the non-Muslims I know? and more...

VERSIONS - PRICING

- *Self-Study Edition (hardcover)*   USD $45.00
- *Self-Study Edition (soft cover)*   USD $27.50
- *Directed Study Edition*   USD $25.00
- *Workbook*   USD $11.00
- *Kindle edition*   USD $09.99

AUTHOR - COMPILER - TRANSLATOR

Abu Sukhailah Khalil Ibn-Abelahyi

BOOK OVERVIEW

- Interactive course book
- Focused upon essential beliefs & challenges
- 4th book in 30 Day Series

AVAILABLE LANGUAGES

English

WHO IS THIS BOOK FOR

All age levels
This course book is intended for both the person who has newly embraced Islaam or that Muslim or Muslimah whom Allaah has blessed to now have the resolve within themselves to truly turn towards their Most Merciful Lord and commit themselves to becoming a better worshipper upon knowledge. It for that individual who, regardless of the direction they came from, wishes to change both the inward and outward aspects of their lives to now move in a direction truly pleasing to Allaah.

PDF PREVIEW   PURCHASE BOOK

https://ilm4.us/30daybook4   http://taalib.com/4147

VARIOUS SUBJECTS

Statements of the Guiding Scholars of Our Age Regarding Books & their Advice to the Beginner Seeker of Knowledge

[Contains A List of over 300 Books Recommended By The Scholars In The Various Sciences Of Islaam]

AUTHOR - COMPILER - TRANSLATOR

Abu Sukhailah Khalil Ibn-Abelahyi

BOOK OVERVIEW

- Taken from words of senior scholars
- Provides road map for Sharee'ah study
- Divided into seven main sections

AVAILABLE LANGUAGES

English

WHO IS THIS BOOK FOR

All age levels

A comprehensive guidebook for the Muslim who wishes to learn about his or her religion with the proper goal and aim, in the proper way, and through the proper books. This question and answer book is for those who seek advice from some of the senior scholars of the current century regarding seeking knowledge, beneficial books, and their warnings against books containing misguidance. Their advice encompasses both modern and classical books in various branches and areas of Sharee'ah knowledge.

"Oh Muslim youth! Oh students of knowledge! Connect yourselves to your scholars, attach yourselves to them, and take knowledge from them. Attach yourselves to the reliable scholars..."

Sheikh al-Fauzaan. - Explanation of Mistakes, pg. 18

WHAT YOU WILL LEARN IN THIS BOOK

Sources and subjects of seeking Sharee'ah knowledge

This book is intended to enable any sincere Muslim to strive to proceed with correct methods and manners in seeking of beneficial knowledge for themselves and in order to guide their families. The scholars are the carriers of authentic knowledge and the inheritors of the Messenger of Allaah. Their explantations make clear for us the way to learn and then live Islaam.

VERSIONS - PRICING

- *Hardcover -7.44" x 9.69"*   USD $45.00
- *Soft cover -7.44" x 9.69"*   USD $27.50
- *Kindle edition*   USD $09.99

PDF PREVIEW   PURCHASE BOOK

https://ilm4.us/seeker   http://taalib.com/79

An Educational Course Based Upon Beneficial Answers to Questions On Innovated Methodologies

of Sheikh Saaleh Ibn Fauzaan al-Fauzaan

> "The person upon the Sunnah has mercy. He has mercy on himself through his following of the Sunnah and standing in its shade. This becomes a cause for his success in this world, the life of the grave, and the next life."
>
> *Sheikh Zayd al-Madkhalee - Sharh Adaab al-Mufrad*

WHAT YOU WILL LEARN IN THIS BOOK

Related to the detailed way we understand Islaam
This course focuses upon the importance of clarity in the way you understand and practice Islaam. What is the right way or methodology to do so? Examine the evidences and proofs from the sources texts of the Qur'aan and Sunnah and the statements of many scholars explaining them, that connect you directly to the Islaam of the Messenger of Allaah.

VERSIONS - PRICING

• *Self-Study Edition (hardcover)*	USD $50.00
• *Self-Study Edition (soft cover)*	USD $32.50
• *Directed Study Edition*	USD $30.00
• *Workbook*	USD $12.50
• *Kindle edition*	USD $09.99

AUTHOR - COMPILER - TRANSLATOR

Abu Sukhailah Khalil Ibn-Abelahyi

BOOK OVERVIEW

- Interactive course book
- Focuses upon principles of the straight path
- Discusses modern groups and movements

AVAILABLE LANGUAGES

English

WHO IS THIS BOOK FOR

All age levels
This course book is for any Muslim who wishes to understand the detailed guiding principles of Islaam as discussed by the scholars throughout the centuries, including the scholars of our age. These principles were initially put in place and practiced by the generation of the Companions of the Messenger of Allaah, may Allaah be pleased with all of them, when Islaam was first established, and have been implemented in each and every century by those Muslims following in their noble footsteps.

PDF PREVIEW

http://ilm4.us/minhaj

PURCHASE BOOK

http://taalib.com/4144

METHODOLOGY & SECTS

The Belief of Every Muslim & The Methodology of The Saved Sect

Lessons & Benefits From the Two Excellent Works of Sheikh Muhammad Ibn Jameel Zaynoo

AUTHOR - COMPILER - TRANSLATOR

Abu Sukhailah Khalil Ibn-Abelahyi

BOOK OVERVIEW

- Interactive course book with diagrams
- Discusses how to study and from whom
- Focuses upon both beliefs & practices

AVAILABLE LANGUAGES

English

WHO IS THIS BOOK FOR

All age levels

This course book is for any Muslim who is looking for an easy-to-follow course- based discussion of not only what it is important to learn but also concise advice on how to study and learn Islaam. Taking selections from two well-known books of Sheikh Zaynoo, may Allaah have mercy upon him, it offers an overview of some of the characteristics and hallmarks which distingushed that clear call our beloved Prophet brought to humanity.

"Indeed I interacted with the people of the different Islamic groups and organizations, and I've come to see that those that stand upon the call of Salafees are those which hold closely to the Book and the Sunnah as understood by the righteous predecessors of the Muslim Ummah..."
Sheikh Muhammad Ibn Jameel Zaynoo - "Methodology of..."

WHAT YOU WILL LEARN IN THIS BOOK

Related to foundation of Islaam & gaining knowledge
This Islamic studies course discusses the different levels of knowledge, important matters related to seeking knowledge, essential study skills, the role of evidence in Islaam, differing and taking from the scholars. Additionally, it explains the central role that the foundation that worshipping Allaah alone should have in our lives, and how that distinguishes every single person.

VERSIONS - PRICING

- *Self-Study Edition (hardcover)*   USD $45.00
- *Self-Study Edition (soft cover)*   USD $30.00
- *Directed Study Edition*   USD $27.50
- *Workbook*   USD $12.50
- *Kindle edition*   USD $09.99

PDF PREVIEW	PURCHASE BOOK
https://ilm4.us/savedsect	http://taalib.com/4141

The Cure, The Explanation, The Clear Affair, & The Brilliantly Distinct Signpost

Book 1: Sources of Islaam & The Way of the Companions-
A Course Upon Commentaries of Usul as-Sunnah' of Imaam Ahmad

"....we know that the beliefs of the righteous first three generations and their methodology is only a single way and path which it is obligatory that we ourselves follow and adhere to. It is that affair, which encompasses within it, that leads to the success of the people." *Sheikh Saaleh Aal-Sheikh, - "Provisions..."*

WHAT YOU WILL LEARN IN THIS BOOK

Related to the independent sources of Sharee'ah guidance
This course book discusses the universal nature and correct beliefs about Islaam as a revealed religion. It also discusses specifically what are the correct evidenced beliefs held by the people of adherence to the Sunnah throughout the centuries about the nature of the Qur'aan, the Sunnah and scholarly Consensus.

VERSIONS - PRICING

- *Self-Study Edition (hardcover)*   USD $50.00
- *Self-Study Edition (soft cover)*   USD $32.50
- *Directed Study Edition*   USD $30.00
- *Workbook*   USD $12.50
- *Kindle edition*   USD $09.99

AUTHOR - COMPILER - TRANSLATOR

Abu Sukhailah Khalil Ibn-Abelahyi

BOOK OVERVIEW

- Interactive course book with 15 lessons
- Focuses upon sources & principles of Islaam
- First book in continuing series

AVAILABLE LANGUAGES

English

WHO IS THIS BOOK FOR

All age levels
This course book is intended for any Muslim who wishes to connect himself to our beloved Prophet. inwardly and outwardly, in order to walk in his footsteps upon knowledge as a worshiper of Allaah. It is designed to help you, as a Muslim, identify the correct sources, principles, and beliefs of the evidenced methodology of Islaam upon scholarship and proofs, in order to be able to distinguished what opposes them from incorrect sources, principles, and false beliefs.

PDF PREVIEW   PURCHASE BOOK

https://ilm4.us/usulbook1

http://taalib.com/62874

The Cure, The Explanation, The Clear Affair, & The Brilliantly Distinct Signpost

Book 2: The Meaning of Worship & Innovation In Islaam- A Course Upon Commentaries of Usul as-Sunnah' of Imaam Ahmad

AUTHOR - COMPILER - TRANSLATOR

Abu Sukhailah Khalil Ibn-Abelahyi

BOOK OVERVIEW

- Interactive course book with 10 lessons
- Focuses upon meaning of worship of Islaam
- Second book in continuing series

AVAILABLE LANGUAGES

English

WHO IS THIS BOOK FOR

All age levels

This course book is intended for any Muslim who desires to understand the guidelines upon which the true life of worship that our beloved Prophet realized was built inwardly and outwardly, and which he taught to his noble Companions. It is designed to help you understand the basic principles and concepts by which the Companions, and those who walked in their footsteps, distinguished the pure Sunnah from religious innovations wrongly attributed to Islaam, upon scholarship and proofs taken from the revealed source texts.

"....As the Messenger of Allaah, may Allaah's praise and salutation be upon him and his family, did not leave any single matter which the Muslim Ummah needed for its success in this world or its success in the next world to come, except that he explained it and made it clear." *Sheikh al-'Utheimeen, "Fatawaa Fel-'Aqeedah"*

WHAT YOU WILL LEARN IN THIS BOOK

Related to the boundaries of worship & of innovation

This course book examines the differences between true worship and false worship, and the conditions for worship to be valid. It discusses the definitions which the scholars have for religious innovation, and clarifies the misconception that some innovations are "good" in Islaam, as well as clarifying what is a "good sunnah" which our Prophet mentioned we are rewarded for.

VERSIONS - PRICING

- *Self-Study Edition (hardcover)*   USD $45.00
- *Self-Study Edition (soft cover)*   USD $27.50
- *Directed Study Edition*   USD $25.00
- *Workbook*   USD $11.00
- *Kindle edition*   USD $09.99

PDF PREVIEW   PURCHASE BOOK

https://ilm4.us/usulbook2   http://taalib.com/71069

CERTIFICATE OF COMPLETION

AWARDED TO:

FOR COMPLETION OF THE COURSE:

AL-WAAJIBAT:
THE FUNDAMENTALS OF ISLAAM

FOUNDATIONS SERIES COURSE (1):
TAALIB.COM

DATE: _____, 144___

This page is intentionally blank as it is the back side of the certificate of completion..

Made in the USA
Middletown, DE
26 September 2023

39365032R00194